SELETAR – CROWNING GLORY

First edition, published in 2002 by

WOODFIELD PUBLISHING
Woodfield House, Babsham Lane, Bognor Regis
West Sussex PO21 5EL, England.

ISBN 1-903953-16-2

SELETAR

Crowning Glory

The History of the RAF in Singapore

DAVID TAYLOR

Woodfield Publishing
~ WEST SUSSEX • ENGLAND ~

Scenic air-to-air shot of a Supermarine Southampton.

RA "Scotty" Powell

Contents

Overhead air-to-air of a Southampton Mkl. Note the lack of restraints and flying clothing.

RA "Scotty" Powell

Acknowledgements

This book, apart from relating significant points in the history of Royal Air Force Seletar, is really the story of the men and women who served at the station over the years, in whatever rank, capacity and whatever their nationality. Help and assistance in the preparation has come from many sources, not least, members of the RAF Seletar Association, to whom I extend my thanks.

Individual thanks are due particularly to the following, most of whom are members of the Association: Colin Brewer, Derek Brookes, Eric Cooper, Bruce Curtiss, Basil Gotto, John E Grady, Bob Hampson, BA Harrison, Peter J Henry, Peter A Hughes, Derek Jones, Malcolm Lancaster (whose father was Clerk of Works in 1946), Ray Mader, AVM Alec Maisner (last RAF CO), the late Syd Manfield, Peter Masters, Ken McLean, Ed Noonan, Stan Ould, Len Parry, Stan Pierce, R.A. "Sandy" Powell (who loaned me his wonderful albums depicting Seletar life in the mid 1930s), Eric Redshaw, Neville Shorrick, Derek Thorpe, Ron Wilkinson, and many whose names have slipped through the net of a failing memory. Many of the above supplied photographs, all, whether intentional or not, revealed snippets of information which attracted my attention enough to have me searching the Internet, the archives at Hendon, the Imperial War Museum, and the Public Records office at Kew in an effort to follow up on their leads. Sometimes I was successful, sometimes not - official records often revealing little but the very basics. It is therefore possible that some people will remember various events as happening not quite as I have portrayed.

Thanks are also due to the Mosquito Association; The Beverley Association; the PRU SEAC Contact Group; Paul Harrison – Kiwi Air Research; Andy Anderson, NZ aviation historian; RNZAF archives; British Airways archives, the *Straits Times* of Singapore; Sqn/Ldr Tony Fairbairn, whose book, *Action Stations: Overseas*, provided inspiration for the title; Peter Elliot of the RAF Museum – Hendon; Dr Christopher Dowling at the Imperial War Museum; Mr Alex Henshaw; Hugh Campbell, for details of the *Tung Song*; the PMA at RAF Innsworth ... the list goes on.

Special mention should be made of John Wood, who made available his father-in-law's collection of memorabilia relating to the Far East Flight. Vernon Lee travelled with the groundcrew

The RAF Seletar Association

Formed in late 1997, the association aims to bring together any of the estimated eighty to one hundred thousand personnel who served at Seletar over the years in whatever category, service or civilian.

For information on joining please contact the Membership Secretary – the author – at: 35 Lower Darnborough Street, Clementhorpe, York YO23 1AR, tel:01904 612542, or via e-mail: dtaylor@deltatango95.freeserve.co.uk

The RAF Changi Association can be contacted via: Mike James, 12 Shiners Elms, Yatton, Bristol BS49 4BY, or at: RAF.Changi.Assn@Telco4u.net out to Singapore in the late 1920's, but he unfortunately passed away a few days before receiving my letter requesting an interview. When sorting through his effects, John came across the letter, and rather than just filing it, he took the trouble to contact me, and so things progressed. I feel sorry to have missed meeting up with Vernon, for, even in his nineties he apparently recalled details very clearly, and was said to have gained much satisfaction when talking about his time with the "Flight."

Extracts from *The Remorseless Road*, and *To the Ends of the Air*, are used by kind permission of Airlife Publishing Ltd and the Imperial War Museum respectively. The note at the start of chapter three is from the Manchester Guardian of 17th September 1928, and is used with the permission of Guardian Newspapers.

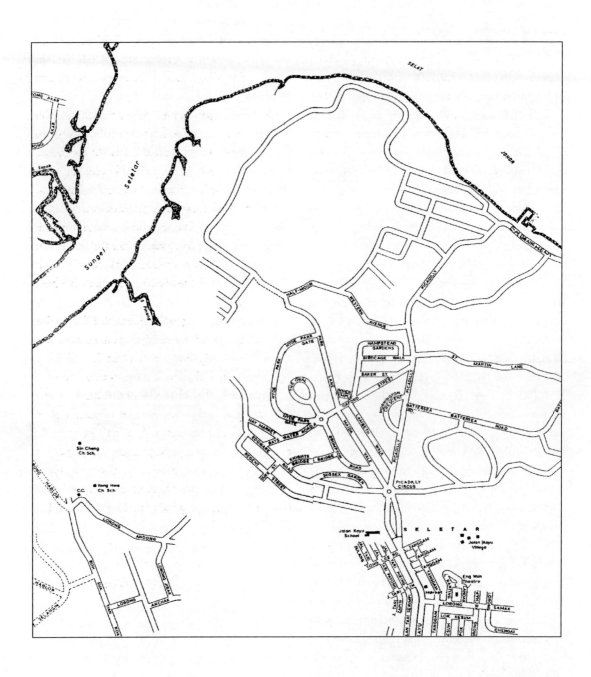

WE WILL REMEMBER HIM

DIED 21.12.2008

Air Vice Marshal Alec MAISNER CB CBE AFC

RAF SELETAR SHOP

Available from: Debbie Attoe: Stroat Farm Cottage, Stroat, Chepstow NP16 7LR Tel: 01594 529693

Lapel badges	£4.50; personalized £6.50 (to order)
Blazer badges	£20
Car stickers	£1.75
Seletar tie	£16.00
Sweatshirts	£26.00 Large. Colours: grey, red, green, blue, white, black.
Sweatshirts V-neck	£25.00 Large. Colours: red, green, black, maroon.
Polo shirts	£19.00 Large. Colours: red, green, blue, white, black.
Baseball caps	£12.00 Colours: red, green, blue, white, black.
Ladies scarves	£19.00 Square or oblong - please state which.
Coasters	£3.60
Keyrings	£3.00
Bottle opener K'ring	£3.80
Bookmarks	£2.00
Fridge Magnets	£3.00
Glass Paperweight	£11.00
Luggage Tags	£3.00
DVD's, various	£7.00 Seletar Through the Ages; Far East Sunderlands; Singapore City & Island.

Seletar Wooden Wall Plaques - available soon
Above prices are inclusive of P&P. Please allow 28 days delivery for polo shirts, sweaters and caps.
Cheques payable to the RAF Seletar Association, please.
All items, plus books & framed pictures are available at the Annual Reunion; a limited amount at local reunions.

OBITUARIES

It is with deep regret and sadness that we have been advised of the passing of the following members. Condolence cards have been sent to their relatives on behalf of all in the Association.

Derek **OAK** (667)	50/53	Arm Sect - Armourer	Deceased Nov 21/08
Eric **WESTGARTH** (219);	50/53	Armourer	Deceased Oct 2008
Thomas Gwyn **OWENS** (412)	57/60	Base Flt - Eng Fitt	Deceased 2008
AVM Alec **MAISNER** (366) ✗	69/71	GD/P - Station Commander	Deceased Dec 21/08
Trevor A **BROOKES** (600)	57/60	JAPIC -	Deceased Sept 16 08
James F **STOWE** (478)	53/56	FEFBW - Air radar Fitt	Deceased Jan 2009
Clifford N **LANE** (881)	56/60-63/66	GRS/AIS -Carp 1	Deceased Jan 22/09
Sydney **SALLITT** (122)	61/63	ATC - Controller	Deceased Nov 30/08
John K B **LEAPER** (235) ✗	46/48	Base HQ - Clerk	Deceased Jan 10/09

FOREWORD

by **Air Vice-Marshal Alec Maisner, CB CBE AFC**

As the last Station Commander of Royal Air Force Seletar, it fell upon me to see the base closed down, at least as far as the RAF presence was concerned. Although a skeleton staff remained there until July, wrapping things up as it were, the base officially closed as an operational MU at the end of March 1971, and I considered it my privilege to address my farewell remarks and to pay final tribute not only to those under my command at the time, but to all those who had served and worked at Seletar

RAF Seletar's last Commanding Officer, Grp/Cpt A Maisner AFC, with Singapore's Defence Minister Mr Lim Kim San, 1971. **Aleksander Maisner**

over the years, both service and civilian. (In fact, one of those civilians who commenced work on the base in 1926, finally retired 44 years later, in February 1970.)

It is due largely to their efforts that this station was able to make a significant contribution to the development of aviation in the area, to Singapore in general, and to the Royal Air Force, Far East. Indeed, Seletar's history is long, colourful, and very distinguished, spanning as it does almost the entire period of existence of our service, since it was in 1921, only three years after the formation of the Royal Air Force, that the British Government took the decision to establish a base on the island.

There is a saying to the effect that life begins at forty; in Seletar's case, the opposite was nearer the truth. Forty-one years after it officially became an RAF Station, it metaphorically closed its gates to end an historic era; though it was closer to fifty years since the idea of building the base had first been mooted, as will be seen by reading in the following pages. Perhaps this manuscript will arouse in many of you memories of some of the more nostalgic moments of your days at Seletar, and some of that magic of the Far East in general.

A. Maisner

Singapore III and palm trees during the Golden Age of flying in Singapore.   *RA 'Scotty' Powell*

Introduction

Crowning Glory seemed a somewhat poignant title for a military exercise, although, as far as the flying squadrons at RAF Seletar were concerned, it turned out to be rather appropriate. Staged in West Malaysia from March 3-12, 1969, the aim of the exercise was to evaluate 28 Commonwealth Infantry Brigade and their associated air support forces in a minor war setting. Upon completion, all the Seletar-based squadrons which had taken part – 66 Sqn (8 x Belvederes); 103 Sqn (6 x Whirlwinds) and 110 Sqn (6 x Whirlwinds) – deployed to Changi, operational flying from Seletar effectively ceasing on March 28th 1969, forty years after it began. From then, until its closure as an RAF base, in March 1971, Seletar's task was as a supply base and Maintenance Unit, providing engineering support and back-up for all aircraft of the Far East Air Force (FEAF), and Army.

Up to 1975 British military aircraft had been based in Singapore almost continually since February 1928, the exception being a period from 1942-45 when the Japanese put in an appearance, although their presence was not exactly, shall we say, by invitation of the local populace!

Seletar was the first RAF base to be constructed in Singapore and for the majority of its years it was the most important. This was certainly true until well after WW2 when Changi changed hands – the Army relinquishing command (albeit somewhat reluctantly) and the RAF taking over – from which point Changi gradually began to assume prominence. Given the immense variety of its activities, Seletar could boast the most colourful history of any base, not only in the Far East but possibly in the Royal Air Force as a whole, for not only did this station see the introduction of flying boats to the area, it was also afforded the privilege of launching the last operational sortie of an RAF flying boat – the Sunderland – along with those of the Spitfire, Beaufighter, Mosquito, Beverley and Belvedere.

This base also played an important part in the development of commercial air routes to and from the Far East and Australasia, playing host to many of the early pioneers during that period which was to become known as the 'Golden Age of Aviation'. Based on these facts alone, Seletar warrants a place in history. Such being the case, I felt it called for a work which detailed not only this history but also some of the stories that people associated with the place and its immediate surrounds over the years might have to tell about it. This objective was partially fulfilled in 1968, with the publication of Wing Commander Neville Shorrick's, *Lion in the Sky* (Federal Publications Sdn Bhd © 036807 – long out of print).

Naturally, as both relate the historic facts, *Seletar: Crowning Glory* closely parallels *Lion in the Sky*, though the greatly expanded story has also been extended to take in Seletar's final years as an RAF base. I've also taken into account, to a lesser extent, other bases used by the RAF in Singapore: Tengah, Sembawang, Kallang and, last to arrive but certainly not least, Changi. They were all closely integrated with Seletar, and they too played an important part in Singapore's aviation history from an RAF viewpoint. The story takes us from the very beginnings in 1921 through to the British withdrawal in 1971 and follows the fortunes of the RAF detachments that, until 1975, formed the British element of the ANZUK agreement.

I have opted for the convention of using numerals in the text only for dates, squadrons, aircraft types, and times – where I have elected to use the military standard, 24 hour clock – though this does not apply in the case of newspaper or personal reports, all of which remain in their original form, even though at times the grammar and terminology may seem, today, somewhat stilted. Times change, as has use of the English language.

Personal recollections are just that, and most, not being the kind of thing to be logged in station or squadron records (F540s), are accepted as being the facts as recalled by memories which stretch back over the years. I thought I had come to know Seletar quite well during my service there in the late fifties, but during the writing of this book I came to realise that I hadn't really known the place – or its story – at all. I also quickly began to realise that official records, though they can tell you a lot, sometimes get confused, and do not always tell the true story.

Another annoying thing about records is that you can't ask them questions.

Being a history – though not written by a historian – I have naturally recorded all the relevant historic facts, though to perhaps lighten things up and make for a more interesting story, I have also taken the opportunity of interspersing the text with many personal anecdotes and recollections of service as it was in the Far East, hoping the reader will tolerate this, at times, somewhat personal input.

Writing this story brought me into contact with many interesting people and I unearthed a great deal of fascinating material. I was reminded not only of my own years at Seletar and in the Far East but also learned of how things were long before my time, hearing stories which caused my emotions to travel through the whole spectrum. I can only hope that this book will invoke in the reader some of those same emotions.

RAF Seletar and the Far East Air Force may no longer be in existence, but the spirit certainly lives on through both the RAF Seletar and RAF Changi Associations.

David Taylor, York, England, March 2002.

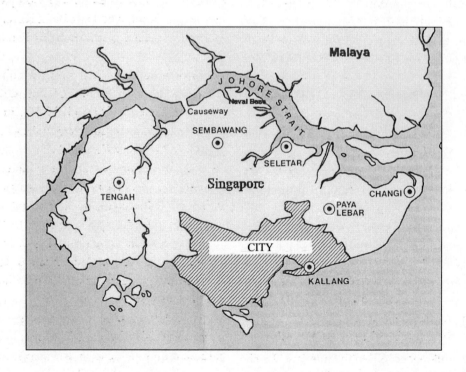

CHAPTER ONE

A Little Background:
Raffles, Threats & Treaties

Singapore; Lion City.[1] Colourful, cosmopolitan, multiracial gateway to Asia. Many cities, indeed many places, lay claim to being "gateways," but Singapore is one of the few that can truly justify such a title. It is now a city whose skyline – along with its coastline – changes by the year. Blink, and yet another old building is no more, another row of shophouses disappears, a few more square kilometres of land are reclaimed from the sea. The old is being swept away by the new. Passenger jets descend into a huge International Airport out at Changi, but the runways at a place called Seletar, to the north-west, are now strangely quiet.

It wasn't always so, and the memories remain. So let us relax, say, in the Palm Court of the Raffles Hotel, Singapore Sling to hand, tropical sun well into its downward arc, air laced with the scents of frangipani, jasmine, and magnolia, and examine some of those memories. And as the atmosphere gently mellows us, as surely it will, let us wallow in a little nostalgia, or, to return to the absolute beginning, possibly, nostalgie de la boue.[2]

• • • • • • • • • •

Temasek, or 'Sea Town' – founded in 1297 – officially entered the pages of world history in 1330, for that was the year Tan Ma-Hsi (as it was then known to the Chinese)[3] first received a mention in any official records. The Chinese writer, Wang Ta-Yuan described it as being an infertile, pirate-infested island, though this was apparently not enough to discourage it from being developed as a trading centre. In fact, it became so successful and important as to attract the attentions of other nations, and the following centuries saw it being ruled by the Siamese, Indians and Javanese. But despite all this, no really significant changes occurred until 1819.

Sir Thomas Stamford Raffles, then Lieutenant Governor of Bencoolen (West Sumatra), vigorously opposed his government's plan to abandon control of the China trade to the Dutch. Raffles, who had started his career as a clerk for the British East India Company in London, was promoted to assistant secretary of the newly formed government in Penang in 1805.

A serious student of the history and culture of the region and fluent in Malay, Raffles served as Governor General of Java (1811-16). In 1818 Raffles sailed from Bencoolen to India, where he convinced Governor General Lord Hastings of the need for a British post at the southern end of the Strait of Malacca. Lord Hastings then authorized Raffles to secure such a post for the British East India Company, provided that it did not antagonize the Dutch. Arriving in Penang, Raffles found Governor General James Bannerman unwilling to cooperate, but upon hearing that the Dutch were claiming all territories of the Sultan of Johore to be within their sphere of influence, Raffles dispatched Colonel William Farquhar, an old friend and Malayan expert, ostensibly to survey the Carimon (Karimun)

Islands (south west of Singapore). Then, disregarding Bannerman's orders for him to await further instructions from Calcutta, Raffles – who knew of Singapore Island from his study of Malay texts – boarded a private trading ship the following night, slipped out of Penang and caught up with Farquhar.

January 28, 1819 saw Raffles and Farquhar anchored near the mouth of the Singapore River. The following day the two men went ashore to meet Temenggong Abdul Rahman – the Malay Ruler who controlled the waters of the Orang Laut (Sea Gipsies), thus effectively controlling Singapore. The Temenggong granted provisional permission for the British East India Company to establish a trading post on the island, subject to the approval of Sultan Hussein. Noting the protected harbour, the abundance of drinking water, and especially the absence of a Dutch presence, Raffles immediately began unloading troops. Clearing the land on the northeast side of the river, they set up tents and hoisted the Union Jack. Meanwhile, the Temenggong sent to Riau for Hussein Shah, who arrived within days. Acknowledging Hussein as the rightful Sultan of Johore, on February 6 Raffles signed a treaty with him and the Temenggong confirming the right of the British East India Company to establish a trading post in return for an annual payment, in Spanish dollars (the common currency of the region at the time) of five thousand to Hussein and three thousand to the Temenggong. Raffles then departed for Bencoolen leaving Farquhar in charge, with instructions to clear the land, construct a simple fortification and inform all passing ships that there were no duties on trade at the new settlement.

The immediate reaction was mixed. Officials of the British East India Company in London feared their negotiations with the Dutch would be upset by Raffles' action; the Dutch were furious because they considered Singapore to be within their sphere of influence. And although they could easily have overcome Farquhar's tiny force, the Dutch did not attack because Bannerman assured them that Calcutta would disavow the whole scheme. But in Calcutta, both the commercial community and the *Calcutta Journal* urged full governmental support for the undertaking. Lord Hastings ordered the unhappy Bannerman to provide Farquhar with troops and money. Britain's Foreign Minister, Lord Castlereagh, reluctant to relinquish to the Dutch "all the military and naval keys of the Straits of Malacca," had the question of Singapore added to the list of topics to be negotiated with them, thus buying time for the new settlement.

The opportunity to sell supplies at high prices to the settlement quickly attracted many Malacca traders to the island. Word of Singapore's free trade policy also spread southeastward through the archipelago, and within six weeks more than one hundred Indonesian inter-island craft were to be found anchored in the harbor, as well as Siamese and European ships. Raffles returned in late May to find the population had grown to nearly five thousand, including Malays, Chinese, Bugis – traders from as far afield as Madagascar, Bali, and Borneo – Arabs, Indians, and Europeans. During his four-week stay, he drew up a plan for the town, and signed another agreement with Hussein and the Temenggong, establishing boundaries for the settlement. He wrote to a friend:

'Singapore is by far the most important station in the East, and, as far as naval superiority and commercial interests are concerned, of much higher value than whole continents of territory.'

And thus it was the seeds were sown? Well, not exactly. Although things did develop apace, it was 1832 before Singapore became seat of Government for the Straits Settlements – the joint colonies of Penang, Malacca, and Singapore – eventually to gain full British Colony status in 1867, to be administered from London. But the seeds, as it were, were actually sown in 1877; Brazilian rubber seeds. These – twenty-two in all – were dispatched from the Royal Botanical Institute in London, to see how they fared in this tropical environment. Alas, eleven years were to elapse – with only nine trees surviving – before HN Ridley, director of Singapore's botanical gardens, discovered a method by which the remaining trees could be developed (a method of tapping the bark which did not kill off the tree). This eventually led to Malaya becoming the world's largest producer of natural rubber.

Rubber, along with tin, brought more traders, Singapore boomed, life became good for the estate managers, and reports of the gracious living enjoyed by the thousand or so Europeans resident in Victorian Malaya, Singapore especially, make for interesting reading.

We are told they tended to remain fairly aloof from the rest of the community. Their spacious bungalows, set in extensive gardens, were clear of the hustle and bustle of the town, though apparently not far enough to avoid being awakened at 05:00 each morning by the sixty-eight-pounder gun, located on the hill at Fort Canning, overlooking the river and Outer Roads anchorage.

At sunrise, the managers (Planters) are said to have rode or walked around their estates, the household employees meanwhile preparing a hearty breakfast for them. They saw little danger in such a stroll, for although tigers did occasionally partake of the odd human, in general they seemed to favour "local fare" when *Homo Sapiens* was on the menu!

The "Planters" worked during the morning, afternoon being a period during which, after a light lunch – the sun now at its peak – they rested. In the evening, whole families would drive along the seafront, and it was reported to have been a pleasant sight to see their carriages returning home after dark, a runner leading the way, flaming torch held aloft. This must have been in stark contrast to the normal mode of transport for the majority: the rickshaw or carrying chair, many of their propulsion units sporting pigtails.

Dinner is described by survivors of that golden period as being something of a feast: soup, fish, imported wine, local beer, chicken or game, curry and rice. To follow: cheese, and the local offerings of fresh fruit; paw-paw, mango, bananas, durian (a popular, and apparently very tasty tropical fruit. But the durian has its down-side – a smell so grave it is banned from being consumed in most public places).

In the mid-1840s, French photographer, Alphonse Eugène Jules-Itier, paid the city a brief visit, and described it thus:

'I remained lost in the thoughts aroused in me by the unexpected sight of the commercial achievement of the English. On this shore where not twenty years ago were grouped a few wretched Malay villages, half fishermen, half pirates, where virgin forest extended to the seashore, where the tiger hidden in the jungle awaited his prey, where a pirate canoe scarcely disturbed an empty sea, has risen today a huge town, bustling with an industrious population. Here the gardens of sumptuous palaces are spread along the water's edge, here a stranger may take a breath of air at dusk, alone and unarmed, as safe from the tigers that have fled into the depths of the jungle as from the bandits who are kept in check by the vigilant eyes of a tireless police; and this hospitable shore has become the centre for ships of all nations.'

Social clubs were founded: Tanglin, and the Singapore Club,[4] and sporting facilities established. A yacht club was opened in 1834, and the racecourse – which in 1911 was to add significantly to the history of the island and our story – first opened in 1843. The cricket club[5] was founded in 1852, and Singapore's first Lawn Tennis Championships were held in 1875, two years before Wimbledon. There was also a hotel named Raffles, which, upon first opening its doors in 1887, boasted twenty rooms. Twelve years later it had one hundred and two, and was the only hotel in the area with electric lights and ceiling fans.

But apart from enjoying the fruits of their labours, the British also contributed a great deal to the country's prosperity, and created a heritage of law and order. However, with the death of the Queen Victoria, shortly after the turn of the twentieth century, Victorian Malaya began to fade away.

It is true to say the colonials *had* initially been upset by news of the Queen's death, just as they were more than slightly disturbed by the signing of the Anglo-Japanese Treaty a little over a year later on January 30th 1902. But although each of these events was to have far-reaching consequences, at the time they barely cast a ripple over the settled way of life of the British in Malaya. The colonialists, believing their interests to be well protected, had, over the years, become somewhat complacent. After all, did not Britain need the rubber they produced? And had not the Royal Navy ruled the sea for the past fifty years?

Little did those colonials realize that these events, especially when coupled to that which occurred in Dayton, Ohio, on December 17th 1903 – the first controlled flight of a heavier-than-air machine by Wilbur and Orville Wright – were to play significant roles in the setting up of what would become the most important air base in the Far East, and the first in Singapore.

Following the occupation of Kiaochow Bay, in 1897,[6] Germany passed the first and second Naval Laws in 1898 and 1900 respectively, in which Minister of the Navy, Admiral von Tirpitz, embarked on the construction of a large German fleet; by which means the Kaiser intended Germany would secure an overseas empire. This led to a bitter and expensive maritime race with Britain, who regarded the German navy as a potential threat to her security, and was determined to maintain naval supremacy.

The British reaction to this German threat was to concentrate her naval strength in the North Sea, hence the treaty of 1902, in which Britain and Japan took to maintain each other's interests in Singapore. In 1905, this treaty was renewed and extended to include India and Eastern Asia, and it is interesting to look back at a somewhat prophetic editorial which appeared in Singapore's main newspaper, the *Straits Times*, dated April 14th 1914: *Our Alliance with Japan may be very good, but we cannot rest content with an arrangement which makes our ally a dominant power in waters where we have enormous interests. In that position she might be tempted to become dangerous...*

This was in response to a speech by Winston Churchill, who was of the opinion that, 'A nation may be perfectly sincere in its friendship one moment, and equally sincere in its hostility at another.'

But the British Government, whose principal concern was the German threat in Europe, could not afford the political luxury of anticipating disaster in some far-flung colony, so no attempts were made to strengthen Singapore's defences. In fact, following the Japanese defeat of the Russian navy at Tsushima in 1905, Britain recalled her Far Eastern Fleet so as to concentrate on home waters.

This had the effect of Britain entrusting the security of her possessions in the Far East – Singapore and Malaya in particular – to the Japanese, enabling them to obtain a considerable amount of local knowledge (which they were to put to good use in later years). A further renewal of the alliance in 1911 meant that from 1902 up to the end of the First World War, Britain depended largely upon Japanese friendship and naval power to police her interests in South-East Asia.

The only incident to affect the island during the First World War happened during February 1915, when Sepoys of the 5th Indian Light Infantry – the only regular battalion at that time based in Singapore – mutinied, putting the Alliance to the test.

The regiment, composed entirely of Punjabi Muslims, was said to be angered by Britain's war with Muslim Turkey and when ordered to Hong Kong, rumours spread that they were actually being sent to fight in Turkey.[7]

During the week of rioting which followed, the mutineers murdered forty people, thirty-five of the victims being Europeans, including officers and men of their regiment.

Although the Japanese Consul in Singapore managed to raise a hundred and ninety special constables, the mutiny was by this time all but over, the Singapore Volunteer Corps (a unit formed in 1914), a detachment of the Malay States Volunteer Rifles, the crews of various allied warships – HMS *Cadmus* fortunately lying at anchor – and the police, having all but restored order.

After the mutineers had been rounded up, forty-one faced a firing squad. One hundred and twenty-five others were imprisoned or sent on active duty elsewhere.

Three months later, in an article praising the response of its readers to a plea for them to join the Volunteer Defence Force, the *Straits Times*, a local paper, was to make reference to this mutiny, advising:

> *... the island was deplorably unprepared for such an event...* It went on to suggest that, *It would be mere childishness to disguise the fact that if one single, capable leader had appeared among the mutineers, they could have marched into Singapore and done pretty much as they pleased.*

Fortunately, Singapore suffered no further humiliation during the term of Japanese protection. Indeed it could be said in retrospect that the Japanese honoured their treaty obligations and protected the island faithfully.

Japan had meanwhile been building up her Navy, and by the end of the First World War had become strong enough to be considered a threat to Commonwealth sea communications. With the Washington Conference of 1921 establishing a Naval Limitation Treaty – restricting the number of capital ships in each of the signatories' navies (Britain, USA, Japan, France, Italy) – this meant that Britain could not now re-create a Far Eastern Fleet, even had she so wished.

Indeed, no attempt had been made to replace this fleet since its withdrawal in 1905, and as the Anglo-Japanese Treaty was allowed to lapse (much to the relief of the Americans, who had advocated just such a move), this meant Britain would now need to shoulder the responsibility of protecting her interests in the area, hence the decision to build a naval base in the Far East, to which the Mediterranean Fleet could move in time of need, choice of location falling fairly naturally upon Singapore.

Singapore's citizens were mildly astounded when, in March, 1911, a Bristol Boxkite, piloted by Belgian, Joseph Christiaens, took off from the Old Race Course in Farrer Park. He'd had the plane shipped out to the island, then assembled it on site. In a demonstration flight, he eventually managed to reach an altitude of a little over one hundred feet; not even enough to clear the island's highest peak – the one hundred and fifty-two foot Bukit Timah (meaning "Tin Hill") – and although the "stunt" did arouse interest and excitement among the public, possibly this lack of performance was one reason why nothing further seems to have materialised from it for another eight years. A handful of men and women were pioneering the air routes of the world, but aviation was still in its infancy, and was seen to pose no threat to the great ocean liners. Nor was military aviation seen as being about to challenge sea power.

In March 1919, the Australian Government managed to stir things up, offering a prize of ten thousand pounds to the first Australian crew to succeed in flying from England to Australia. The subtext contained a clause to the effect that the flight must be completed in less than one month. Captain Ross Smith, along with brother Keith and flight mechanics, Sgt's Bennett and Shiers, beat six other contestants, their Vickers Vimy bomber, G-EAOU – the crews' interpretation of this registration being "God 'Elp All Of Us" – taking 28 storm-ridden days to complete the journey from Hounslow to Darwin.

Good press copy indeed. But even back then it seems the newspapers occasionally felt the need for added zest in their stories. Upon arrival in Pisa, a violent rainstorm and a waterlogged airfield delayed the machine's departure next day until it could be extracted from the boggy ground. When it came, the take-off was reported as being sensational, viz:

> "A *mechanic held down the tail until the engines were running and the aircraft was moving off, after which he made a running jump for the cockpit, being hauled aboard even as the machine became airborne.*"

Daring and adventurous? Yes indeed, but fairly common back then. Sgt Bennett was holding down the tail to guard against the possibility of the aircraft nosing over in the soggy ground, releasing it only when the pilot signalled him to do so. Once the aircraft started rolling he would leap aboard as best he could. Holding down the tail was a task normally performed by the ground crew, but with no ground crew on hand, it became the aircrew's responsibility.

Captain Ross Smith's arrival in Singapore on December 4th, 1919, was a milestone in the history of aviation, and we again turn to the *Straits Times* for this description of the landing, the first by an aircraft arriving from overseas:

Sailing steadily from the north and flying fairly low, the aeroplane came. It was noted that the engines were comparatively quiet, not being audible until the machine was fast approaching the race course. Coming over the east end, the machine flew the whole length of the ground, affording a splendid view to everybody. Then, making a complete circle, flew far away to the south. Returning, it passed over the west end, gradually descending, and made a splendid landing in the centre of the course. Going to the east end again, it swung round and came slowly along, to stop finally opposite the stewards' stand and close to where a group of officials were assembled.

The spectators cheered continuously as the machine was coming to earth, and three final cheers were given as it drew up.

From this point on, those early aviators and aviatrices came in a steady stream, landing on the racecourse initially; Cobham, Hinkler, and later, Kingsford-Smith. But although the island became an en route port-of-call for the adventurers and record breakers, its own aviation development was still proving to be extremely slow. Paradoxically, although a good deal of flying was taking place in China, Java, and Siam, there was no civilian flying at all in the Settle-

ments – despite the fact that there were reportedly some sixty ex-First World War pilots now living in Singapore, most of whom would no doubt have been more than willing to take to the air again. But, with the rest of the world slowly beginning to accept the challenge of aviation, Singapore, it seemed, was just not interested.

The adventurers and intrepid aviators managed to keep hopes alive, and most of them were extremely confident of the future. As Alan Cobham pointed out upon his arrival in Singapore in 1926:

'We have got to that stage in aviation when, provided you have sufficient organisation, petrol supplies and so on, you can keep on flying round the world without a stop.' [8]

But our story really begins in 1921. With the British Cabinet reaching the decision to establish an up-to-date naval base in Malaya, they also resolved to take things a stage further. By now recognising the growing importance of the aeroplane, both in and out of warfare, agreement was also reached on the setting up of an airfield and flying boat base in Singapore.

The two sites were approved in 1923, both being situated to the north of the island, well clear of the exposed southern coast and Keppel Harbour. The thinking was along the lines that, with the north coast being well protected by the Malayan jungle, any attack on the island was sure to be from the south.

The air force base was to be east of the naval base, at a place located between Sungai Seletar, to the west, and Sungai Punggol, to the east. It would eventually become known as Seletar – a Malay word meaning, 'leading to the straits'; the very straits that were destined to become – thirty six years later – the RAF's last operational flying boat base.

CHAPTER TWO

Survey & Approval:
An RAF Presence

Twenty-six year old Gerry Livock once more circled his aircraft over the swamps and forests of northern Singapore, a routine flight, part of a, by now, routine job: a photographic survey. Flight Lieutenant GE Livock was the senior pilot with a flight of Fairey IIID float planes which were parented by the seaplane carrier HMS *Pegasus* – or "Peggy" as she was affectionately known by her crew.

Soon it would be over, and he would depart for England, hopeful, perhaps, of getting in some serious cricket – a sport at which he was quite an accomplished player.[9] Little did he realize that Seletar would become a second home to him over the following years, and that 43 years later he would be invited to return, on what would for him be a very sentimental journey.

● ● ● ● ● ● ● ● ● ●

It was on April 20th, 1924, that the odd-looking ship, *Pegasus*, festooned with a complicated array of cranes and other equipment, nosed her way alongside the oiling wharf in Singapore harbour. The RAF flight, under the command of Squadron Leader EL Tomkinson, had formed at Mount Batten a few months previous to this, undertaking preparatory work: the fitting of vertical cameras to the aircraft, and of ironing out any teething troubles. Joining *Pegasus* – captained by Commander (later, Rear Admiral) HG Rawlings, RN – the expedition departed England on March 24th, 1924, their instructions explicit: to carry out a large scale photographic survey in the Far East, the first ever attempted by the RAF. Indeed, this was to be the first RAF group to arrive in the area, or to cross the equator.

A short while after berthing, the first of *Pegasus'* aircraft, N9634, was prepared for flight. The procedure called for pilot and crew to climb aboard – in this case, Flt/Lt Livock, Lieutenant Ashby, RN, and Corporal Fish, RAF – fire up the four hundred and fifty horsepower Napier Lion, carry out their checks, and signal when ready. The RAF officer on deck would then signal the crane operator – by means of flags – for the aircraft to be lifted off its trolley and swung over the side. On receipt of another signal, the aircraft was lowered until its floats were just touching the water when, upon yet another signal, the observer, standing on top of the fuselage, pulled a quick release. The aircraft dropped into the sea, taxied clear, then took-off on what was to be the first RAF flight in Singapore.

Communication between crew members was by way of a rubber speaking-tube, the "earphones" of which were sewn into the flaps of their "solar-bowlers" – a half-sized topee, worn in lieu of a flying helmet, for, quite erroneously, it was then considered almost certain death to go out in the sun without adequate head protection.

On completion of the sortie – a harbour crane hoisting the aircraft ashore for its compass to be swung – Flt/Lt Livock became the first RAF officer to set foot on the island.

Due mainly to poor lighting conditions, the survey took far longer than expected. A low mist would usually obscure the ground early on, clouds often forming below one thousand feet as the mist burnt off, sky invariably overcast. Things would generally improve towards evening, but by then the light was fading dramatically.

But it wasn't all work. The rubber industry was reported to be booming, expatriates rolling in money. Planters invited the survey crew to shoot on their estates, and as Gerry Livock tells it, 'Parties, armed to the teeth, would disappear into the "Ulu" – as the jungle was referred to locally – though they seldom brought anything back. Although we did one day catch a huge stingray in our net when fishing. Lifted aboard "Peggy" by crane, it was found to weigh slightly over one thousand pounds. And this was from the area in which we would swim!'

In those days, such famous old hotels as the de l' Europe and Raffles[10] were at their peak, steeped in memories of Kipling, Conrad, Maughan and the romance of the east.

"And I soon found my way to the cricket club," recalls Gerry Livock.

But the pioneers of *Pegasus* did not find Malaya to be complete paradise, for the hot, steamy, tropical climate often made life unpleasant. All kinds of ailments were suffered, prickly heat topping the list. 'A plague of cockroaches threatened to overrun the ship,' recalls Livock, in his book *To the Ends of the Air*.

'These filthy little pests got everywhere in their thousands, even in our caps hanging on pegs outside the wardroom during meals... However, some genius devised a simple means of keeping them out of our cabins. Cigarettes on board were sold in tins of fifty, and the empty tins were baited with pieces of banana or dry bread and placed at the entrance to any opening such as air grating or holes for piping. The rims of the tins were made slippery with a smear of butter, and the stupid cockroaches slid into the traps and couldn't get out again. One of the duties of one's servant was to empty the generally full tins each morning.'

On June 26th, 1924, the Causeway linking Singapore and the Malay Peninsular was opened to traffic, three of the Fairey IIID's flying over in formation during the ceremony, taking photographs of the event.[11] They also took the Sultan of Johore's three sons for a flight. Prudence, one would assume, for thereafter, they carried with them during their survey flights, a chit from the Sultan which, in Malay and English, apart from giving them permission to overfly his terrain, requested that his subjects offer help, should the aircraft *be obliged to make a forced descent*.

'Also carried,' says Gerry Livock, 'on advice from the planters, was a first aid kit, parang, small tool kit, rations, cooking utensils, flares, revolver, and a length of rope – for lowering ourselves out of the branches of tall trees – necessary precautions when flying over this tiger and snake infested dense jungle, so we were advised.'

As the expedition had come to Singapore to conduct aerial surveys and tropical flying tests over the Malayan peninsula, HMS *Pegasus* did not remain in one place for long. Her anchor was soon hauled up from the Singapore mud, and she was heading up the east coast of Malaya. Later on, flights were made at places as far apart as Kuala Lumpur, Port Swettenham, Penang, Sarawak, and Hong Kong – where Livock chalked up another first, his Fairey floatplane being the first RAF aircraft to land in the colony; Nov 4th 1924. Whilst there he represented Malaya in an inter-port cricket tournament, scoring centuries against both Kowloon and Hong Kong.

Then, finally, on January 16th, 1925, from six thousand feet, Flt/Lt Livock, with Flying Officer Rankin as photographer, completed two survey flights over the proposed air base site at Seletar. And on the 10th of February 1925, they completed a mosaic of the future air and naval bases. It was during these runs that they inadvertently took some highly secret photographs of oil tanks and gun positions, copies of which were later to appear in a Japanese photo shop. There were some awkward questions to be answered as a result of that, but the cause of the leak was never discovered.

HMS *Pegasus* departed for England shortly after completion of the Seletar survey, arriving home in March 1925, after having completed a most successful and historic voyage. This was also to mark the beginning of the RAF's long association with Singapore and the Far East. The expedition, according to Gerry Livock, had been 'Full of interest, and lots of fun. Singapore, Malaya, Hong Kong, Borneo, with many of the places visited never before having seen an aeroplane. On top of this, it was crowned with complete technical success, strangely enough.'

Shortly before HMS *Pegasus* had set sail at the start of this voyage, a unique political event had taken place in England – the coming to power, in January 1924, of the first Labour Government, under Mr Ramsay MacDonald.

The Socialists had for some time been totally opposed to the construction of a base in Singapore and upon attaining power immediately issued orders for all work on it to cease. Sir Lawrence Guillemard, then Governor of the Straits Settlements, successfully managed to ignore the Cabinet's decision, work on clearing the area continuing. *Pegasus*, too, managed to complete her assigned task, and this was attributed to the fact that *her* orders had been issued before Labour assumed power.

Although many other projects were subsequently cancelled, the Sea Lords had "apparently" overlooked *Pegasus*, which sailed quietly on her way. Thus Commander Rawlings was able to proceed according to *his* instructions, and by the time the cruise was over, the Socialists were no longer in office, their term lasting a mere ten months!

By November 1924, the Conservatives were back, and they naturally decided to "resume" work on the base, meaning that scarcely any time was lost at all, the base slowly beginning to take shape.

It had been 1923 when the Straits Settlements Government had ceded the original site as a gift to the Air Ministry, the Government having acquired it from Singapore United Rubber Plantations Ltd. It was an undulating stretch of land which rose from the foreshore, the one hundred and forty acre coastal fringe being mangrove swamp. The remainder of the site, apart from limited areas of coconut palms, fruit trees and vegetable gardens, had been planted with rubber trees, though with weeding having been discontinued for the past eighteen months, secondary jungle now flourished, there being some extremely thick undergrowth.[12]

A few aborigines had lived in the Seletar area for many years, belonging to a race about which very little is known. This particular group were said to have been called the "Orang Seletar," a nomadic folk who roamed the northern shores of the island, attempting to eke out a simple living along the coastal waters and rivers. They are thought to be the original Orang Laut (Sea Gipsies), encountered by Raffles in 1819. Mr JT Thompson, who surveyed the area many years ago, has left for posterity the following vivid account of these people:

> They possess no weapons, either offensive or defensive, and their minds do not find a higher range than necessity compels. The satisfying of hunger is their only pursuit. Of water, they have an abundance without searching. With the sarkab, or fishing spear, and the parang, or chopper, they eke out a miserable existence from the stores of the riverside forest. They neither dig nor plant, yet live nearly independent of their fellow men, for to them, the staple diet of the East, rice, is a luxury. Tobacco they procure by the barter of fish and a few marketables collected from the forest and coral reefs ....

> .... They hunt the wild hog but refrain from snakes, dogs, iguana and monkeys. In the three great epochs of their individual lives, we find no rites or ceremony enacted. At birth, the child is welcomed to the world only by its mother's joy; and marriage – a handful of tobacco and one chupah (half a coconut shell) to one another confirms the tie. At death, the deceased are wrapped in their garments and committed to the parent earth. Their tribe, though confining its range to thirty square miles, may still be considered to

be wanderers. In their canoes, barely sufficient to float their loads, they skirt the mangroves, exhausting one spot then searching for another. To one accustomed to the comforts and artificial wants of a civilized life, theirs, as a contrast, appears to be extreme. Huddled up in a small boat hardly measuring twenty feet in length, they find all the domestic comfort they are in want of. The personal appearance of these people is unprepossessing, and their deportment lazy and slovenly, united to much filthiness of person.

According to various sources, the "Orang Seletar" either drifted off to more peaceful creeks on the mainland, the remainder becoming absorbed in the population, or they were resettled by the Sultan of Johore, Abu Bakar, at Sungai Pulai, in SW Johore. Said to be still very primitive, they live on boats, or huts in the mangrove swamps, earning a living catching fish and crabs for the Johore Bahru market.

The tasks confronting the engineers who carved out the first RAF station in Malaya from this rough territory – given prevailing conditions – must have been hellish, for the acreage lay one and a half miles off the nearest road, up a snake-ridden track suitable only for bullock carts. It was a rough and often dangerous trek, but the only alternative was by launch – when the tide was favourable – and as this entailed wading through three hundred yards of mud, it was none too popular. The nearest road suitable for motorized traffic was at Paya Lebar, about five miles distant. In between lay thick jungle, and all that the word entailed.

By 1927 things were well under way, and come March that year about one hundred acres had been cleared and drained, with ditches in place. Gerry Livock, meanwhile – promotion to Squadron Leader having ruled him out of a flight to the Cape (though he did make a trip to Cyprus, and on to the Middle East) was once again in the area, having just completed an exhausting journey during which, between Calcutta and Singapore, he selected forty-three sites suitable for the refuelling and servicing of

both land and seaplanes. He had travelled to Calcutta on the SS *City of Nagpur*, and from there, owing to a lack of roads or railways, by coastal steamer and Government launch. From Penang down, the journey had been by car.

On arrival in Singapore he drove out to Seletar, and recalls 'the rubber trees were being cleared to make the landing ground. There was a little slipway on the beach, and alongside it, an "attap" hut which was later to become our Squadron Headquarters.[13] There were no other buildings; no hangers, no quarters, and I was the very first RAF officer to visit the site.'

On April 10th, 1927, Mr CE Woods, often described as the "man who built Seletar Air Base," arrived in Singapore to take up the post of Principal Works and Buildings Officer, RAF Far East. His job was to prepare for the arrival of four flying boats that were due in Singapore early the following year, The Far East Flight. With this in mind, initial work was directed towards the services connected with this flight.

Construction of the slipway had progressed well: Forty feet wide, it stretched over two hundred and fifty feet out into the Straits of Johore, sliding gently into the waters. Working between tides, this concrete edifice was built in just six weeks – a magnificent feat. Once dredging operations were complete, the intent was to extend the length of the slipway considerably.

Roads presented some problems, the original means of access being nothing but an eight feet wide track. But within eight months over a thousand yards of firm main roads had been built, along with many others that were temporary. Some of this blacktop was necessarily constructed over what had originally been mangrove swamp, much infill being required, no less than fifteen feet in one particular area.

In spite of numerous difficulties, the whole area – with the exception of ninety acres of mangrove – had been cleared come December, access with the Yio Chu Kang Road being established in January 1928. A temporary building had also been constructed, the extended slipway was almost complete, and a concrete apron had been laid for use by aircraft whose arrival was imminent. There was a temporary office, guardroom, dining room and kitchen, along with a supply of fresh water.

Many encounters with wildlife were reported – cobras, pythons, crocodiles – but the most unusual was said to be a pair of cobras, one of which was reportedly discovered among the papers in the Chief Engineer's office, whilst its mate was found wrapped around the right leg of a visiting surveyor when he awoke after a night's sleep on site. It is reported that he refused all offers to stay there ever again!

The real foundation for progress was attributed to the highly successful anti-malarial measures which had been implemented, a further one hundred acres being acquired to help achieve this; absolutely essential, with malaria being a killer disease. The main valley, running north-south, was used as a catchment area for the smaller ravines, most of the water being channelled to the sea by way of open drains and culverts. In a comparatively short time the area was well drained, an important factor in maintaining the health of the labour force.

In addition to preparations for the Far East Flight, another major task was to commence in 1927: the creation of an area on which land planes could set down. Floppy-leaved banana trees and rioting creepers were to become things of the past in the area selected, enormous amounts of felling and cutting taking place throughout.

On the aerodrome itself, over a million tons of earth were shifted. Top soil was removed to a depth of twelve inches, being piled nearby until the necessary felling and cutting were complete. It was then relaid, the resultant surface being turfed with the local buffalo grass.

As Singapore is occasionally subjected to torrential rains, drainage was of prime importance. Constructed as an inverted saucer with the runway on top, monsoon drains were located every few yards around the circumference. So efficient was this, that within half an hour of a heavy downfall – airfield resembling a lake – the surface was once more transformed into a hard green airfield.

"Concrete Lizzies," the real workforce behind the building of Seletar. These ladies, and many more like them, shifted whole hillsides during construction of the camp. RA *"Scotty" Powell*

Taking over two years to complete, the scheme was on a scale not then precedented in Malaya, and so successful was it that Seletar was used as the role model for many of the other airfields which were destined to appear up and down the peninsula.

The plans called for two hangars to be erected, each two hundred and fifty feet in length. Sliding doors at either end gave a clear opening of one hundred and twenty feet in width by thirty feet in height. The seaplane hanger was situated opposite the slipway, on the beach, the hangar for land-based aircraft being close by the landing ground.[14]

The first structure required 45 thousand tons of earth to be removed, and due to the difficult nature of the ground, the foundations of the seaplane hangar required concrete piles to be driven to a depth forty feet. Alongside the slipway, a pier was built. This featured a narrow-gauge railway which carried a five ton travelling crane, necessary to transport the thousands of tons of steel and other heavy equipment from the barges which brought materials to the site.

Looking back, one can imagine scenes of immense activity, for it was truly amazing what had been accomplished in so short a time; a great feat of engineering. Especially so considering the lack of machinery. Mr Woods' was assisted by seventeen British engineers and supervisors, along with a labour force of fifteen hundred

Chinese and Malays, and around five thousand Indians.

It is said that the road leading to the site was named after the man who created the Seletar Air Base, Mr Woods – a fitting tribute to the accomplishments achieved by him – but that, at his request, instead of being known as Woods Road, the Malayan translation of Jalan Kayu was substituted. Yet according to the Singapore National Archives, the road was so named because firewood was stacked at the roadside. I would suggest the former to be the more obvious and accepted explanation – after all, the road was not even in existence before Mr Woods had it built.

Six hundred acres of land had been cleared and converted into a flying station by early 1928, and although far from complete, it was now ready to receive its first visitors, the Supermarine Southampton flying boats of the Far East Flight. These four aircraft were already en-route, a

journey which many were to rank as one of the greatest flights ever made, though not the Air Ministry. Unfortunately, for some obscure reason, the Ministry refused to accord this flight any publicity whatever. Little mention of it was made at the time, and forty years were to slip past before it began to be given its true place in history. So let us now return to those days.

The original Main Gate. Once the boundaries were extended this became site for the Chartered Bank.
Ken McLean

One of the first permanent buildings - still in use. The Station HQ was built in 1931, replacing the stilted hut that now became 205 Sqn HQ, later, the Seletar Y C.
RA "Scotty" Powell

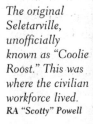

The original Seletarville, unofficially known as "Coolie Roost." This was where the civilian workforce lived.
RA "Scotty" Powell

CHAPTER THREE

Making History:
The Far East Flight

This is the greatest flight of its kind ever attempted, and it has been carried through without any mishap and with only the most trivial mechanical troubles. The arrival in Singapore completes a total distance of 23,000 miles. *(Manchester Guardian, 17th September 1928.)*

● ● ● ● ● ● ● ● ● ●

Group Captain Henry Cave-Brown-Cave, DSO DFC, had been selected to assume control of the most important flight ever undertaken by the Royal Air Force. Having been fully briefed at the Air Ministry and, being the serious-minded, conscientious forty year old that he was, there was no doubt that he would carry out his instructions to the letter.

The year was 1927, and the RAF was proposing to take a flight of four Supermarine Southampton flying boats – to become known as "The Far East Flight" – by stages, from Felixstowe to Singapore, then on to Australia, a route which even Imperial Airways had not yet considered developing: indeed it would be another two years before their routes extended even as far as India. In fact, the crews themselves considered the possibility of all four machines completing the journey as being remote indeed. [First to Australia, © GE Livock, *Air Pictorial*, Vol 30, April 1968.]

The RAF *had* flown similar aircraft down the Cape route, and Sqn/Ldr GE Livock, second in command, and senior pilot on this flight, *had*

taken two of these aircraft to the Middle East and back. But, despite being very experienced, he, along with Cave-Brown-Cave, and the project's lead navigator, Flight Lieutenant PE Maitland, AFC, had been pouring over maps and charts at Felixstowe for some months. After all, a trip along the relatively well-known Mediterranean route was a far different proposition to a twenty-seven thousand mile haul halfway across the world. Even the aircraft differed from the version he had flown previously; the hulls were now constructed from duralumin, as opposed to wood, and two of the aircraft had been fitted with experimental, metal airscrews, again in place of wooden ones. (By the end of the flight, all would be fitted with the metal version, the brass leading edges on the wooden blades showing signs of lifting.) No change in the open cockpits though; they offered little protection from the sun and rain, none at all from engine noise. Communication between aircraft would be by Aldis lamp or hand signals, only two of the machines being fitted with w/t sets.

The main aims of the exercise were, (a) to gain experience in working a flight of flying boats on a mobile basis; (b) to collect further information on possible seaplane bases along the route; (c) to gain technical and operational experience in the development of flying boats; and (d) to fly the flag, considered to be very important in the days of empire.

That was what Henry Cave-Brown-Cave had been told, officially, but he probably assumed there was much more at stake than those precise objectives. The last war had demonstrated the effective the use of flying machines, but questions were still being posed as to which form these machines should take. Until the fatal crash of the R101 – yet three years in the future, but which was eventually to decide the issue once and for all – some were pushing for the development of the dirigible.

There was even disunity among the heavier-than-air supporters, one group being of the opinion that flying boats would have little practical or strategic value, being dependant, as they were, on sheltered waters. It was also argued that to fly such an aircraft over vast stretches of land, was to be taking unnecessary risks. Thus, from Cave-Brown-Cave's point of view, this trip was not only the most important of his career, it was to be a "make or break" effort. The aeronautical eyes of the world – airlines in particular – would be upon the Far East Flight, and the future shape of flying may well depend upon how they fared in the coming months.

They were ready to depart Plymouth on the17th of October, three days after leaving their Felixstowe base, but first the group would pose to have their picture taken. The fact that these photographs could possibly one day be of some historical significance obviously never occurred to the press, only the representative of a local paper bothering to turn up. The reason for this lack of interest was almost wholly due to the attitude adopted by the Air Ministry. Possibly with thoughts of failure in mind, they did not wish for the publicity sought by other record-breaking aviators, who at the time were flying to all corners of the globe. This was purely a service affair, not a stunt.

Crew selection had, naturally, been of paramount importance, for this was certainly no training flight. Each aircraft was to carry a week's supply of food and water, along with cooking facilities, sleeping bags and an inflatable dinghy – handy for getting ashore, but also found to be useful as a bed, or, when inflated and left out in the rain, a bath. The Officer Commanding the expedition was in many ways an ideal choice. A very experienced pilot and highly qualified engineer, he would be unlikely to allow anything to interfere with the technical success of the venture, even though public relations exercises and socializing – both of which were likely to feature strongly – were not really his forte.

At 09:00 hours, on the dot, Sqn/Ldr Livock gently eased his aircraft off the water to lead the formation on their great adventure. His selection, too, had been almost inevitable, for he was one of the most experienced and capable flying boat pilots serving in the RAF at that time. As well as taking part in that Far East survey of 1924, and the Mediterranean flight, he had also, in 1926, completed an overland survey between Calcutta and Singapore, selecting forty-three prospective landing sites for both land-based and seaplane-type aircraft; knowledge that was to prove invaluable. In fact, it was during that 1926 survey – when spending Christmas at Mergui, Burma – that Gerry Livock first received news informing him that he was to be senior pilot on the Far East Flight.

The departure formation was to be maintained throughout the trip, with S1149 heading the pack. S1150, piloted by Flight Lieutenant DV "Andy" Carnegie, AFC, took station on Gerry Livock's port side. Partnering Flt/Lt Carnegie was an ex-Cranwell cadet and junior member of the team, Flying Officer GE "Nick" Nicholetts. To starboard was S1151, flown by Flt/Lt CG Wigglesworth, AFC, popularly known as "Wiggie." Another superb sportsman, who, like Gerry Livock, often represented the RAF at cricket. "Wiggie" was probably the most popular member of the party, possessing as he did, that greatest of assets, a Yorkshire sense of humour. Sharing the aircraft with "Wiggie" was another seasoned flying boat pilot, one with extensive engineering experience, Flying Officer SD Scott.

The Commanding Officer, piloting S1152, positioned himself directly behind, and slightly below the leader, Cave-Brown-Cave being accompanied by Flt/Lt HG Sawyer, a skilled aviator and another athletic type, often representing the service at hockey.

It is interesting to note that all these pilots survived their flying careers. Flt/Lt PE Maitland, AFC, a quiet and efficient man, rose to become an Air Vice-Marshal before retiring after the Second World War. Cave-Brown-Cave and "Andy" Carnegie also made AVM, the latter ending a long and interesting career as AVM David Vaughan Carnegie CB CBE AFC (RAF) Chief of Air Staff, Royal New Zealand Air Force, from 1951-53.

It was as a Flying Officer that Nicholetts, along with Sqn/Ldr Gayford, was to break the world's long distance record in the 1930s. They flew a Fairey Monoplane, an aircraft specifically designed for long-distance fight. Captured by the Japanese in Java during the Second World War, Nick was to spend three years as a prisoner. By the time of his retirement, he was Air Marshal Sir Gilbert Nicholetts.

Also retiring after the War, Air Commodore C.G. "Wiggie" Wigglesworth, AFC died in 1962.

A base party of three officers and twenty-three other ranks had been sent on ahead to set up facilities for servicing the aircraft. The officers, Flt/Lt's Freeman (engineering); Horwood (stores and pay); and Cheeseman, MBE (maintenance and handling), becoming known as Freeman, Hardy & Willis – after the footwear chain. This was said to have been in reference to the fact they were to be mainly surface bound, though no doubt the Engineering Officer's surname had a bearing on the matter. It was reported to be a very happy team all round.

The complete aircrew list was as follows:

S1152 Grp/Cpt Cave-Brown-Cave DSO DFC, (Squadron Commander); Flt/Lt HG Sawyer; Cpl Coyne, (fitter); LAC Nelson, (W/T).

S1151 Flt/Lt C.G. Wigglesworth; Flt/Lt SD Scott; Sgt Hart, (rigger); Sgt Semple, (fitter).

S1150 Flt/Lt DV Carnegie AFC; F/O GE Nicholetts; Sgt McMeeking, (fitter); Cpl Myers, (fitter).

S1149 Sqn/Ldr GE Livock DFC, (Flight leader); Flt/Lt PE Maitland AFC, (lead Navigator); Sgt Cushing, (fitter); LAC Williams, (W/T).

The first leg was to Hourtin, near Bordeaux, a distance of three hundred and eighty miles, and although the weather en route deteriorated badly, the aircraft arrived safely, after a flight of five hours. Adopting a procedure which was to become characteristic of the entire journey – making no attempt to break records – they departed for the South of France two days later. The flight across the Mediterranean was supposed to be via Crete, but upon learning that their fuel had yet to arrive, they made a last minute diversion to Athens. From the Greek capital they continued without mishap, following the coastline, by stages, to Alexandretta (now known as Iskenderun), Turkey, close to the border with Syria. As flying boats normally stuck to the coastal route for safety reasons, the leg to Baghdad posed a danger, taking them over high ground, and across two hundred miles of desert. Down-draughts and a full fuel load combined to create problems when clearing the cloud-covered mountains, and once over, they were faced with strong headwinds and dust storms, visibility being reduced to a few hundred yards at times. Realizing they did not have enough fuel to reach Baghdad in these conditions (average speed, forty-five knots), they set down on the river Euphrates, at Ramadi, where fuel was available at the RAF emergency landing ground. Refuelling was by means of drums, the fuel poured, via a chamois filter, into a central container, from where it was pumped by hand into the tanks, each aircraft carrying its own pump. They took thirty gallons each, departing next morning to arrive at Hinaidi in time for breakfast.[15]

Following the Euphrates all the way to the Persian Gulf, they again took the coastal route, this time to India, calling in at Bushire, Persia. Here, because of the fear they may be importing the plague from Iraq, the authorities quarantined the aircraft, refusing to allow the crews ashore; although this didn't stop hordes of officials braving the plague to come out and have a look around. The Royal Navy took pity, inviting the officers to dine and sleep aboard HMS *Enterprise*.

Karachi, the next destination, was reached on November 18th, another historic milestone: covering four thousand eight hundred and fifty nautical miles in seventy-three hours flying time, they had completed first formation flight from England to India. (Pakistan did not exist prior to 1947).

The schedule in Karachi called for a stay of over three weeks, during which the aircraft were beached one at a time. Airframes and engines were thoroughly examined and overhauled, the Freeman, Hardy & Willis team achieving wonders.

Flt/Lt S. Freeman, had already distinguished himself by being an ex-Royal Naval Air Service mechanic who had become commissioned, and had learned to fly, whereas Flt/Lt Cheeseman's main claim to individuality being that he was the only total abstainer and non-smoker in the party. It was said that in spite of this "defect," he managed to carry out his work quietly and efficiently at all times. Flt/Lt Horwood, an extremely capable ex-Army officer, was in charge of the all-important pay arrangements. Needless to say, the officers had made the most of their prolonged visit, much to the delight of the local nurses, and the numerous sports clubs in the area.

The aircraft of the Far East Flight had white-painted hulls, and to distinguish one from the other they also had respectively none, one, two, and three black bands painted round the hull. It was during beaching after the long stay at Karachi that an interesting discovery was made: although that age-old enemy of shipping, the barnacle, had the same affinity for the hulls of flying boats, they were seen to favour the black paint rather than the white, the black bands being more thickly coated. The more bands, the more barnacles, which seems a bit hard on S1151, number three in the flight. Number four, S1152, Cave-Brown-Cave's aircraft, carried no bands.

December, and everyone set off again, the aircraft departing on the 18th, en-route for Ceylon, via Bombay, where they were to spend their first Christmas away from home.

'In some ways, the flight down the west coast of India, to Ceylon, was the most interesting and certainly the most entertaining of the whole cruise,' says Gerry Livock.

'Although there were no apparent onward communications, word had somehow filtered ahead that the "Flying Ships" would soon be appearing, and hundreds of natives packed the beaches to watch us pass by. Upon seeing this, the Commanding Officer decided to give them something to talk about, for he suspected not too many of them would have seen an aircraft before.

'Turning the flight around, we flew in formation a few hundred feet overhead. The natives watched in awe, then, roaring with excitement, chased after the aircraft until we disappeared from view.' (In actual fact, town authorities along the Flight's route had been advised by the Port Officer at Mangalore of the approximate dates and times the aircraft could be expected to pass overhead.)

The Flight arrived in Colombo on the final day of 1927, and the airmen of the flying crews were able to get some proper rest for the first time. In two parties, they were sent ashore to the delightful and luxurious Naval Rest Camp, up in the hills at Diyatalawa. The officers, too, had an enjoyable stay, and were entertained royally. In return they showed hundreds of local people over their aircraft. One of their visitors, a journalist, astounded even the broad-minded travellers by entitling his article, "Boudoirs of the Blue," after becoming infatuated with the domestic arrangements on board.

Colombo harbour was notorious for fouling the hulls of ships, and after a stay of twelve days it was found that aircraft were not immune to this phenomenon; those barnacles again! As Gerry Livock said, 'It was lucky there was plenty of room, for take-off from there was double the normal run.'

On January 12th, they set off along the east coast of India, and in an interesting chapter of his book, Gerry Livock recalls how well received they were, and in particular, the numerous experiences and adventures which took place at virtually every port of call. But it was at a place called Chilka that they had their most interesting encounter.

'The aircraft were moored a few hundred yards from the Rajah of Khalikote's palace, and we gave the Rajah a flight over his domain. We were treated to a mock sword fight, visited a Hindu temple which was covered with what to Western eyes could best be described as a mass of obscene figures, and took part in a bear hunt. Much to my relief,' said Gerry Livock, 'we failed to find any bears.'

The crew's accommodation in the Palace, we are told, featured a sitting room which counted among its furnishings one of those "What the butler saw" machines, which showed "feelthy pictures." The assumption was that this had been specially installed for the visit!

On the last day at Chilka, Sqn/Ldr Livock missed a shooting trip so as to show the Ranee over a flying boat, a difficult task given that all the ladies of the Palace were in strict purdah. So far, not one of the officers had even glimpsed a female around the Palace. Livock describes how things went.

'It was a rather complicated process getting her aboard, as all the locals had first to be driven back from the road which led down to the jetty. The Ranee slipped out of a heavily-curtained Rolls Royce into a barge. She them emerged, heavily veiled, from the closed cabin and climbed into our rubber dinghy, which I rowed for the last few yards to the aircraft. Once on board, the Ranee threw back her veil and asked for a cigarette. After looking around and asking many questions, this beautiful and intelligent lady replaced her veils, and the complicated manoeuvre of returning her to the seclusion of the palace was successfully completed.'

While the flight wended its way along the Indian coastline, the base party travelled overland from Karachi to Calcutta, sailing from there directly to Singapore, arriving on January 11th 1928. They were to be the first airmen stationed at Seletar, though they were not initially accommodated there. As the various messes and accommodation were still under construction, the airmen were temporarily housed with the

Duke of Wellington Regiment at Tanglin Barracks,[16] whilst the officers were accommodated in the city. The net result was a daily journey to work of around twelve miles, which, in an unfriendly climate and rudimentary conditions, made life extremely arduous.

Vernon JW Lee, an airman who travelled out with the ground party, kept a meticulous diary of the trip. He describes their arrival at Tanglin and his first sight of Seletar, to which they travelled on January 14th, thus:

'The Duke of Wellington Regiment has very fine barracks, and we welcomed the fine weather again. Had quite an interesting morning, we went and saw the RAF Base at Seletar. We had a good walk over the aerodrome to be, it should be a wonderful place in a few years' time. Our slipway is finished and ready to haul up the flying boats. It is nearly a one hour ride to the base at Seletar, through rubber plantations.'

The diary entries continued for some time, covering the period up to the flight's arrival date. During this time he tells of having very little to do apart from, 'tinkering with vehicles and working on the "motor boat" which we will use once the aircraft arrive.' There is mention of having seen a Chinese funeral – 'very quaint', and of there being many motor smashes – 'a total of 9 in 4 days.'

Friday Jan 27th was described as a day they had all been looking forward to: I received "Credit" (pay) of $18, or £2-2-0.

Jan 20th, 1928, and mention is made of an aircraft called "Red Rose," which was being flown to Australia by a Capt Lancaster and a Mrs Miller. (*Avro Avian; the first light aircraft to complete the journey from England to Australia, Oct '27 to March '28.*) This had apparently crashed upon landing in Singapore and was being repaired at Seletar: 'All new parts except the fuselage.' The aircraft finally departed on March 8th. Red Rose had not landed at Seletar, for the honour of being the first land plane to touch down there is mentioned in a diary entry for October 7th 1928: 'The "Spirit of Australia" arrived. Unable to take-off from the racecourse with a full load of fuel the aircraft had flown over to Seletar, the first machine to land on the drome.'

The entry for February 28th, 1928 merely states: 'Flying boats landed at 5. Everyone OK. Brought back the Governor of the Singapore from Port Swettenham.' (Actually, Governor of the Straits Settlements, Sir Hugh Clifford. Departure from Port Swettenham had been postponed a day at the Governor's request so as to allow himself and his staff to be able to travel down with the Flight.)

Feb 29th: 'Machines brought up for cleaning and operations started.' After this the entries are few and far between, although on May 8th: 'Machine tested. Went for a trial flight around Seletar, up 20 mins.' And on October 12th, 1928: 'We moved to Seletar into the new barrack block, the finest quarters I have ever been in.' So it seems the hard times were over.

Things were not always pleasant for the aircrews either. In Calcutta, for example, conditions ashore were so primitive that the Commanding Officer moved everyone from the official quarters into an hotel. Reading about it, one could get the impression that the whole trip was an enormous joy ride. They were often treated royally, true, but for a good proportion of the time those crews were living in aircraft which were fitted with few basic luxuries whatever.

The designer of the aircraft, RJ Mitchell – creator of the Schneider Trophy winners, and later to become even more famous for the Spitfire – had gone to considerable lengths to make the Southampton as comfortable as possible for the four man crew, two officers and two airmen. Even so, life aboard would appear to have been quite primitive by today's standards. [As a look around RAF Hendon's magnificently reconstructed hull will reveal.]

On completion of a typical day's journey, the crew would normally change into their working kit at six in the evening: khaki shirt and shorts, or overalls. Supper would typically consist of the tinned variety: stew, potatoes, peas, and if they were lucky, bread and butter. This could be followed by tinned fruit. Exotic local dishes provided the occasional change of diet but basic meals were usually the preferred option.

After the meal, log books would be updated, and a thorough study of the next leg made, on completion of which, everyone would turn in, for although the aircraft were fitted with electric lights, excessive use caused too much drain on the batteries.

Bed could mean a sleeping bag laid out beneath the pilot's seat, or a folding bed on the deck, certainly no Dunlopillo-type luxury here. Nor was a flying boat on the water conducive to a peaceful night. The aircraft moved about, even in calm conditions, frequently jerking at their moorings.

To take advantage of the daylight hours, and in case of any delays, take-offs were always early morning affairs. The crew would rise well before dawn, and after a mug of hot tea would set about their allotted tasks. Toilet facilities were, superficially, very good, a neat lavatory having been installed down at the tail end. Unfortunately, as this was liable to leak during taxying, it was usually left well screwed down, more primitive methods resorted to. This could prove embarrassing if the locals had paddled out in their canoes to see them off!

Breakfast would be a fairly rudimentary affair, often taken in silence for, as Livock recalls, 'At such an early hour, the atmosphere was not conducive to talking.' Preparations would then be made to get underway; preflight checks, unshackling and stowing the mooring pennant, starting and checking the engines. With all four aircraft ready, Sqn/Ldr Livock would turn into wind and bring both Napier Lions up to full power.

Once airborne, the crew members would fall into a steady routine: changing places every hour or so, resting when they could. This continued until they arrived at their destination, by which time, having endured several hours in an open cockpit, with the engines roaring barely feet away, they'd be stone deaf. They tried to overcome this in many ways, but even the plugging of glycerine-soaked cotton wool in their ears and the wearing of helmets with ear flaps proved ineffective. It would take hours for the effects to wear off, which could be awkward, especially when officials had come alongside, wishing to chat to the crew.

Upon alighting, each aircraft would make for a pre-positioned buoy, deploying sea anchors en-route, one either side. These effectively acted as brakes, reducing momentum to a level at which the buoy could be captured; another use was as a crude means of steering. The aircraft was then secured by means of a pennant wire, the engines shut down; flight over, another stage complete.

But the day's work was not yet over, for the aircraft had now to be refuelled – a long and tedious process, considering the amount involved – two hundred and fifty gallons per aircraft – and the method used. Only then would the exhausted crew be available to wade through the numerous receptions and entertainments which were thrust upon them. Life was never easy.

From Calcutta, they routed through Rangoon, Mergui (also in Burma), and eventually, to Penang, Malaya, where they arrived on February 16th. There was to be one further stop, February 27th, at Port Swettenham, west of Kuala Lumpur.

On Tuesday February 28th, 1928, the Flight departed the mangrove-fringed river at Port Swettenham, on the last leg to Seletar. Over Malacca they descended to fly along the sea front, and once again hundreds of the inhabitants rushed out to view the spectacle.

Flying at a height of around one thousand feet, they managed to maintain an average speed of eighty-five mph for the trip. Continuing along the west coast of Malaya, only one slight detour was necessary when they encountered a thunderstorm.

At Singapore they made a one hundred and eighty degree turn over the island before heading back to Seletar, to arrive overhead at 17:10. Here they were welcomed by several hundred Singaporeans who had gathered at the RAF base, and what a unique sight those four aircraft, flying in formation, must have made.

One after the other they alighted on the Johore Straits, opposite the air base, taxied in and made fast to their buoys. A launch then went out

and brought His Excellency Sir Hugh Clifford and his staff ashore, they having flown down with the Flight from Port Swettenham.

Thus was completed the first RAF flight from England to Singapore. Including the month spent at Karachi, they had been travelling for four and a half months, had covered nine thousand five hundred miles in one hundred and forty flying hours. In spite of the Air Ministry's reticence, this feat made headlines in the world's press. The unanimous view was later summed up by the *Daily News* of 30th June, 1928, when, in a special feature, they described the journey as being *'The Greatest Flight in History'*, even if it was wrongly headlined as being *16,500 miles by Naval Squadron*. It went on to say: *These giant air boats – veritable "ironclads" of the sky – have hulls built entirely of metal*, and suggested the flight was *outstanding proof as to the reliability of the British flying boats and their Napier engines*.

Next in line was the flight to and around Australia, a route that was virtually unknown.[17] But first there was work to be done, as Sqn/Ldr Livock later described:

'A set of landing wheels for each aircraft had been shipped out to Singapore, and all four aircraft were hauled onto the concrete apron at the air base. There were no hangars, and the mechanics had to work on the aircraft out in the open in the blazing heat. At the time of our arrival, Seletar was still in the early stages of construction. There were no officers' quarters and no barracks for the airmen. The flight office, or HQ RAF Far East, was a small native attap hut built on stilts over the water. The workshop and stores were also of matting, as were the airmen's quarters. It was all very primitive and inconvenient, but I think everyone enjoyed the feeling that they were pioneers out in the wilds.'

As well as for inspection of aircraft and engines, the stopover in Singapore was also timed to allow the Australian winter to set in, when they could expect favourable winds, the Indian sectors having been timed to coincide with the N-E monsoon for similar reasons.

Whilst up slip at Seletar, it was noted that a couple of swifts were building their nest at the top of S1151's main struts, but it was decided not to disturb them. The nest actually remained there during the air test, birds aboard! They then travelled with the aircraft to Banka Island and, after a trip ashore, rejoined for the next leg. Unfortunately, the nest fell to pieces during a forced landing off Sumatra,[18] the birds last seen heading for shore. Gerry Livock later wrote this up as an article for *Country Life*, but the Air Ministry refused permission for it to be published, on the grounds that it would be bad publicity for people to be given the impression that RAF aircraft were so badly inspected that birds were able to nest in them.

Two and a half months after arriving at Seletar, the same crews set out for Australia on May 21st. They flew along the Indonesian island chain: Sumatra, Java, Bali, Sumbawa – where they refuelled – then on to Kupang, in Dutch Timor and on south. Landfall in Australia was on the west coast, at Roebuck Bay, Broome. After Broome came Port Hedland, described as looking like a film set.

They followed the west coast down to Perth, then barely a small provincial town. After a stopover in Perth – where, due to fever, Livock was forced to remain when the flight departed – they continued south to Albany. Here, after catching the train down, Livock rejoined for the journey east, to Adelaide, Melbourne and Sydney.

Leaving Sydney, they followed the coast north and east, all the way round to Darwin, heading back to Seletar on September 1st, via the Dutch East Indies.

The tour had been an outstanding triumph for the flying boat, whose value had been proven beyond dispute. Grp/Cpt Cave-Brown-Cave had led his team successfully and without any major mishap. All over Australia the airmen had received overwhelming hospitality. At Melbourne in particular, they had the time of their lives, being given virtual freedom of the city. Every single comment was eagerly seized upon, and perhaps the Commanding Officer should have taken heed of an incident at a Perth reception, where he had casually remarked upon the perceived beauty of the West Australian ladies. This made headlines the next day as, "World Fliers think Perth girls wonderful," prompting one Australian to comment, 'You've got yerself into grive trouble talking about Perth girls being pretty. You wite till yer get to Sydnee. Why the girls there'll cutcher brices!'

The Sydney encounter with the press was nowhere near so amusing. With the famous New South Wales hospitality in full swing, the Group Captain was unlucky enough to have his hotel room invaded by the tough Sydney pressmen, before he could bathe and change, which is where his diplomacy let him down. Being quite naturally annoyed at having his privacy disturbed, he told them he had nothing to say, and was anyway too busy to be interviewed. The reporters vented their spite in the stories they wrote. One newspaper in particular chose to make virulent attacks against the visitors. *The gallant birdmen became stuffed shirt pommies overnight*, stated one issue, whilst another featured a childish row of ugly faces across the top of a page, under which was written, Cave-Brown-Cave-Brown-Cave-Brown-Cave. The Group Captain did however receive a lot of sympathy as result of this, the Governor and his Lady going so far as to state that it was an honour to be slanged by the Sydney Press.

September 15th found the Flight once again circling over Seletar, next day's *Straits Times* describing their arrival as follows:

The droning of the great twin-set Napier engines was heard over the air base shortly before ten o'clock, and a few minutes later the graceful outlines of the flying boats, familiar to Singapore people after their appearances over the city last March, were seen. The Flight circled in formation over the Straits and came down in line, making a perfect landing. The weather was dull but fine, and there was no wind. The boat which contained Group Captain HM Cave-Brown-Cave DSO, DFC, and which had a tattered and faded Air Force flag fluttering from its struts, immediately taxied to the slipway. The tide was high and most of the two hundred feet length of this concrete structure was under water. A cheery, "Good morning" to Flight Lieutenant Freeman, commanding the Base party of the Flight – whom the flying men had last seen in Melbourne – and they immediately set to work to get the machine ashore. The spectators then had an opportunity to appreciate the size of these machines at close-quarters. Its all-metal hull fifty feet long, its wings covering a span of seventy feet, and weighing seven tons, the ease with which the first flying boat was brought on to dry land was remarkable. Chassis fitted with monstrous wheels were speedily attached, thirty airmen and Tamil coolies hauled on a rope, and the machine was safely ashore.

One person missing from the welcoming party was Mr Woods, who was convalescing after a severe attack of typhoid.

So ended the main task of the Far East Flight. One further trip had yet to be completed – five thousand miles to Hong Kong and back – but first, in line with Air Ministry orders, one aircraft (Gerry Livock's S1149) was returned to England to allow a detailed examination to be made by Supermarine, after which it became a star attraction at the Olympia Air Show of 1929. A replacement aircraft (S1127) had meanwhile been shipped out to Seletar, this being reassembled upon arrival and painted with its one black band, thus bringing the flight back up to strength.

Preparations went ahead, but conditions at Seletar were still difficult. As the hangars were not yet complete, crews faced the task of overhauling aircraft which stood on the concrete pan under a fierce tropical sun. There was also a daily rainstorm to contend with, which didn't help matters, the men being continually soaked, either with sweat or rain. A particularly difficult task lay in replacing hundreds of corroded rivets. This called for the riveter to lay on his back on the hot concrete, there to hammer each rivet into place. It is reported that a party of visitors to Seletar watched the rivetting taking place while another airman fried eggs on the bare concrete nearby.

The China Sea section of the cruise began with visits to Kuching and Labuan, two locations in which RAF bases were to be developed in later years. After this, the aircraft were flown via the Philippines to RAF Kai Tak, Hong Kong, being welcomed by a flight of Fairey IIID land planes. (Following that *Pegasus* survey of 1924, Kai Tak became an RAF base in March 1927, the first in the Far East.)

The return flight began on November 29th, taking a southern route along the Indo-China coastline, then overland to Bangkok. The final leg eventually took them from Penang to Singapore, where, on December 11th, they landed safely back at Seletar.

For Grp/Cpt Cave-Brown-Cave the trip had proved to be a triumph. The same crews had flown and lived together for fourteen months, yet there had been scarcely a word spoken in anger. He had led his men through twenty-five different countries and they had covered over twenty-seven thousand miles at an average speed of eighty

S1127, the replacement aircraft for S1149 - shipped back to Supermarine for detailed examination - is brought up slip for servicing.

Vernon J W Lee collection

Superb Gerry Livock shot of the FEF at anchor on the River Euphrates at Hinaidi, 07:30hrs 8th Nov 1927.

Imperial War Museum Ref: Q81995

mph, much of it over largely unknown territory. All this had been achieved with the bare minimum of radio facilities, and mostly without the use of any accurate maps whatsoever. In fact the entire voyage had to a certain extent been a daring experiment; and it had succeeded magnificently.

January 1929: the Far East Flight disbanded to become 205 Squadron. Grp/Cpt Cave-Brown-Cave departed for England, leaving Sqn/Ldr Livock to assume command of both the station, and the newly-formed squadron, Seletar's first. On February 28th, Chief of Air Staff, Lord Trenchard, wrote personally to Sqn/Ldr Livock, congratulating him on his AFC, the first medal to be awarded at Seletar. Year's end saw Cave-Brown-Cave return, to assume command of RAF Singapore, by which name Seletar was known when it officially became an RAF station on January 1st 1930.

Heinz 57 to hand, W/Op LAC Williams prepares dinner aboard Supermarine Southampton S1149. 1927.
Imperial War Museum Ref: Q82023

A 205 Sqn Southampton
at anchor off a Malayan
beach. *RA "Scotty" Powell*

A group of 1935 airmen
model the latest line in
working dress - beret by
Bell helmets perhaps. The
aircraft is a Hawker
Horsley.
RA "Scotty" Powell

Gerry Livock's Fairey IIID is recovered aboard HMS Pegasus after a survey flight over the Seletar area in 1924.
Imperial War Museum *Ref: Q82189*

Jean Batten arrives at Seletar in Gipsy Moth G-AARB,1934/35.
RA "Scotty" Powell

Ill-fated Australian of the 'Golden Era' Jimmy Melrose was to disappear whilst engaged in the search for "Southern Cross" over the Bay of Bengal.

RA "Scotty" Powell

Typist turned aviatrix Amy Johnson arrives at Singapore's only airport in 1930, the joint military/civil facility at Seletar. Her aircraft the DH Gipsy Moth G-AAAH - which she named Jason.
RAF Museum Hendon AC 71/23/30

Douglas Fairbanks Snr passes through Seletar with Lady Ashley his travelling companion (below). **RA "Scotty" Powell**

Regular Singapore visitor, Noel Coward particularly enjoyed his visits to the Seletar Yacht Club. **RA "Scotty" Powell**

CHAPTER FOUR

Asian Airport: Record Breakers, Personalities & Scheduled Services

"Looking into the future, I expect to see Singapore become one of the largest and most important airports in the world. It is on the direct route to Australia and is bound to develop as a nodal point for air services in the course of time."

• • • • • • • • • •

S o said Sir Cecil Clementi, Governor of the Straits Settlements from 1930-31 during a speech to the Legislative Assembly Council Proceedings, Singapore on 31st August 1931.

If only he could see Changi today...

It was whilst the Far East Flight was on its way to Hong Kong that Seletar airfield had its first civilian visitor – October 7th, 1928 – the *Spirit of Australia*, a Ryan Brougham (*Spirit of St Louis* look-alike) which carried the registration G-AUIX. It was piloted by Captain Frank Hurley, an Australian, and F/O Moir, two of a number of adventurous aviators pioneering the air routes of the world at that time, and this was just the beginning. Following in his wake, many others called in over the next nine years. Seletar, as well as being an important refuelling point for the world's greatest pilots, was also to assume the role of becoming Singapore's first international airport.

With no dedicated landing ground previously available, the island had lagged well behind as far as international air traffic was concerned. Now, upon completion of Seletar's grass strip, and with permission being granted for the airfield also to

be used for civil traffic in 1929, things were about to change. Assisted by the Straits Settlements Government, local enthusiasts had grouped together to form the Singapore Flying Club, which in itself played an important part in the development of civil aviation in the area.

The official instructors were military pilots stationed at Seletar, with Flight Lieutenant Carnegie becoming captain of the "first seaplane club in the British Empire, and particularly the first in the tropics," for, despite the newly completed strip, the club's activities were for some years largely limited to seaplane flying, utilising a floatplane version of the De Havilland Cirrus Moth.

One of Seletar's earlier civilian visitors – landing there in the aircraft that was to become synonymous with his name was the man who would become known throughout the world as "Smithy." Sir Charles Kingsford-Smith is generally recognized as having been one of the greatest pilots of his time. (The story goes that Kingsford – originally a Christian name in the family – was tacked on whilst the family were living in Canada when Smithy was just five. The street in which the Australian Smiths lived also housed six other Smiths, so to make the postman's job easier, the surname was hyphenated.)

In recognition of his services to aviation, Smithy was honoured with a knighthood by King George V in June 1932. Despite this, official recognition by an Australian Government was a long time coming, Smithy's portrait being selected to grace the new decimal currency twenty dollar note in February 1966. His name is also perpetuated in Sydney's international airport; the name being changed from Mascot to Kingsford-Smith.

Smithy's first visit to Seletar, apart from being unplanned, was in his most famous aircraft, the tri-engined Fokker VII monoplane which he had named, *Southern Cross*. In this, he and his friend, Charles Ulm, had flown from Darwin – on the north-west coast of Australia – direct to Singapore. Unaware of the construction taking place at Seletar, they made for the old race-course, which had until recently been used by all aircraft intending to land on the Island. However, with the racecourse out of commission, *Southern Cross* began circling the area, its crew engaged in a desperate attempt to find a landing ground. Personnel at Seletar, lacking communication with the aircraft, used their initiative. They lit a huge petrol fire, which soon attracted Smithy's attention. Heading north to investigate, a quick pass soon reassured him, and he descended to make a flawless landing. Despite having spent the last nineteen hours in the air, the two men now insisted on a late night out to view the sights.

Next morning, *Southern Cross* departed Seletar at the crack of dawn, narrowly averting disaster in the process. Heavily-loaded take-offs with minimal margins were one of the hazards of pioneering flights such as this, and even though they used the full length of the airstrip, they cleared the ditch at the end by mere inches. Trail blazing was certainly not for the faint-hearted!

Smithy's next visit to Seletar was in October 1930 when, on a solo record-breaking flight from England to Australia – in an Avro Avian named *Southern Cross Junior* – he covered the ten thousand plus miles in nine days and twenty-two hours, breaking the existing record by a margin that was measured in days.

Numerous fliers made attempts on this record during the next few years, almost all calling in at Seletar; exciting times for airmen based at the camp. Amongst the visitors were to be seen the likes of Jim Mollison, Bert Hinkler, Francis Chichester – also eventually to be knighted, and

first man to sail around the world single-handed – Charles Ulm himself, and HF Broadbent, to name but a few. Although, at the time, it's unlikely that any of these names would have been familiar to the RAF personnel, the fame came later; they'd probably have been looked upon as adventurers. But not Kingsford-Smith, for he became a regular and familiar visitor, not just to the RAF station, around the island, too. Flights during which Kingsford-Smith was likely to have landed at Seletar:

■ Australia – UK, June 25/July8 1929. Southern Cross – Fokker VII.

■ UK – Australia, solo, Oct 9/19 1930. Southern Cross Junior – Avro Avian.

■ UK – Australia, (assist airmail) April/May 1931, Southern Cross.

■ Australia – UK, solo, Sept 24/Oct 7 1931. Southern Cross Minor – Avro Avian

■ Australia – UK, 1st airmail, Dec 3/16 1931. Southern Star – Avro X (Fokker VII built under licence by AV Roe. ANA, the airline set up by Smithy and Ulm, favoured this British-built version so as to avoid paying the import duty that was required on foreign aircraft, ie, the Fokker.

■ UK – Australia, airmail, Jan 7/19 1932. Southern Star.

■ UK – Australia, solo, Oct 4/11 1933. Miss Southern Cross – Percival Gull.

Then there were the ladies who were to attract world interest in the thirties. The first aviatrix to touch down at Seletar was probably the best known of them all; the future Mrs Jim Mollison.

At the age of twenty-seven, and with only eighty hours experience to her name, Hull-born ex-typist, Amy Johnson, set out from Croydon in her second-hand Gipsy Moth, *Jason*, a brave attempt to fly solo to Australia. And although she failed on the London-Australia record, it is worth recording that she broke the existing record to India, making Karachi in six days. From there on,

Charles Ulm (L) and (Sir) Charles Kingsford-Smith (R) alongside Southern Cross. Obviously a posed photograph; they certainly didn't fly dressed like this. Tom McWilliams, their Radio Op, is between them.
Vernon J.W. Lee collection

things did not go well, her legendary battles against all odds now part of aviation folklore.

Mid-May 1930, saw her heading towards Seletar, and the people of Singapore awaited news of her progress. Her arrival, escorted by two Moth floatplanes of the Singapore Flying Club, was reported by the *Straits Times* in an article, headed simply "Miss Amy Johnson":

> *There was no fuss or bother at Seletar, no frenzied shouting, no wild running about, no vast crowds getting in the way of the machine, or mobbing of the weary pilot. The two hundred people who gathered at the 'magnificent' Royal Air Force aerodrome – which by the way, Miss Johnson praised to the skies as the finest she has so far met in the East – welcomed the lone flier for all the world as though she had just come over by car from Johore to make the presentation at a school prize-giving.*
>
> *As she stepped from her travel-stained Gipsy Moth, everyone clapped hands sedately and the men then gravely raised their topees, while their womenfolk waited their turn to hold her by the hand and whisper their mixed congratulation and heart-felt sympathy. Miss Johnson responded to these kindly overtures with a happy, radiant smile, which clearly indicated how thoroughly at home she felt – despite the contrast between her oil-stained flying kit and the bright "confections" of*

> *Singapore ... Miss Johnson has been exceedingly unlucky.*
>
> *The monsoon has, this year, established itself much earlier than usual and she ran into storms which normally she would not have encountered so early in May. Her fight against blinding rain of tropical intensity, and head winds of gale strength, had her blind, groping 10,000 feet up amidst clouds more dense than a London fog for a pass through the mountains of Moulmein, her nerve-racking experience when following the south coast to Singora only 50 feet up without goggles, and with sheet rain tearing the eyes from her head, and finally her horrifying ordeal at Singora ...(where she had to take-off from a crowd-lined road, with little forward visibility) read like chapters from a modern Iliad of the air. She cannot beat Bert Hinkler's record now (15½ days at that time) but she has won for herself a niche in aviation history which will ensure that her name will live forever. Singapore is proud to have known her for a few short hours.*

Amy Johnson eventually made a perfect landing at 13:55 hours on a Sunday afternoon. After seeing her aircraft into the hangar, issuing instructions on refuelling and re-oiling, she left to clean up and have a meal in the Officers' Mess. A special recreational hut had been re-arranged for her use and she spent the night there. Thereafter known as 'the Amy Johnson hut' it was for many years used for Sunday evening services.

With the following day's forecast being very bad, a delegation headed by the Officer Commanding, Grp/Cpt Cave-Brown-Cave, pleaded with her to delay her departure. Amy confessed later, 'It was considered madness to go on, but I had already lost time and was determined to continue. My worst trouble began soon after leaving Singapore. Over the Java Sea, storm and rain beat my plane down until it only just skimmed the waves. I expected every minute to be my last. It only required the plane to touch a wave and – goodbye! I would not take on the trip again in monsoon time.'

Amy managed to battle through, touching down in Australia on May 24th, covering the ten thousand three hundred and forty miles from England in nineteen and a half days. The news was celebrated by the whole world, and congratulatory messages, including one from the King and Queen, poured in. Amy Johnson, shortly to be honoured with a CBE, had become the first woman aviator to fly solo from England to Australia.

By November 1934, Englishmen, Scott and Black, flying the DH88 Comet racer, had reduced the record to just seventy hours and fifty-four minutes. The following year, Sir Charles Kingsford-Smith set off on what he had said would be his final attempt. He was accompanied by co-pilot, Tommy Petheridge, in the Lockheed Altair he had named *Lady Southern Cross*. (All Smithy's aircraft carried similar names: *Miss Southern Cross* was a Percival Gull, with *Southern Cross Junior* and *Southern Cross Minor* being Avro Avians.

Departing Hamble, England, early on the morning of November 6th, 1935, they arrived in Greece eight hours later. They continued to make good time as far as Baghdad, but a sudden sandstorm on the leg to Allahabad dropped them behind schedule. Next day, *Lady Southern Cross* set out for Seletar. She overflew Calcutta's Dum Dum airport at nine that evening, and was later reported as flying on course over Akyab, Burma. She was never seen again.

On the morning of November 9th, with no news having been received of the aircraft's position, search parties were organized. Two of 205 Squadron's Singapore III flying boats (which had only recently replaced the Southamptons of the original Far East Flight) and four of the 36/100 Squadrons' Vickers Vildebeests, took off from Seletar. Numerous ships and other aircraft also helped scour the waters of the Bay of Bengal, without luck. The Altair was last sighted by HF Broadbent, who had reported it passing him over the Bay of Bengal. He said 'jets of flame were spurting from *Lady Southern Cross'* exhausts, and that things looked serious.'

Australian pilot Jimmy Melrose abandoned his solo attempt on the England- Australia record so as to help. Melrose searched for four days – on the fifth day he too disappeared.

A widespread search continued over the next two weeks, but eventually, Air Commodore Sidney Smith, AOC RAF Far East, reluctantly recalled his aircraft, the presumption being that by now the missing airmen were dead.

These tragedies naturally made headlines around the world, but people were reluctant to give up hope. For some time, many believed a miracle might occur, and that the missing airmen would turn up. The Australian Government even had fifty thousand leaflets printed in five native dialects, having them scattered over vast areas of jungle. A reward of five hundred pounds was offered for information on the whereabouts, dead or alive, of Kingsford-Smith and Petheridge. The aircraft and its occupants were never seen again.

These disasters affected morale at Royal Air Force Seletar. They had done what they could, to no avail; a personal friend was gone forever. Australian newspapers carried black banner headlines, and a whole nation mourned . Kingsford-Smith's exploits had provided the inspiration for many other aviation pioneers to follow in his footsteps, perhaps none more so than Jean Batten. Her first flight had been with Smithy, in *Southern Cross*, thus sparking her interest in aviation; the New Zealander eventually became another famous aviatrix to visit Seletar when she made her record-breaking flights in 1934, 1936 (all the way to New Zealand), and again in 1937 when, in a staggering performance, she flew from Darwin to Lympe, Kent, in just five days, eighteen hours and sixteen minutes, smashing the existing record set up by HF Broadbent five months earlier.

Once again London went wild, giving Miss Batten an enthusiastic welcome. Huge crowds lined the streets to celebrate her achievement in what was generally regarded to be a man's job. Commenting years later, an air force officer who was at Seletar in the thirties is said to have paid the following tribute to Jean Batten: 'I've served in two wars, the first in the infantry in France, but in my memory, she was the bravest human I have seen.' (After disappearing in her later years, Jean Batten CBE, was to die in Majorca in 1982. Unknown locally, she was committed to a pauper's grave, the world unaware for five years. In her will, discovered later, she had requested a cremation in London, her ashes to be interred at Auckland Airport. Due to the nature of her burial, this was no longer possible, although her most famous aircraft, Percival Gull, G-ADPR, is now displayed in the Jean Batten terminal at Auckland International airport.)

Whilst these pioneers were capturing the headlines and the imagination of the world, the airlines had been watching, waiting, developing. Once it became apparent that the journeys were possible, commercial interests came to the fore. Services were already well established in Europe and the United States, then the Dutch East India Company was granted permission from the Straits Government to start a service to Malaya, using the runway at Seletar. By early 1930 the arrangements were complete and on February 11th the first commercial flight landed in Singapore. A powerful, three-engined Fokker F18

of the Dutch East India Airways Company carried a cargo of flowers and fresh fruit from the Java highlands. It also carried the first airmail to Singapore, along with eight fare-paying passengers. The seven hundred mile, seven hour trip from Batavia (Jakarta), revolutionized communications in the area. As the famous Dutch pilot, Mr JJ Moll[19] said, 'In other words, air transport makes it possible to travel from Singapore to Batavia in seven hours, as against thirty-eight hours by the fastest steamship service. When the regular service is started I anticipate that the time will be cut by another hour and a half.'

An appreciation of the airfield at Seletar was made by Mr H Niewenhuis, the manager of the Dutch East India Airways Company, who stated: 'I would like to say now that it is the finest landing ground I have ever seen. Mr Woods, who is responsible for it, has certainly done wonders to turn hilly jungle into such a perfect landing ground. I think he must be very proud of his splendid achievement.'

The Java Air Service was officially inaugurated at Seletar the following month, in the presence of the Governor of the Straits Settlements, Sir Cecil Clementi. Then, in April 1930, the Singapore Government announced it had

Kallang airport's official opening on June 12th 1937 drew a 27 aircraft contingent from Seletar, all visible in this photograph: four Short Singapores overhead, the rest little more than specks. **RA "Scotty" Powell**

decided on a site for a civil aerodrome which would form the final link in the chain through Malaya. Due to the site being low-lying and swampy, completion was expected to take four years, so in the meantime, commercial traffic would utilize the facilities at RAF Seletar.

The service was a great success, and plans were soon in hand to try something more ambitious. Eventually, on April 4th, 1931, the first mail bags bound for Singapore were dispatched from London. Mail was also picked up en-route on this experimental flight, and twelve days later the first British air mail landed safely at Seletar. The aircraft used was the Imperial Airways, DH66 Hercules biplane, *City of Cairo*.[20] On April 16th, the *Straits Times* printed a vivid description of the aircraft's arrival:

The sun was setting in a blaze of glory over the RAF aerodrome at Seletar yesterday afternoon, when a crowd of some 300 to 400 people, all tense with excitement at the expectant arrival of the Imperial Airways Hercules aeroplane which was carrying the mail from England to Singapore, heard in the distance, the drone of engines of the Goliath of the air. Some five or six minutes later it swept down with all the grace of a "chummy" Puss Moth.

It was a magnificent sight. As the plane drew nearer, and the drone of the engines developed into a mighty roar, we could see (writes a Straits Times representative) that here was a species of aircraft bigger than any that had previously landed on Seletar aerodrome .

She circled the 'drome once, and having got her bearings, sank gracefully to earth, outlined against a typical Malayan sunset, some 200 yards from the fringe of the awaiting crowd. Almost instantly the crowd moved forward, but as quickly there came a full-throated roar from the "City of Cairo's" triple engines, and the spectators stepped back as the plane taxied towards the awaiting petrol lorry.

It was at this moment that the spectators began to realize what a span of 79 ft 6 in, and an overall length of 56 ft, really means in an aeroplane. Some 60 or 70 Europeans gazed in silent admiration, while a large crowd of Asiatics looked upon a scene which amazed them.

The postal authorities were taken by surprise, too, for they had not received confirmation of the aircraft's departure from Alor Star, on Malaya's northern border. Despite this communications failure, Malaya heartily welcomed the experimental flight, expressing the desire that it would become a regular

Captain Parmentier refuels the commercial DC2 at Seletar during the 1938 England-Australia Air Race in which he finished 2nd to the Black/Scott DH88 Comet, a purebred racer. **RA "Scotty" Powell**

Swimming pool, 1935 - a fenced off area in the Straits, directly in front of the yacht club. Note the rather precarious-looking walkway, the only means of access.   *RA "Scotty" Powell*

weekly service. Stamp collectors, meanwhile, endured several frustrating hours, but at least they did not suffer the anxious moments their antipodean colleagues were to experience, disaster almost putting an end to the whole venture.

The *City of Cairo* left Seletar with fifty thousand letters destined for Australia. Unfortunately, the aircraft encountered strong headwinds and ran out of fuel, making a forced landing in Dutch Timor. There were no casualties on this trial flight, and the mails were saved. Our old friend, Charles Kingsford-Smith, later delivered these safely, flying over in *Southern Cross* to pick them up.

As the air services developed, so the facilities at RAF Seletar improved, the Government of the Straits Settlements eventually placing an order for a large modern hangar to be erected. This all-steel structure was over three hundred feet long, one hundred and sixty feet in width, with a height of thirty feet to the cross girders. The hangar was first used by the Dutch airmail aircraft, being taken over by the RAF once the civil airport at Kallang opened. (Later used by Seletar's first Maintenance Unit, No 151, it still survives today.)

It was a November day in 1932 that the Air Service managed to attract an unexpected visitor

to Seletar. This created great excitement, at least for the few fleeting moments he was actually on the base; Douglas Fairbanks, Senior, one of Hollywood's leading idols of the time, decided he was in a hurry. Arriving in Singapore by sea, he was rushed ashore by fast launch, driven to Seletar, and bundled aboard a plane bound for Java. Even though it all happened quickly – news spreads rapidly among servicemen – hundreds managed to catch a glimpse of the celebrity. Fairbanks had been on his way to shoot a film, before joining his wife, Mary Pickford, in Egypt. Strange that he just happened to be travelling with a Lady Ashley. Now, after seeing a photograph of Lady Ashley, I wonder just who it was those airmen were really after a glimpse of?

But the air base was now a major airport, and during this period, a host of other stars and celebrities also passed through Seletar. Noel Coward was one of the most famous. As a frequent visitor, to both the base and the yacht club, he was often a guest of the Air Officer Commanding, staying in the house which, in later years, would be occupied by the Station Commander.

Charlie Chaplin and Paulette Goddard also staged through Seletar, as did Mrs Lawrence – mother of Lawrence of Arabia – and Chief Scout, Lord Baden-Powell. Such people – along with various Maharajahs, Princes, Sultans, Prime

Ministers and even Kings who used the airlines – ensured that Seletar's military community never became bored.

As the amount of civil traffic steadily increased, so another milestone in Seletar's history was recorded: May 3rd 1933, KLM's Fokker F18, *The Pelican* – a sixteen seater – arrived from Batavia at 16:30 hrs. Seletar thus became a staging point on the world's longest air route of the time – Batavia to Amsterdam. It was now possible to travel from Singapore to London in just seven days. This auspicious occasion was marked by the presence of the Governor, and two hundred guests, along with many others, KLM having issued invitations to the public in Singapore.

In June it was the turn of Imperial Airways, when *Astraea*, an AW15 Atalanta class aircraft touched down when on a special "goodwill" flight to Australia. The inaugural scheduled service between London and Singapore, again using the AW15 Atalanta class aircraft, was to arrive in December. Though it carried no passengers, the aircraft did bring a large consignment of mail from Europe and places en-route to Singapore. The return trip was scheduled for December 31st, this time, also carrying passengers: one hundred and eighty pounds sterling one way, three hundred and thirty-four return.[21] Another year was to pass before the service was finally extended all the way to Australia.

Not that this had any effect on the military side at Seletar, for a tour was a tour – up to five years in those days. Anyway, no serviceman could even contemplate that kind of money. Airmen took leave locally, those with transport probably touring around Malaya, for there were excellent Government run rest houses dotted about the place, some quite palatial, all very cheap.

Organization by the airlines at Seletar was to become streamlined and efficient. The following verbatim description of what happened when an airliner made a scheduled night landing, appeared in the *Straits Budget*:

On the landing ground at the RAF Base, which serves as a civilian aerodrome as well, *night flares are laid out in "L" formation; all is ready for the plane.*

Ambulance and fire Brigade stand by in case of emergency. The red Post Office van is waiting for the mails. The landing staff stroll about with their eyes on the cloudy sky. Then just above the horizon a pinprick of light is detected. At first it looks like a red star, but it is moving nearer.

'There she is,' someone remarks, and now the hum of the engines can be heard very clearly, and soon, very soon, the plane has begun to encircle the aerodrome.

She is high up tonight – nearly 2,000 feet – but she quickly comes down as she flies gracefully around. Then there is the most spectacular moment of all as shortly before landing the pilot lights flares to help him to land.[22] Still a few hundred feet up but quickly coming down, the plane moves on with the flares throwing a bright white light downwards from the wings. She seems to be on fire.[23] The machine banks and, with her flares still burning, runs into the stretch of landing ground. Illuminated by the aerodrome lights, she lands down the long arm of the "L". Towards the foot, she is down, bumping ever so slightly.

Very soon the plane is manoeuvring across the aerodrome. The ground staff rush to help and tonight they decide to haul her with ropes up the slipway [sic],[24] towards the hangar, instead of letting her taxi under her own power. In the hangar, lights show the massiveness of the monoplane quite clearly. In the darkness outside, she looked like a broad-winged bird swooping to earth, but now she looks more like what she is – a giant passenger-carrying airliner. No passengers this trip, but officials are soon checking the mails. One bag of mail, apparently for the air base, is taken away on a bicycle. Small parcels and small bags are carried out of the plane and laid out for the Post Office van. A precious cargo which has been brought from England in a ten-ton machine for forty cents per half-ounce.

The Martin and OSA Johnson Sikorsky S39CS amphibian, now renamed 'Spirit of Africa & Borneo' makes an appearance at Seletar in September 1935. They had to call in at Singapore to apply for permits to visit Borneo, the aircraft being delayed with a fuel problem. **RA 'Scotty' Powell**

Fokker F18 used during the future KLM's inaugural service linking Batavia (Jakarta) in the Dutch East Indies and Malaya - Singapore, Seletar. **RA Powell**

An unusual visitor. A US Navy Grumman JF2, known as the "Duck". This one, tail number 9524 was based on the minesweeper-converted-to-seaplane-tender USS Heron, operating out of the Philippines **RA Powell**

DH86A used by Qantas on routes between Singapore and Darwin during 1935. **RA "Scotty" Powell**

A regular Australia to England service began on December 10th, 1934, opened in Brisbane by His Royal Highness the Duke of Gloucester. A week later, Imperial Airways were flying east from Seletar, thus completing their route through to Australia, a trip that took four days.

The following February saw Qantas (Queensland and Northern Territories Aerial Service) assume control of operations on the Darwin-Singapore sector with DH 86A aircraft, and from 16th May, 1936, the company began operating a twice-weekly service from Brisbane to Singapore-Seletar. For the first three months, most of these flights were operated by Imperial Airways, until the Australian airline was able to supply its own crews, Jimmy Youell, a pilot of some renown, often to be found at the controls.

With all this activity taking place, things were becoming somewhat hectic on the base, but that was about to change. Work had been progressing on the new civil airport at Kallang for some years, and Seletar's role as an Asian airport – as opposed to a pure military base – was almost at an end.

November 21st, 1935 saw a flight of Hawker Ospreys off the aircraft carrier, HMS *Hermes*, over the Kallang area when they were caught in a tropical storm. The Ospreys, pride of the Fleet Air Arm (at this time, still under the control of the RAF), encountered extreme turbulence.

They managed to avert disaster by landing on the as yet unfinished airfield, thus becoming the first aircraft to use Singapore's civilian airport.

Another fierce storm, in March 1937, was to afford the great Dutch pilot, Captain K D Parmentier, the honour of landing the first civilian aircraft at Kallang. He was flying a KLM DC3 airliner from Batavia to Seletar, en-route to Europe, when a radio message informed him that the weather had deteriorated, and he should not attempt a landing at Seletar due to the airfield being awash. The only remaining option was the new and empty airfield to the south, and after completing a cautionary circuit, Parmentier touched down.

On June 12th, Governor of the Straits Settlements, Sir Shenton Thomas (after whom Singapore's financial district, Shenton Way, was later named) completed his address, fired a signal rocket, and declared the civil airport to be officially open. Imperial Airways had flown the Governor over from Seletar, accompanied by an escort of twenty-seven service machines, flying over to participate in the display which followed the opening. Next day, all airline movements were transferred to Kallang, leaving Seletar to assume its intended role, that of a military base.

The station had played an invaluable part in the development of civil aviation, not only in

Hawker Osprey makes a low pass over the Padang during a parade, St Andrews in the background.

SELETAR – CROWNING GLORY

Singapore, but in the expansion of routes to the Far East and beyond. Her availability had enabled Singapore to benefit from the rapid growth in air transport, and to become the hub for flights to this part of the world, development that could have been seriously impeded had not the facilities at Seletar been available. Statistics, published for 1937, show this growth vividly. In 1934, eight hundred and ninety-six passengers passed through Seletar, with slightly over twenty-one thousand pounds of mail being dispatched overseas from there. The figures for 1936 read: two thousand and ninety-five passengers, and almost fifty-three thousand pounds of mail.

Aviation was to be the cause of dramatic changes in Malaya, perhaps even accelerating the urge towards nationalism. It certainly offered an improved way of life of the European community who, previous to the introduction of air travel, had been lucky if they could take leave in England every five years – their alternative being a trip to the Cameron Highlands, where the air was fresh and cool. Out on their plantations, they were unlikely to see a fellow European for months on end, so Singapore, with its grand hotels and lifestyle, became the Mecca to which a pilgrimage was made whenever possible.

The boom in aviation changed all that. Now the wealthy began travelling *through* Singapore, on the way to visit England. English newspapers were now days old, rather than weeks or months. With these changes came a change in outlook. Change was no doubt inevitable, but there is equally no doubt about the part Seletar had played in this change. In fact, in her civilian guise, she had exceeded all expectations. So much for the civilian side of things; let us now turn our attention to affairs of a military nature.

The gang "Up country" in Malaya enjoy a cooling dip. RA "Scotty" Powell

Scotty Powell and friends set out in his Lea Francis for a weekend in Malacca. Owning a car of any kind was a guarantee that you would have plenty of friends. RA "Scotty" Powell

Before and after shots of Hawker Horsley floatplane S1445 making a not too successful touchdown...

RA "Scotty" Powell

Aerodrome and Marine Airport Facilities: Karachi to Singapore.			
Conventional Signs LL. Landing ground suitable for all weathers L. Landing ground uncertain in wet weather. E. Emergency landing ground. C. Customs. H. Hangar.		*Conventional Signs* P. Refuelling. W. Wireless Telegraphy: long and/or short wave. M. Meteorology. A. Accommodation. T. Telegraph or telephone.	
Aerodrome and Alighting Area	Situation and Size	Accommodation	Remarks
Singapore. (Seletar.) LL., A., T., P., M. C., H., W. Sheet No...............0.7 No. of sheets............8 Date issued.....30.7.34 Authority.................G.S Date replaced or amended.........15.2.36	*Long.* : 103° 52' E. *Lat.* : 1° 25' N. *Altitude*: 10 ft. *Size*: Diameter 1,000 yds. 7 miles N. of Singapore town.	*Aircraft*: R.A.F. hangars; one civil hangar. *Personnel*: Hotels in Singa- pore.	*Markings*: Centre circle and angle flats. *Surface*: Excellent grass surface through- out the year. *Obstructions*: Hangar and camp build- ings to the E.; trees up to 40 feet high, and Officers' Mess to S. W/T masts to E. and S. *Refuelling*: A.P. Co's underground in- stallation on aerodrome. *Lighting*: Flares only. *Meteorological*: 1st order station; complete weather reports available. *Wireless*: Call sign: G.E.O. Wavelength: 333 k/cs D/F. None at present. Marconi Adock to be installed.

This sheet is the property of IMPERIAL AIRWAYS.

Seletar memorabilia.

CHAPTER FIVE

Settling In: Politics, Rebellion, & Showing the Flag

"I doubt whether there were many people who realized when they were enjoying the social activities of Singapore, Kuala Lumpur, and Rangoon, that they were seeing the last flickering lights of the way of life immortalized by Kipling."

(from *With Prejudice*, by Marshal of the Royal Air Force, Lord Tedder.)

• • • • • • • • • • •

One of those occasions when history was seen to repeat itself occurred in 1929, for June of that year saw Labour being returned to office, with a reduction in defence spending again being declared as their main aim: "A vigorous pursuit of disarmament," was how they termed it. Once more, overseas commitments were targeted to bear the brunt of such pruning. In fact, the left-wing element favoured total withdrawal from the Far East; in a time of mass unemployment, along with a crisis of national proportions, a view that was thought to be supported by a large percentage of the population.

Luckily, having no overall majority in the Commons, and with contracts for the development of bases in Singapore having already been signed and sealed, Labour were somewhat restricted on this front. Still, expenditure on Seletar was cut to the bare minimum, work on developing the base slowing considerably. So it was – at a time of growing international tension, with many countries openly rebuilding their military might – that Britain's politicians were

again seen to be burying their heads in the sand. As Prime Minister, Mr Ramsay MacDonald, was reported to have told the United States in January 1930: 'During the First World War, Britain produced no less than three thousand three hundred front-line aircraft, and with three hundred thousand personnel in service, had created one of the strongest air forces in the world.' He then went on to say, 'After the war, this powerful weapon was virtually scrapped, and today, the front-line strength of the Royal Air Force is no more than seven hundred and seventy-two machines, with manpower at thirty-one thousand. The air fleets of the other great powers far outnumber us. Could there,' he asked, 'be more striking evidence of a will for peace in the British people?'

But events were moving fast, the leaders of certain countries either not willing, or able, to heed these self-sacrificing gestures from Britain. The National Socialists were gaining power in Germany, whilst in Italy and Spain it was the Fascists. Extremism was the word in Japan, and in Burma the discordant voice of a religious fanatic was to be heard, his appeal apparently timed so as to profit by the nationalistic fervour which was beginning to embrace various other countries in the area. And it was to Burma that some of Seletar's aircraft were soon to be deployed.

On July 10th, 1930, the CO at Seletar received a cable from the Air Ministry advising that a civil aircraft was reported to have been in difficulties one hundred miles south east of Akyab. It continued: "Assist search by sending flying boats. Take reasonable steps without undue risks."

'Without undue risks!' Sqn/Ldr Livock was said to have retorted. 'To fly fifteen hundred miles through some of the worst weather in the world to look for a Moth in jungle-covered mountains!' But fly he did, and after twenty-four hours fraught with danger they landed at Akyab, only to be informed by a harassed District Commissioner that the airmen had been found; one alive, the other having died in the jungle. He then added: 'I do wish you people wouldn't come *doing your stunts* here at this time of the year.' Livock says he was too tired to point out that, while perhaps agreeing with him about the civilian pilots, our flight hardly came in the category of suicidal folly. This was certainly true. For after a series of adventures brought on by cyclonic weather, they were not to arrive back at Seletar for eight days. Much of that time having been spent anchored on a river, miles from civilization and out of radio contact; in itself a worry to the authorities at Seletar.

The murder of a forest officer on December 30th, 1930, was to signal the start of the Burmese rebellion; a seemingly half-baked, ill-organised rather comical affair that eventually turned into anything but.[25] It was, in fact, the beginning of Burma's fight for freedom from British rule. It was also to provide Seletar's squadrons with their first real enemy.

The uprising was led by an ex-monk called Saya San, who lay claim to great magical powers. Collecting together a few followers from the villages around the Tharrawaddy, he had them tattooed with a special mark between their shoulder blades. He then sold them pills which, he claimed, would make them invulnerable to bullets.

The amazing thing about this rebellion was that, despite the suicidal attacks on British machine gun positions resulting in numerous deaths, support for Saya San actually increased. To many indigenous Burmese, he became a romantic figure, the conflict dragging on for over a year.

Inevitably, it seemed, Sqn/Ldr Livock was again in the thick of things almost immediately. En-route from Seletar to India – to report on the suitability of a certain stretch of water for flying boat operations – he landed in Rangoon the following day. Here he was approached by Mr Leach, Chief Secretary to the Burmese Government, and asked if he would overfly rebel-dominated areas to "show the flag." Unofficially, Livock and his crew flew a couple of sorties before departing for Delhi. Whilst there, he requested, and received, the AOC's permission to step up operations on the return trip. A series of observation and leaflet-dropping flights were made over the following days; hundreds of leaflets showering down from the skies. Apart from offering "A reward of five thousand rupees ... to anyone bringing in Saya San..." They also advised that "The rebellion in Tharrawaddy has been suppressed. Many of the rebels have been killed and many more captured. Do not believe those persons who say they are able to make you bullet-proof by means of charms and incantations. There is no drug and no charm which can protect you from the guns of Government. Come in quickly and hand over your arms. The Government only wants to punish the leaders who instigated and misled you into rebellion. Those who do not surrender their arms will be punished. If you continue to resist, the aeroplanes will come back with bombs and guns."

The Burmese Government saw these leaflet-dropping sorties (the first in South-East Asia) to be highly effective, but given that a majority of the population were illiterate, this would seem to have been way off the mark. In fact, it was possible that Saya San actually benefited from the raids by way of increased prestige. 'Look,' he was said to have told his followers, 'I wave my hands and their bombs turn into harmless pieces of paper!'

Gerry Livock, upon asking an interpreter to question a captured rebel (whom they had named, Horace), on how they had reacted to the appearance of the flying boats, said he'd been rather chastened to hear they hadn't been at all alarmed. 'Saya San had announced that all he had to do was to point a finger and the plane would be brought down,' said Horace, which raised a laugh amongst the aircrews. But a few days later, with two VIP's on board, Livock reported a strange happening whilst flying over rebel-held territory. All was going well when the steady beat of the engines suddenly changed to a discordant roar, the starboard engine losing revs. He immediately set course for the distant Irrawaddy, and upon completing his turn pushed open the throttles. To his surprise, both engines responded instantly, running smoothly. Later, a thorough check of the starboard engine revealed no fault whatsoever, and Livock says he often wondered whether or not Saya San had waved a malicious finger in their direction.

But, according to his book, Gerry Livock hints at life not being too bad, reference being made to cruises up the Irrawaddy, visits to Mandalay, and discussions over "a few sundowners."

The first land-based aircraft to be stationed at Seletar arrived in Singapore during this time.

These were the all-metal Horsley torpedo bombers destined for 36 Sqn, and within days they too were dispatched to Burma, to assist operations. Two more aircraft, en-route from Calcutta to Seletar, also found themselves diverted to Rangoon, and for several days, reconnaissance flights were made over the Tharrawaddy district. But although large crowds of people were to be observed, no action was taken. All the aircraft returned to Seletar on April 9th.

Saya San was eventually captured, and the rebellion brought under control, but it was to be some years later before the rebel leader was tried. He was convicted and executed.

Back at Seletar, all seemed well. But out on the world's stage the political situation was seen to be rapidly deteriorating, extreme nationalism assuming prominence. By 1933, the European nations were becoming increasingly wary of the political party which had gained supreme control of Germany; the Nazis. In Asia, too, Japanese policy had taken an entirely new turn. From being a strong supporter of the League of Nations, and the Naval Limitation Treaty of 1922, Japan was now showing herself to be an

Good air-to-air of Hawker Horsley S1613.

RA "Scotty" Powell

independent, aggressive nation; annexing Manchuria in 1931, attacking Shanghai a year later.

British Chiefs of Staff reacted quickly, advising the Government to reverse its defence policy. They stressed in particular that "It would be the height of folly to perpetuate our defenceless state in the Far East." Thus it was decided that – with Germany looking more dangerous by the day, and Japan an aggressor already – Britain should re-arm.

But policy for the defence of Singapore seemed to be extremely short-sighted. It was assumed that, in the event of trouble, as it would take the British battle fleet seventy days to reach the area, Singapore only needed to be able to defend herself for this period; the "Britannia Rules the Waves" syndrome was not yet dead. So it was that fortifications were arranged with an attack from the sea in mind – batteries of heavy guns being mounted so as to command the seaward approaches. The Royal Air Force's role in the defence of the island, though seen to be necessary, was thought to be of secondary importance, which accounted for the build-up at Seletar being a comparatively leisurely affair; not until December 1933, was Headquarters Far East Command separately established on the station. The following month (Jan 1934) saw the arrival of No.100 Squadron, commanded by Sqn/Ldr Lewis G. Le B. Croke, with their Vildebeest torpedo bombers, bringing unit strength up to three squadrons.

Leisurely, maybe, but, returning to the base in 1932, after surveying the Palawan Passage, off the Philippines, Gerry Livock recalls his thoughts at the time:

'As I circled Seletar before coming down to land for the last time, I remembered how, in 1925, Bud Rankin and I had photographed a patch of jungle, mangrove and rubber that was to become the RAF station. Now that patch had been cleared and new buildings were almost hiding our old bungalows. There was even a large parade ground being laid down where bands would play and troops would drill. That large red building was the new palatial mess, where officers wore mess kit for dinner. Mess kit!

It was time I said goodbye.' And so, it turned out, he did, not to return for thirty-five years. (Maybe this statement reveals a flaw in Gerry Livock's character as far as the Air Force was concerned, for, despite a long service career, he was never to advance to Air rank, one of the few Far East Flight aircrew not to do so. Another reason could have been that he never married.)

The final paragraph of *To the Ends of the Air* says it all for Gerry Livock: 'I pulled back the throttles and slowly glided down over the new hangar, over the old attap hut, and then sank gently onto the waters of the Johore Strait. Taxiing slowly to a mooring buoy I flicked off the main switches, and the engines wheezed and sighed to a stop. I stood up in the cockpit and took off my flying cap. Suddenly everything seemed to have gone very quiet.'

• • • • • • • • • •

It was in 1931 that thoughts were given to establishing a second RAF base in Singapore, that at Tengah, to the west, responsibility for the supervision of its development falling to Seletar.

Burma apart, operations throughout this period were of a strictly peaceful nature: survey and meteorological flights, long distance cruises, combined exercises with the Army and Navy, the inevitable tasks of escorting and transporting VIP's. But in amongst what should have been interesting and uneventful work, Seletar was to experience its first aviation accident. On Thursday 17th February 1931, the pilot of a 36 Squadron Hawker Horsley, Flying Officer SA Davies and his passenger Corporal V. Boyce were killed when their aircraft dived into the ground from a height of around seven thousand feet. No definite conclusions were reached as to the cause of the crash.

The dangers of flying over Malaya had been stressed by the AOC, India, Air Marshal Sir W Geoffrey H Salmond just three months before, in November 1930. This was when, visiting with a flight of two Wapitis and a Hinaidi in connection with the impending move of 36 Sqn from Karachi to Seletar, he had offered the opinion that, because of the unpredictable weather conditions in the area, aviators would have a need to take extreme care.

A period of nineteen months were to pass before disaster struck again. Seletar's second serious accident was 205 Squadron's first; two more airmen losing their lives. This time, the pilot and other members of the crew surviving, an accurate account of the accident was filed.

On September 15th 1932 a 205 Sqn Southampton crashed at Pulo Ubin after making a standard descent and levelling out at what the pilot estimated to be a height of fifty feet. Early altimeters were not totally reliable and, with a flat calm sea, from which a brilliant tropical sun was reflected, judgement was likely to be impaired. In fact it was, for in reality the aircraft was only at about twenty feet above the surface. Hitting the water sooner, therefore much harder than expected, the machine immediately overturned. Another Southampton, en route to an air-firing exercise over Blakan Mati, spotted the wreck and landed to pick up the survivors.

From this point on, accidents seemed to happen all too frequently, and it is sad to recall that up to the outbreak of hostilities with Japan, aircraft from Seletar were involved in no fewer than fifty serious flying accidents. These resulted in fifty-seven fatalities and twenty-three injuries; an average loss of almost six aircraft per year between 1933-41: statistics that were particularly dispiriting when applied to the Torpedo Bomber (TB) squadrons, their average alone amounting to four aircraft per year.

Faced with a growing number of tragedies, it was decided to modernize Seletar's equipment. In April, 1935, a year after the arrival of 100 Squadron with its Vildebeests, 205 Squadron converted from two engines to four with the latest line in flying boats – the Singapore III – their crews at last sheltered from the elements in the luxury of an enclosed cockpit. This was another triple-finned biplane, built by Short Bros, its R-R Kestrel engines arranged in tandem pairs, two pushers and two pullers. [The R-R Kestrel was in fact the engine used to power the prototype ME109, its intended engine not then ready.] Three months later, 36 Squadron was to switch from the Horsley to the Vildebeest, but not

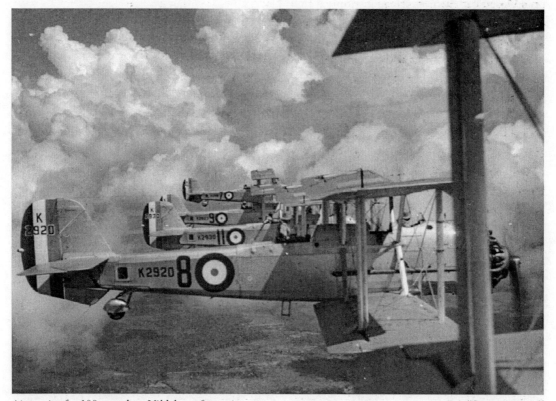

Air-to-air of a 100 squadron Vildebeest formation.   *RA "Scotty" Powell*

What a way to go! Recently demised Sultan of Kedah's body is returned home for burial. Under Muslim law this has to take place within 24 hrs of death & Alor Star is a long way from Singapore.
RA "Scotty" Powell

before one of the squadron's Horsleys was to fulfil the role of Royal hearse. This unusual event occurred when the Sultan of Kedah died whilst on a visit to Singapore in April of that year. With the coffin heavily wrapped in sacking, it was literally lashed beneath the fuselage and between the undercarriage struts, for a somewhat undignified return to his home in Alor Star, North Malaya. It was the only way in which the body could be returned for burial within the limited time specified by Muslim law. Hardly to be classed as part of the everyday routine into which Seletar's squadrons had once again settled.

It was in early 1935, during the course of these equipment upgrades that a most tragic of

accident was to occur. Although not taking place at Seletar, it did involve what were to be Seletar-based aircraft, the new Singapore III flying boats for 205 Sqn.

Four of the aircraft had departed England in January, bound for the Far East. They were flying from Naples to Malta when disaster struck as they crossed high ground near Messina, Sicily. A description of events was given to a Reuter's correspondent in an interview with an eye-witness, being duly reported in the *Straits Times*.

I was digging on my mountain-side terrace about 9:30 this morning when I saw a big aeroplane burst out from the clouds which were clustered around the top of the mountain. The machine was slanting terribly, one wing was right down, the other right up. It seemed to sweep the side of the mountain with its lower wing. Suddenly there was a puff of smoke, followed almost instantaneously by a tremendous explosion. The machine burst into flames before it hit the mountain. Then it seemed to break into pieces and fall down the hillside. I rushed to the spot and saw two men half-burned in front of the machine. The wreckage was blazing fiercely and it was quite impossible to get near her. I rushed to the village and called the Carabinieri (police).

100 Squadron Vildebeest on the airfield in front of the Officers' Mess.
RA 'Scotty' Powell

The report continued...

An Air Ministry statement declares that there were eight occupants of the machine and that all of them are dead. The machine was flying from Naples to the RAF base at Calafrana, Malta, on a further stage of its flight from England to Singapore. The aircraft was flying in fog.

This accident became an almost overnight sensation in the press, the routing which forced the aircraft to fly over such dangerous terrain being strongly criticized . It was said the Singapores had been refused permission by the Italian Army to fly directly down the Straits of Messina, a restriction which was opposed even by the Italian Air Force, but an Air Ministry spokesman stated, 'It is a route demanded by international agreement to avoid flying over prohibited areas.' No mention was made of the fact that Italy was at the time engaged in a war in Ethiopia, troopships sailing out of Messina.

This accident was at first reported to have tragic and unexpected consequences, for on February 21st, 1935, not long after the crash, two sisters, Betty and Jane Dubois, committed suicide by leaping from a hired plane while it was flying over Upminster. It was reported that they been engaged to Flying Officer Forbes and Flight Lieutenant Beatty, pilots of the aircraft that crashed at Messina. In a letter, found in their plane upon landing, one sister was said to have written, "I think you know Charles and I were going to spend our lives together and I must keep my part of the bargain."

It was later confirmed that Jane and Elizabeth Dubois – daughters of the US Consul General in Naples – had booked all the seats on a flight to Paris, and had leapt from it to their deaths. Suicide without a doubt, but police said the letter contained nothing that would indicate there was ever a question of an engagement to any members of the Singapore's crew.

The remaining aircraft eventually arrived at Seletar, one of them carrying the recently appointed Commander of the Royal Air Force, Far East, with them: Air Commodore AW

Tedder, later to become Chief of Air Staff. Until Far East Headquarters moved into the Union Building in Singapore city – April 1st, 1937 – Air Commodore Tedder lived on the base at Seletar, occupying the bungalow which was later to become official residence of the station's Commanding Officer.

The aircraft to claim most lives at Seletar was the Vickers Vildebeest. Yet when the first station magazine, *The Straitsman*, appeared on July 1st, 1934, the following tribute was paid to the aircraft, under the heading "Ode to a Beeste."

The Vildebeest, a quaint old bird,
Of rather gaunt appearance,
Between its tummy and the ground,
Has heaps of buckshee clearance.

It sports a hump upon its back,
has legs so long, like Tamils,
A flight lined out across the 'drome,
Looks like a string of camels.

Found in Malaya and Iraq,
It flies in hefty circles,
Its motive power is stuck in front,
And loudly it capurtles.

Unlike the usual type of bird,
It lays its eggs whilst flying,
They vary both in size and weight,
And cleave the air, a-sighing.

The Vildebeest's patriotic claims,
Are painted on its chassis,
Red, white and blue, a tasteful hue,
So dignified and classy.

But this "quaint old bird" had rather a unfortunate record when it came to involvement in crashes. On May 23rd, 1936, a mid-air collision between two Vildebeests of 36 Squadron resulted in the deaths of four airmen. Two years later, eleven men of 100 Squadron died in three crashes in consecutive months, the worst of these being in June, 1938, another mid-air collision accounting for six more deaths. Hardly the fault of the aircraft, unless it was related in some way to all-round vision, or lack of! Whatever, by this time, morale on the two torpedo bomber squadrons was at a low ebb.

But not all the crashes were to end in disaster. A 100 Squadron Vildebeest was to cause a widespread search to be instigated when it crashed into a hill in the heart of Johore's jungle. This search had been in operation for several days, when the crew, led by the pilot, Pilot Officer Hobler (eventually AVM Hobler), made an unexpected re-appearance. Miraculously escaping serious injury, they had worked their way through the jungle until they stumbled across the railway tracks. These were to lead them to the nearest village, and survival, and their aircraft became the first to be successfully salvaged from the Malayan jungle when, the following month, Sqn/Ldr G le B Croke, and party of seven men, made the twelve-mile trip to the crash site. Seriously hampered by swamps, humidity, and a green hell, they eventually reached the scene of the accident, and, after dismantling the machine and packing the pieces in rattan bags – made on the spot by the locals – they set off on the return journey. Amazingly, the complete aircraft was salvaged, engine included! Quite a task when one imagines the conditions, and the equipment available; mainly manpower.

But, despite these accidents, and the grief they caused, Seletar was reported as being a delightful posting. One reason for this lay in the building programme; the standards of working and living accommodations being subject to progressive improvements. Initially, a vast labour force was contracted to clear the site and construct the necessary buildings. Supervision of this was not always an easy matter, and working conditions were often dangerous. Snakes and crocodiles were prevalent, Malaria rampant, and tigers still roamed the island as late as 1940. Coolies were killed in accidents, and trouble would occasionally break out between the various "Tongs". But, except for one such incident, when a man died, these disturbances rarely got too far out of hand.

Thanks to the dedication of the Works Directorate employees, and the able Mr Woods, Seletar quickly took shape. What was to be aptly described as a "miracle," had been created from jungle, mangrove swamp, and a rather neglected plantation.

The first building to be erected was an attap hut, to be used by the Station Engineer. It remained on site, near the army signal compound – close by the Shell garage – until at least 1968. The thirties' guardroom is today well inside the station boundaries, and was once home to the Seletar branch of the Chartered Bank. The first hangar, used by 205 Squadron to begin with, and, much later by 1124 Marine Craft Unit, was still in use at the turn of the century. As mentioned previously, station headquarters originally occupied the site upon which, later, was to be located the Seletar Yacht Club, close by the top of the slipway.

By June 1935 there were one thousand six hundred and fifty-two Asians living on the camp, in an area then known officially as "Civilian Lines," ("Coolie Roost" to the airmen of the day). Many other Asian employees lived outside, travelling in to work every day. Around two hundred married quarters were built in 1936, these to accommodate locally employed artisans and their families. A number were also available for single artisans and labourers. This whole area, later to become known as "Seletarville," was a civilian cantonment within the perimeter fence. It housed Indians, Malays, Chinese and Eurasians. Slowly, a community within a community grew up there. No rent was charged for the quarters, nor was a charge made for the water and electricity used by the occupants. The area boasted its own medical centre, where a doctor held a surgery for two hours each morning. There were shops for provisions, tailoring, and "dhobi." There were also coffee houses, several canteens, and churches: C of E, Catholic, a Mosque, and one for other denominations.[26]

Unfortunately, British servicemen were not so well placed when it came to the matter of married quarters. Up to 1929 – with the exception of one or two senior officers – all married personnel were obliged to live off the station, the officers, as far away as the city itself. No hardship there, it seemed, for there was never a shortage of wives wishing to join their husbands on this overseas tour.

According to service records, first on the scene was the wife of Far East Flight pilot, Flt/Lt Wigglesworth. Wiggie's wife arrived in 1929, their son, David, being the first recorded RAF baby to be born in Singapore.

Up to 1933, Seletar was a single posting for airmen – senior NCOs and other ranks – with no accommodation available for families. But, on March 31st, 1933, with the building programme in full swing, twelve families (one warrant officer and eleven airmen) arrived by sea to take up residence on the station, thus establishing Seletar's first "married patch" at the newly completed houses in Birdcage Walk. These families consisted of wives and pre school children only; with no schools at present available, elder children had to remain in the UK to continue their education.

Until barrack block "A" was completed, airmen had to make do with wooden huts, "bashas," or tented accommodation. And what a relief it must have been to make that move, for, as anyone who has served at Seletar can vouch, those barrack blocks, designed especially for the tropics, were reasonably comfortable.

The officers, meanwhile, had taken over the three bungalows previously occupied by the officials of the Works and Buildings department, one becoming their mess, though by all accounts its inhabitants were rather unconventional in their ways, possibly emulating the habits of the local plantation managers. Mess kit was said to encompass such as grey flannel trousers and cricket shirts, and it must have been a fairly small mess, for this bungalow was later to become the Station Commander's residence. With a permanent mess building being erected towards the end of 1930, Seletar at last began to take on the look of an orthodox Royal Air Force Station.

So what was life really like back then? Well, in a letter to the *Voice* (Seletar's third and last station magazine), dated January 1971, Herbert R. Shawyer provides a little insight into the 1931/32 era.

Entertainment was extremely limited on an LAC's pay of thirty eight shillings per week, inclusive of ten shillings flying pay, *(one hundred and ninety pence, out of which he contributed fourteen pence for extra messing)*. Parties of four would travel to town by taxi. There we could go to the "flicks" or bars. Occasionally we could afford to visit one of the "Worlds" and buy a book of dance tickets, to dream of romantic affairs with lovely Eurasian hostesses.

The usual overseas tour was for five years, with no hope of getting home for leave periods. There were no service aircraft capable of regular UK – Far East flights, only Imperial Airways or KLM.

It was a chargeable offence to be out in the sun without a topee *(pith helmet)*. We wore flannel shirts with ventilation holes under the arms, short sleeved and cut around the neck, the edges bound with white tape. At the end of the work period we all felt and smelt a bit high – no deodorants then, and if there had been we would have been viewed with the utmost suspicion had we used them.

When on cruises we were privileged to wear khaki shorts and shirts, but even this was too much at times. I recall cooking an evening meal off Mergui, the perspiration dripping off me as I juggled pots and pans over the primus, unable to stand upright. We were besieged by a swarm of greenfly. These fell into the pan, along with drips from me. This gave me a certain amount of satisfaction when passing the food up to the officers taking it easy out on the centre section beneath an awning.

Apart from the preparation of meals, the W/Op was also responsible for the daily inspection of rigging and airframe, mooring up, drogue control and slipping the buoy, all this in addition to his normal task of communications, and assisting the fitter when refuelling up to five hundred gallons by hand, using the zwicky pump fitted to the fuselage. All in all, a bit of a dogsbody.

Of course, this was only when the squadron was away on cruises, which happened frequently enough, but there was always sufficient adventure content to make it all worthwhile.

Working hours at Seletar were from 07:00 through to 12:30 – a five hour day – which, in a tropical climate, contrasted sharply with the 07:30 to 16:30 put in by later occupants of the station, albeit given a much improved working environment.

In the thirties, afternoons were treated largely as siesta times, except to the odd enthusiast who insisted on being typically English – as in Noel Coward's "Mad Dogs and Englishmen." After all, it is highly likely Singapore was the place that gave inspiration to those words. In the evenings – when they could afford it – many officers would dine in the Swimming Club in Singapore city. Occasionally, on a Saturday night, they would dispense with formality and head for one of the big amusement parks, the three "Worlds" – New, Happy, and Great.

By some unwritten convention, other ranks seemed to favour the Happy World, whilst officers, immaculately dressed in jackets and ties, would frequent the New World, both groups partaking of all the inexpensive luxuries which the city offered by way of entertainment. Particularly popular were the dance halls, where hostesses were readily available; four dances per dollar. Also contained within the precincts of the "Worlds" were bars, cafes and markets. Chinese drama and singing were featured, along with a diverse selection of cabarets and sideshows – where "impossible feats" were performed! Almost unlimited entertainment on one site, so an outing to one of the "Worlds" was often the highlight of the week. Reminiscing on those far-off, pre-war days, servicemen in Singapore recall that the amusement parks were a meeting place for all walks of life. Everyone was attracted eventually, and it was not unknown for a young officer to be detailed to escort distinguished visitors there.[27]

Another plus-factor associated with the 'Worlds' was their lack of a dress code. Whereas establishments such as Raffles and the top hotels demanded that you wear a jacket and tie and lesser hotels didn't demand but preferred that you did, the "Worlds" didn't much care whether you even owned a jacket and tie! But it *was* a service requirement that airmen wear long-sleeved shirts after dark when the mosquitos came out to play.

But the cost of living was extremely high, and the pay not generous enough to allow either junior officers or airmen to live a life of luxury. Indeed, for the airmen, a trip down town in the station lorry was all most could usually manage, "private car" travel to Singapore costing four dollars. (It was against the rules to use public transport, not seen as befitting for an expatriate – the white man's burden and all that.)

The station itself offered little in the form of ready-made entertainment, although there was always something for those active enough to seek it. A swimming pool of sorts was built on the edge of the Straits, a wooden pile enclosure that was probably good enough to exclude anything untoward, though it's doubtful if this included the sea snakes which abounded thereabouts. And despite its location rendering it fairly inaccessible, it did prove to be extremely popular, especially for moonlight bathing in the cool of the evening.

Sport was also popular; a very high standard seemed to be guaranteed at Seletar. RAF players were often to be found in the Colony's representative sides, making quite a name for themselves on the island. The airfield itself was used initially, after flying had ceased, naturally, but once the sports field had been built, there always seemed to be something going on.

Leisure hours would be spent either in the bar, horizontal on your bed, or reading; the station library stocking a varied selection of books. Church services on the station were held monthly, but transport was available every Sunday to take men of all denominations to the churches in Singapore.

A local leave centre was established within the confines of the station, the idea being that here one could spend a holiday on the beach, away from the worry of duty. Its wooden huts were equipped with standard issue beds, but there was no reveille, or "lights out," and the only contact with the station was at meal times, or during NAAFI breaks. From all reports it did not prove to be at all popular.

The facilities improved with time, a golf course providing added interest. Families were also taken into account, and on September 25th, 1933, the first schoolmistress was engaged to teach the younger children.

But the most outstanding development of all, at least from a social and sporting point of view, had to be the Seletar Yacht Club. A meeting of interested parties in December 1933, resulted in the club being formed and twelve Moth type boats being ordered from Thornycroft of Singapore, at a cost of fifty dollars each, ownership being divided equally between officers and airmen.

The club was officially opened in February 1934 by Air Commodore S.W. Smith, OBE, AOC Far East . Wing Commander Burling – Seletar's Commanding Officer at the time, and the person largely responsible for the scheme – was appointed the club's first Commodore.[28]

A large attap hut, carried bodily to the water's edge by three hundred coolies, became the first boathouse. Sail-lockers, storerooms and changing rooms were formed from packing cases in which the Horsley bombers had arrived at Seletar.

Before long, it seemed like everyone was taking to the water, and a larger type of boat became a prime requirement. The Commodore himself ended up designing a boat to suit local conditions, a twelve foot dinghy known as a Pram. Fashioned from locally available teak, these boats were built in large numbers by Thornycroft, Singapore, for they were also ordered by the Army (at Changi Garrison), and Navy (at Sembawang), as well as by clubs in Sumatra and Karachi. Racing the Prams became popular, and many happy hours were spent at races between the various clubs.

After the original HQ Far East building was finally vacated by 205 Squadron, it became the new Club House, featuring a popular little bar run by an amiable Tamil called Ahmad. Over-looking the Straits was a verandah, the roof of which was lined with silvered, aircraft fabric, where members and visiting VIP's often signed their names. Eminent among the latter were those of the Lord and Lady Mountbatten; Under Secretary of State for Air, Sir Phillip Sassoon; Prince Aly Khan; the King of Siam; Jean Batten; and Mr Noel Coward, who was a rather frequent visitor. Great skill was required to sail a dinghy in the Johore Straits, with its fast currents and loose shipping, and to own a helmsman's certificate – difficult to obtain – was the mark of a competent sailor.

The Seletar Yacht Club thrived over the years, serving its members well,[29] many people retaining fond memories of the place. But obviously not all, for I suspect, especially back then, divisions were formed, as is hinted at by the following ditty, written in 1935.

Not A Chance.
I want to join the yacht club,
Where men are men, I'm told
I'd cheerfully pay my monthly whack
To join that unique fold
I want to wear a trilby,
Like some of them I've seen
The colour doesn't matter much
Gee whizz! I'll say I'm keen
I want to drink a brandy dry,
And pay for it weeks hence
I'd finish with the canteen beer;
Destroys the finer sense
I want to say, 'What ho! Old bean,'
Instead of 'whotcher mate'
And talk of wind and tack and helm
Of racing up to date
I want to feel the thrill of speed,
Of racing at knots three
A moth, a dinghy, either will do,
As long as it's trouble free.

On July 1st, 1934 – the month the station's first magazine, *The Straitsman*, put in an appearance – Mrs Sidney Smith, wife of the AOC Far East, declared the outdoor "Talkie" cinema to be open.

For a guide as to the size of the station's compliment in those days, we can turn to the monthly lists which were produced detailing all postings in and out; one page! And those lists point to something else that changed over the years: most of those being posted out were not going to the UK. Upon leaving the Far East it was usual to go first to India for a spell, then to the Middle East, literally working your way home in stages, hence the five year tour.

One of the more popular outings for yacht club members in the thirties was an evening sail across to Punggol Point. A group of boats could often be observed making their way over to visit the Japanese restaurant which was located in the bay at Punggol, and the Japanese must surely have gleaned a certain amount of useful information about the station during these visits.

The relationship between Seletar and the Japanese military was seen to be extremely cordial – on an official level – with frequent meetings taking place, although these appear to have been well biassed towards the Japanese. On 27th March 1931, Wing Commander AC Wright, AFC, was presented to Vice Admiral Seizo Sakonji when His Imperial Japanese Majesty's Training Squadron visited Singapore. In February 1934, Japanese officers from the vessel, *Kuma*, visited the base, and a month later, Seletar played host to a Japanese Admiral along with other officers, the Naval Training Squadron again visiting Singapore. Records show this Training Squadron to have returned to Singapore yet again in March 1935. Visiting Seletar this time was Rear Admiral Nakamura, accompanied by His Imperial Highness Lieutenant Commander Asoakira – a Prince of the Royal Family – a number of other officers, along with the Japanese Consul General in Singapore.

Elsewhere, some very senior officers were airing their anxieties in public. In fact, Marshal of the Royal Air Force, Sir John Salmond, made a particularly big impact on the Singapore scene, when, in an article in London's *Evening Standard*, he wrote:

At Singapore there are fewer than thirty shore-based aircraft, whereas Japan has stated to the League of Nations as far back as 1931, that she possessed three hundred and twenty-nine aircraft on carriers, and six hundred first-line planes...

At least a hundred shore-based bomber and reconnaissance aircraft are required at the strategic point in Singapore, which remains a grave temptation as long as it is practically defenceless.

To which a *Straits Times* editorial replied:

The dissemination of false views of the situation only serves to cause alarm at home and elsewhere, without misleading in the slightest degree those non-British people who are curious about our defences.

But there is little doubt the Japanese were fully aware of the strategic capability available at Singapore, their frequent visits, along with the espionage net they had set up in Malaya, no doubt keeping them well informed. And although the security forces were no doubt abundantly aware of the situation, there was little they could do to combat it. The large number of civilian workers alone must have posed a serious security risk, and no amount of supervision could ensure that information was not being offered for sale.

There were many stories doing the rounds, most eventually confirmed, some not: The Chinese junk manned by a Japanese crew, caught taking soundings around the harbour area; The Japanese tennis club which imported large amounts of cement, ostensibly to build new courts, but was later found to have been shipped out to one of the offshore islands, possibly for the construction of gun emplacements; The barbershop in downtown Singapore, popular with servicemen because it was staffed by very attractive young Japanese girls. These girls were apparently very happy to engage in chit chat, especially if the serviceman had downed a few beers. 'When you go on manoeuvres?' and such like. Innocent sounding questions, but pretty little ears could take in a lot of seemingly insignificant data. There were also reports that mail passing through Headquarters was being very expertly tampered with. Seletar had anyway been subjected to a great deal of close scrutiny, the Japanese Government apparently more aware of the fact than their British counterparts, that if a war was to be won, then air superiority was essential. They were no doubt by now well aware of the fact that Seletar, with its three squadrons of outmoded aircraft, was the sum total of British air power in the Far East.

A more realistic state of the relationship between Seletar and Japan could be derived from the flight which began on January 10th, 1936. Three aircraft of 205 Squadron – the Singapore III flying boat – left on a goodwill mission which was eventually intended to take them up to Japan itself. Unfortunately, much of the so-called goodwill was shattered even before the flight departed. Not a result of the general deterioration in the world situation, but the Japanese insistence that the aircraft should not carry cameras, and that the flight was required to follow a very specific route to their destination, keeping well clear of the Japanese coastline.

Led by the Air Officer Commanding, Far East, Air Commodore Sidney Smith, the cruise was fraught with difficulties, and numerous hazzards were encountered. At Kuching, Borneo, their fist stop, a seven hour storm – reputedly "the most violent in history" – delayed their departure. Then, on the leg from Kudat – Sabah – to Manila, the lead aircraft, flown by Wing Commander Scott, suffered an engine failure, the aircraft being left to await a replacement engine. A dense bank of fog delayed things in Hong Kong, and a second engine failure saw another aircraft awaiting a replacement engine, this time in Amoy, China. Here they found themselves subjected to close scrutiny by the crew of a Japanese destroyer, the vessel departing less than twelve hours after the aircraft had left. Meanwhile, Wing Commander Scott's aircraft, serviceable once more, re-joined the flight en-route to Shanghai, but deteriorating weather forced them down in a sheltered bay at Nam Kwam, sixty miles south of Weanchow. Nam Kwam was said to be a pirate stronghold, and as this was the first visit to the area by any kind of aircraft, the crews were no doubt disturbed to find themselves surrounded by numerous native craft, shortly after anchoring.[30] But as the tide gradually receded, so the craft headed for the beach. But it was not yet over, for with the tide at low ebb – flying boats settling into the soft mud – back they came, using a novel form of transport; similar in construction to a children's

Air-to-air of a Singapore III. Note the tandem, push-pull engine layout.   **Ken McLean**

scooter, but with the wheels removed, they skied out across the mud. But all was well, it appears they were just curious.

The flight eventually arrived in Shanghai on February 26th, only to be told by Vice Admiral Oikawa, the senior Japanese Naval Officer in the area, that the onward section of the cruise to Japan had been cancelled, a violent political disturbance having broken out in Tokyo, being offered as the reason.

Given this state of affairs, the Chinese Government invited the party to extend their visit to Shanghai, and numerous functions were laid on. General Wu Te-chen, Mayor of Greater Shanghai, held a reception on February 27th, to which he invited all the leading citizens, including General SK Yao, Chairman of the China National Air League. Air Commodore Smith was presented with a beautifully engraved silver plaque, depicting a Singapore III flying over the Civic Centre building in Shanghai. An attached plate carried suitable inscriptions in both English and Chinese. In addition, General Yao presented a marble sphere, mounted on a pedestal. The sphere was about six inches in diameter, and the pedestal bore an inscription in Chinese giving details of the presentation.

The return flight to Singapore went according to schedule, the aircraft arriving back at Seletar on March 10th, 1936, having flown five thousand six hundred nautical miles during the twenty-nine-day cruise.

Perhaps the following newspaper reports give an indication that, even in the mid-thirties, people were alive to the possible threat of an invasion, even if the Air Force's contribution in preventing such was not seen as being too significant.

The most important sea, land and air man-oeuvres ever undertaken by British forces in the Far East are to begin in Singapore on a date that is being kept secret, says Reuter. Officially it is stated that the primary objectives are to test the defences of the fortress. Twenty-six naval units from the China Station will take part, and air squadrons are expected from Iraq.

This next is probably dated more towards the end of the decade, or early in the forties.

If mustard gas is dropped on Singapore there will be considerable difficulty in detecting it by smell, because it is like garlic – one of the town's most common smells.

This was pointed out by Major A.J.C. Beveridge, of the RAMC, states British United Press.

Another difficulty the major foresees is the curiosity of the native population. 'They will walk straight into contaminated areas,' he says.

With approval for the development of an airfield at Tengah having been granted back in 1931, progress had been leisurely, to say the least,

Singapore III flying boats up slip for servicing. Note period ground transportation. **Ken McLean**

Vildebeest formation over the troopship Somersetshire in Singapore's Keppel Harbour.   **RA "Scotty" Powell**

for it was 1937 before work actually began. The first aircraft to officially touch down on its grass strip was that of the Landing Fields Inspector, in July 1939. Two years later, with the threat of a Japanese invasion imminent, a tarmac runway was laid. And although site clearance and building began at Changi, on the east coast, at about the same time as Seletar, it had been developed as an Army base, for the Royal Artillery.[31] It also played host to regiments of the Gordon Highlanders, and the Royal Engineers, who built it over a period of fifteen years. It was the job of these same engineers to destroy the place once it became evident that its artillery had been so sited as to be useless when it came to the actual defence of Singapore; fifteen years of wasted effort.

With progress on re-armament outside the UK being alarmingly slow, the Straits Government decided to lend a hand, the Straits Settlements Volunteer Air Force officially coming into being at Seletar on March 25th 1936, with which a variety of aircraft began to appear on the station: Avro Tutor, Hawker Hart, Osprey and

Audax. January 1937 saw the total number of squadrons at Seletar rise to four when 230 Squadron arrived, bringing with them five more Singapore III's.

● ● ● ● ● ● ● ● ● ●

Perhaps these excerpts from a piece featured in the first edition of the Seletar's second station magazine, *Apa Khabar*, dated March 1939, may give us a little insight as to the feelings that Seletar was capable of generating. As with most good fiction, one assumes the author, Hiram K Pilsner, to be writing from experience:

In the grey light of the tropical dawn, figures were to be seen moving around the hangar, and soon the quiet of the morning was disturbed by the whine of a starter. An engine broke into life, stuttered, then settled down to a low hum of power. As the sky lightened, the sleek form of a Vildebeest moved out of the shadow of the hangar, towards the aerodrome. Another and another followed. Engines were run up and tested until space was vibrant with the song of power. Then, like a camel caravan against the skyline, they moved into formation on the field. As one machine, they passed smoothly into the sky and headed north. That night their crews sat together on the steps of their attap dwelling and watched the last rays of the sun gleam across a golden sea, touching the palms with red and lighting up the hilltops with a ruddy glow. Waves lapped gently against the smooth beach and waving palms rustled an accompaniment to the cries of the night-hawks. They had truly tasted the night-life of the orient.

• • • • • • • • • • •

Many days were like that, but things could also be very different, as related by Ken McLean, at the time, an LAC with 230 Squadron.

'It was quite a thrill to learn I was to fly on a four week "cruise" of the China Seas, and that our aircraft (K6918) was to be the flagship, carrying as it did the Officer Commanding Far East, Air Commodore Tedder. The remainder of our aircraft's crew consisted of the captain (Sqn/Ldr); pilot – the Squadron Commander (Wg/Cdr); Sgt navigator; Cpl and LAC fitters; wireless op (LAC), plus myself (rigger) and a Government surveyor. Quite a range of ranks, all told.

'Our three Short Singapore Mk III flying boats departed Seletar on March 8th 1937, setting course for Indo China – as it then was – and Cam Ranh Bay, a rather sparse, drab-looking shoreline, I recall. (Something that was to change dramatically during the sixties and seventies war in Vietnam.) A cruising speed of ninety knots, at two thousand feet, meant a trip of over eight hours, and preparing meals over a primus stove, in cramped conditions, ensured that every leg would be an adventure in itself.

'After landing and anchoring in the calm waters of the bay, we were to be faced with our first problem – APU failure. This auxiliary power unit – driven by a small two-stroke situated in one of the engine nacelles – was a very important item, not only in the refuelling process, in other aspects, too: it served to charge the batteries, run the bilge pumps, and recharge the air accumu-

lators which were used to start the four Rolls-Royce Kestrel engines. Despite all attempts, no amount of effort at repair seemed to have any effect, so we resigned ourselves to refuelling by hand. Four gallon tins had to be manhandled on to the upper wing, to be poured into the tanks via a funnel, a very slow, tiring, work-intensive process. With a normal fuel load of 786 gallons, or the more likely 1266 gallon overload, that pointed to around three hundred tins. This of course made for a late finish, and so no trip ashore.

'Take-off next morning was as smooth as the previous day's had been – air pressure reserves fortunately remaining high enough to start the engines – and it was well into the afternoon before the first hint of bad weather came.

'Our destination was to have been Hong Kong, but as evening closed in so the weather deteriorated further. Heavy rain and strong winds evidence we had been caught in one of those fierce, sudden storms that occasionally blow up along this coast, and the order was given to standby for an emergency touchdown. Following the coastline, we searched desperately for a sheltered area in which to set down, an island appearing which seemed to offer just such a possibility. In far from ideal conditions, each aircraft landed as close to the shore as seemed safely possible, in the lee of Tong Ho, about eighty miles from Hong Kong. With the sea state increasing dangerously, with waves actually breaking over the lower wing and hull, it was now deemed essential to taxi closer inshore, and to find a suitable place in which to drop anchor, hopefully to ride out the storm.

'With the anchor out – K6918 was using an experimental version this trip – we found ourselves to be still drifting towards a very rocky and angry looking shore, yet the other aircraft seemed secure. The reason for this became clear once we recovered our anchor, or what remained of it; the flukes had broken off. The experimental anchor was obviously a failure, our only hope now was to taxy clear of that shore. With the engines not having been cut – they never were until a secure mooring was confirmed – we began to move away from the coast, but ever increasing seas meant we were unable to taxi into open waters. A dilemma.

With taxiing back and forth being ruled out due to the danger of us being swamped in the turns, and fuel levels anyway low after a full day's flying, it seemed take-off was the only remaining option. The captain therefore opened throttles, maximum permissible boost. We were about to gamble our power against the angry sea, a frantic struggle in which it felt the aircraft was being shaken to pieces... and then the sea won. All four engines – having taken on so much water – cut in unison; we slumped back into the sea's clutches. Now another frantic struggle ensued, the Cpl fitter on the engine panel fighting to get those propellers turning, to no avail. The air pressure dropped to zero before so much as one engine fired up. With the aircraft again drifting towards the shore, we were once more faced with a no-choice situation: hand cranking – similar to a car, only the handle went into the side of the engine panel. Eddie (the LAC fitter) and myself pulled ourselves up through the hatch and onto the slippery, windblown, heaving fuselage, clutching at flying wires and anything else that afforded a hand-hold as we scrambled towards the engines. Had fate not intervened last night, denying us a trip ashore, our spirits could well have been dulled, but now, boosted by a surge of adrenalin, we turned as never before, fear giving us added strength.

Now I was thankful of those ugly rope-soled sandals with which we'd been issued for this trip; another trial, but one that worked, for, if you'll excuse the pun, they stood us in good stead on that soaking, pitching surface. I was thankful, too, for Ginger, on the engine panel, for he was somehow successful in his quest to start all four engines. We now returned to the hatch and thankfully slithered down the ladder, securing the entry behind us even as full power was once more applied. We picked up speed, bouncing and shuddering in the violent seas, everyone grimly hanging onto something; it was now or never. Then came one of those quirks of fate which happen only rarely, and it was to be our saviour. A huge wave that seemed about to end it all, chose instead to catch us just right, heaving us into the air. There was a frightening, sickening downward lurch, then it held and we were clear, airborne. Luck, skill, fate? Who knows. All that mattered was that fifty storm-tossed, dangerous minutes later, the lights of Hong Kong hove into view. Within the sheltered waters alongside the airfield at Kai Tak, we were soon safely moored to a buoy. And by the time destroyers of the Far East Fleet departed to stand by the aircraft left at Tong Ho, we slept the exhausted sleep of those who have by good fortune survived a fight for life.

Fixing the beaching gear to a Singapore III. The serial (K3593) identifies it as a 210 Sqn aircraft.   **Ken McLean**

'The other aircraft arrived the next day, and after exercises off Hong Kong the cruise continued to the Philippines – where we stayed at an American Air Force base, and boy, could those old sweats knock it back! They certainly saw most of our lot under the table, and we thought we could hold our own with anyone. From Manilla we flew down to Borneo – Sandakan; Kudat; Jessleton; Miri, where raging flood waters threatened to hole the boats with debris, only the constant use of boat hooks fending off the swirling tree trunks. Then it was on to Kuching and back to Seletar.'

As for the return to Seletar, Ken recalls it vividly:

'Here I see again the sly grin on the face of Air Commodore Tedder as he awaits the dinghy that is to take him ashore, warning me, with a twinkle in his eye, that his pennant must not come down until he had stepped off K6918. Then, as the dinghy moved away, a wave of the hand signified that the cruise was over, and thank you. It could all have ended so differently.'

The above incident was reported in the March 10th, 1937 edition of the *Times*, who – back then when the data was likely to be slightly worse than second-hand – could probably be excused for getting things a little wrong, producing an extra aircraft from somewhere.

• • • • • • • • • •

FLYING BOATS SAFE AFTER ADVENTURE

The four Singapore III flying boats of No 230 Squadron which left Singapore on Monday for Hong Kong, had to take shelter in a bay off the small island of Tong Ho, about 50 miles from Hong Kong and three of them remained there last night.

On Monday the squadron, accompanied by Air Commodore AW Tedder, flew from Singapore to Kamrahn Bay, Indo China. Early yesterday it set off to complete the journey to Hong Kong, where it was due to take part in combined exercises. Bad weather compelled it to take shelter, and when conditions improved slightly, the boat in which Air Commodore Tedder was flying took off and completed the journey to Hong Kong. Our Hong Kong correspondent telegraphs that the British destroyers *Duchess* and *Westcott* are standing by the three flying boats. There is some anxiety lest the flying boats should break adrift in the darkness. The weather is very thick, making flight over high hills dangerous.

It says something of service protocol in those days that even in the somewhat cramped conditions aboard the aircraft, for most of the time strict demarcation was observed between officers and men. Unless being addressed directly, "permission to speak" often needed to be sought before one of the other ranks addressed an officer.

Another point to be illustrated by a story Ken told me was the value of seemingly insignificant articles to the local populace, and the authorities' insistence that the "colonialists," carrying as they did, the "white man's burden," were seen to be fair – at least as far as the military went.

'The whole camp was unexpectedly paraded one day, best KD, rifles, the lot; officers and men. It turned out to be an identity parade for a prostitute who had been relieved of a bar of soap by her "client." After drawing a blank at Seletar, the base at Sembawang came next, and then on to the army base at Changi – where the culprit was finally uncovered!

So ended a period of adventure and discovery, where the important role had been to "show the flag." There were to be no more flights to Japan, and the years which followed were those of an uneasy peace and growing apprehension.

Sad remains of a very Short Singapore!
RA "Scotty" Powell

Yacht Club, the early days - circa 1938. This site had previously played host to the original Station HQ, and later, 205 Sqn HQ.

Ken McLean

After a land acquisition programme, the new maingate under construction in 1939. The original gate was now well inside the station boundaries.

Eric Redshaw

The cinema moves indoors, but if it rained you would have trouble hearing the soundtrack!

Ken McLean

Seletar's torpedo section serving 36 & 100 Sqns.

RA "Scotty" Powell

A familar sight, until March 1959. Sunderlands at their moorings on the Straits of Johore. Seletar had been associated with water based aircraft from March 1928 to May 1959; the last of the RAF's flying boats operated from there.   *Author*

A pair of photo recce Spitfires somewhere over Malaya.   *Peter A Nunn*

CHAPTER SIX

The Storm Clouds Gather:
Sunderlands and a Declaration of War

Today, when it is realized that air power supplements rather than replaces sea power, few could be so rash as to suggest that Singapore will become more famous for its air squadrons than for its naval base; yet the role of Singapore as an air base is going to be a vital one if war spreads to the Far East.

(Extract from *The Eastern Graphic*, written on October 1ˢᵗ, 1941.)

● ● ● ● ● ● ● ● ● ●

It was on June 22nd, 1938 that No.230 Squadron – a relatively new arrival at Seletar – took delivery of yet another type of flying boat, eventually to be regarded greatest of them all. Seletar had already witnessed many exciting moments in aviation history, but with the possible exception of the arrival of the Far East Flight, nine years earlier, nothing could surpass the awe-inspiring, yet graceful sight of the latest aircraft to arrive over Singapore: the Short Sunderland, a gigantic silver monoplane.

One of these magnificent aircraft – the first Sunderland to be accepted for overseas service – settled elegantly onto the Straits of Johore on that June day. Its captain, Flight Lieutenant William A Hughes, and crew (all of 210 Squadron, Pembroke Dock), had, in a gentle, thirteen day flight, brought into South-East Asia one of the finest aircraft ever built. Henceforth, with the exception of the war years, Sunderlands of various marks were to be based at Seletar right through until June 1959, a period of over twenty years, making it the longest serving aircraft type

in the Royal Air Force, Far East. These last aircraft, belonging to 205 Squadron (Sunderland Detachment) for the final months of their lives, were the last of a long line of flying boats to be operated by the Royal Air Force – the end of an era.

By September 1938, shortly before Chamberlain's "Peace in our time" declaration of the Munich agreement, 230 Squadron's strength had risen to five aircraft. Four of these had been donated by the Sultans of the four Federated Malay States, and it was thought that a fitting gesture would be to name the aircraft after the States concerned. Thus a series of unique ceremonies was to take place in Lumut, Perak (September 30ᵗʰ); Port Swettenham, Selangor (October 19ᵗʰ); Kuantan, Pahang (October 21ˢᵗ); and finally, in Port Dickson, Negri Sembilan, the *Straits Times* carrying a report on the latter...

Saturday was the most important day in the recent history of Port Dickson. From shop houses along both sides of the 50-yard long main street, the gold, black and red flag of State hung side by side with the red, white and blue of England. From the top of the aircraft moored a few yards from the jetty, Yam Tuan (the Sultan) released a State flag. The aircraft's bow displayed the name, Negri Sembilan, *in Jawi characters.*

Hundreds of people including a large proportion of Malays in their brightly coloured Hari Raya clothes, watched from the jetty and the waterfront, and cheered as the great aircraft took off and roared above them. His Highness was in the aircraft and it was his second flight, his earlier experience being in an open plane at Seletar.

The success of the aircraft was toasted in champagne at a reception at the railway station. The Sunderland returned to Singapore in the afternoon, a journey that took less than an hour.

Following the introduction and crew training, 230 Squadron carried out the same tasks as Seletar's three other squadrons – No's 36, 100 and 205 – ie, reconnaissance, practice bombing, transportation of personnel, and "showing the flag." But it was in this latter role that the Sunderland looked so impressive, being a great source of pride to the British.

In his book, *Flying Boat*, Kenneth Poolman states:

> *Every Sunderland of the Royal Air Force was fitted with a socket in the eye of the bows to take a pukka flagstaff, to which the Union Jack was bent on the necessary occasions, being hoisted at sunrise and dipped at sunset with varying degrees of decorum according to the character of the skipper. And a proper white canvas awning could be rigged on stanchions which fitted into sockets on top of the Sunderland's hull. With flag flying, snowy awning spread and silver paintwork gleaming in the tropical sun, a Sunderland of the Far East Air Force conveyed the dignity and power of Imperial Majesty every bit as well as the tiddliest gunboat in the Royal Navy.*

Servicing Sunderlands was an advancement on earlier types of flying boat, engines now being set in the leading edge of the wing rather than up between the wings, as on the bi-plane types. To facilitate servicing, the wing leading edge alongside the engines featured hinged sections. When lowered, these formed platforms on which to stand when working on the engines.[32] But as with all flying boats, tools needed to be secured were they not to be lost forever. Oops!.. Clink.. Plop..

Damn and blast! Look out, fish, here she comes: 5/16 x 3/8 Whitworth o/e. Inventory holders were never easy to find!

Even with the aircraft up slip an airman's life could be fraught with danger, for on their beaching gear the hull was a long way off the ground, the shoulder wing even more so. One airman was discovered in what was thought to be a pool of blood after falling thirty feet to the ground. Fortunately, his injuries were superficial, the "blood" found to be nothing more than the contents of the tin of red paint he had been carrying.

Eric Redshaw, posted to Singapore and 230 shortly after the arrival of the first Sunderlands, gives us another slant on what life at Seletar was like at the time.

'One job was to repair the cockpit roof over the pilot's head. The perspex panels had shrunk in the tropical heat, leaving wide gaps. Apart from allowing the ingress of copious amounts of rain, there was a danger of these panels being sucked out or blown in when airborne, and with no spares available it was left to us riggers to fashion replacements from aluminium, not an easy task given the double curvature of the roof. The panels were sealed with a Bostik-type material, messy, and difficult to make neat.... Corrosion was, of course, the big enemy to look for.... but we could feel for our opposite numbers on 205 Sqn, next door; the Singapore III's had miles of control cables to check, splice and renew. A lot of friendly rivalry of course, but pride respectfully in your own outfit.'

Apparently, boat guard was the preferred choice out of all the duties to be performed, just as it was in my time. Out there on the briny you were unlikely to be troubled by mosquitoes, and the fishing was great. There were bunks to lie down on, to be lulled to sleep by the gentle motion of the swell, and a radio to listen to, provided you knew how to power it up. (Airmen in later years had the advantage of transistor technology.) Yes, if you had to pull a duty, this was the one, provided the aircraft didn't take it into its mind to sink whilst you were aboard; one of the reasons for your presence, as well as to ensure that any ships kept well clear of the moorings. (In later years, during the Malayan 'Emergency', there was also the matter of possible terrorist attacks to be taken into account.)

Relating to off-duty hours, Eric says, 'Those peacetime days passed pleasantly enough. Plenty of sport available; sailing at the yacht club, swimming in the Straits off the beaches within the base perimeter (the pool came later). After tea, 16:00-16:30, one usually thought to go into the city: cinemas, the dancing places, bars, restaurants etc, depending on one's current finances, of course. The PSI (Public Services Institute) bus was the cheapest means of transport, but you were limited by the departure times. PSI taxis were the preferred method, although these had to be booked, so were not readily available. To make the fare reasonable, these were shared. Such parties would go to league, or inter-service soccer matches at Anson Road stadium, there being keen rivalry between both teams and spectators. Once in a while, dinner would be taken at Kallang airport (which had quite a reputation for good food), where you could sit and watch the airliners come and go. There were nice beaches for picnics and swimming, parks and gardens to stroll in; the Botanical Gardens had monkeys in amongst a riot of colour, and band concerts were a regular feature. There was Chinatown and the Singapore River, environs around which we were warned to watch our step!

'We were expected to use taxis in town – to uphold the "white man's position", as it were, but since us "service white men" were paid and taxed to UK standards, this rule was pretty hard to adhere to.

'Cheaper socializing was available on base, the Married Families' Club for tombola and dances, with drinks at much lower prices. The various messes also ran dances now and then. Then there was the kampong (native village) just outside the camp gates, (this would be Jalan Kayu) where one could browse around the trinkets and knick-knacks, or get fitted out with civvy clothes expertly made by the Chinese tailors. Later on, when uniform was ordered to be the walking-out dress, these were usually made up too. This enforced change from civilian attire to service KD brought about embarrassment for not a few! In civvies you *could* well be an officer, so as to dazzle the fair sex, or compete with the young "Tuans." No doubt the sudden demotion to Cpl, LAC or even AC2 took some explaining in some cases.'

These happy days came to an end for Eric, not because of his posting to 100 Squadron, in November 1938 – 'The Vildebeest seemed a far cry from the lofty Sunderland, but I could still thrill to the distinctive sound of four Pegasus' in fine pitch, as a 'boat' made its long take-off run along the Straits' – but was due entirely to the following:

So the story goes, when Wing Commander GM Bryer, OBE DFC was Officer Commanding 230 Squadron, he was to play a central part in a very dramatic moment in the history of the RAF.

It was customary for officers to attend Dinning-In Nights on no fewer than four or five evenings a week. In the Officers' Mess at Seletar – reputed to be one of the largest in the Air Force – everyone would dress in Full Mess Kit, Sundays excepted, when they were allowed to wear lounge suits. They would gather in the Dinning Hall to enjoy their evening meal, with traditional entertainment to follow.

September 3rd, 1939, had been a stormy day, with thunder, lightning and heavy rain. Now the atmosphere was oppressive, which tended to make tempers a little short. The formal ritual was well under way when an outsider broke the golden rule of all Messes; he entered the assembly and approached the CO. But protocol was dispensed with seconds later when, in the ensuing hush, the Wg/Cdr rose to his feet and solemnly announced, 'Gentlemen, we are at war.' Then, in a memorable moment, everyone stood and drank a toast to victory. It seems probable that Seletar could have been the only RAF Station to receive the declaration of war in so dramatic a fashion.

Just three months earlier, 230 had lost their first Sunderland (the second to be lost in the RAF service), when L5801 crashed on take off from the Johore Straits. That had been in peacetime; things would be different now.

The station was immediately caught up in war fever. Aircraft suddenly sported two-tone green camouflage, their guns were now loaded with live ammunition, and real bombs replaced the practice version. But for 230 this was the end as far as Seletar was concerned. A month after war was declared they left Singapore for a short spell at Koggala, Ceylon, before heading off for the Mediterranean theatre. Later, they were again to be Ceylon-based, returning to Seletar at the end of the war. Once again they were to remain only a few months, before departing to England, the first time the squadron had been to the UK in ten years.

Long after their departure, 230 Squadron were found to have left behind an interesting memento at Seletar; buried in a long-forgotten grave it was to remain intact for twenty-two years – although sometime during the intervening period, the original wooden headstone had been replaced by one of stone.

It was in June 1959, when two airmen were clearing an overgrown area in preparation for that ancient ritual known as AOC's Inspection, that the site was re-discovered. They carefully unearthed the remains of the rough grave, and what they found was a hatchet and a sealed bottle. When opened, the bottle was found to contain documents which recorded that the hatchet had been buried with due ceremony at 21:00 hours on June 19th, 1937. The burial had apparently been conducted with great solemnity, correct protocol being observed by squadron members. 210 Squadron, their sister unit at Pembroke Dock, had evidently presented 230 with the hatchet upon their departure for Singapore; to commemorate the squadron's good feelings towards 210.

The papers detailed the Parade Orders and a Roll of Attendance; those who served the internment in an official capacity. Two officers and two NCOs had formed the hatchet-bearer party, other NCOs had been responsible for the pyrotechnics, photography, and minute bell. Two further squadron members served as "grave diggers." The torchlight procession had assembled and slowly marched to the burial place. The ritual complete, a headstone commemorating the occasion was placed in position.

The following poem, also contained in the bottle, had been especially written for the occasion.

We brought this axe from Pembroke Dock,
A present from our pals,
Who seem to like us very well,
Although we pinch their gals.

210 Squadron drink their beer,
In gloomy Pembroke Dock,
While we swipe Tops in Singapore,
Each night at 6 o'clock.

Our thoughts this night go out to you,
In wild and woolly Wales
And to dear old Snozzle (you know who),
And friend, Chief Warden Jones.

The hatchet now goes underground,
Escorted by all ranks,
We've had a lot of fun all round,
So many, many thanks.

The final verse has now begun,
Our hatchet's day is o'er,
And in this soil so parched and dry,
T'will rest for evermore.

And, thanks to those airmen of 1959, it did, at least up to 1971 – probably still does. After listing and photographing, the contents were returned to their resting place, the grave expertly restored, headstone freshly painted. Is it today still "rusting in peace" as the original headstone had advocated?

A postscript to this is that there had been a second burial alongside the above mentioned grave. But as this had been a not so elaborate, hastily arranged affair, its remains were probably less evident. This must have taken place a few short weeks before 230's departure to Koggala. It concerned the Malayan phrase "Tidak apa" (or,

(above) The original headstone marking the spot where 230Sqn buried the hatchet" in 1937.
(below) The grave after the hatchet's 1959 airing & reburial.   Peter J Henry

Perhaps inspired by the squadron's hatchet burying escapade of two years previous, the ceremony was to follow a similar pattern.

On the evening of September 4th 1939, a group foregathered near the head of the slipway. There, on a small catafalque, rested the coffin of T'dapa. LAC (later Sqn/Ldr) Syd Manfield takes up the story.

'We proceeded in an orderly or disorderly procession – suitably supported spiritually, or perhaps liquidly, by lashings of Tiger beer – to the grave side, which was next to the grave where the hatchet was buried. A suitable oration, composed and delivered by Henry Austin from an ornate scroll was followed by the firing of a volley – actually a pile of Chinese firecrackers. Then, to the accompaniment of "much weeping, wailing and the gnashing of teeth," or was it something else? T'dapa was interred, together with lots of *objet d'art* of the period; largely consisting of empty Tiger beer bottles.

'The Wake was held in the adjacent grounds of the yacht club, and my most vivid recollection of that particular "thrash" is that of F/O Garside at the piano singing "The King of the Cannibal Islands."'

This ceremony was also reported in Apa Khabar, Vol.1 No3. [In the archives at Hendon.]

Syd Manfield also tells a story of the Christmas dinner of 1938, when the then Station Warrant Officer, "Topper" Brown, was actually to be seen riding a bicycle up and down the tables in the airmen's mess. That never happened in my day!

Although the departure of 230 Squadron meant that Seletar was once again reduced to three squadrons, numerous other units began to materialize. An anti-aircraft co-operation unit had been established towards the end of 1938, and this, under the command of Squadron Leader OS Hurry, DFC AFC, was using the De Havilland 82B Queen Bee, radio-controlled target drone (suitably modified Tiger Moth's). In October of 1939, a spotter unit, was formed to assist in defending Singapore, and in June 1941, the Engineering and Equipment wings were amalgamated to form 151 Maintenance unit

in service parlance T'dapa); roughly equivalent to the Spanish, "Manana," which, contrary to popular belief, does not mean "tomorrow," but, more accurately, "not today." Hence, when upon hearing about the outbreak of war, Wg/Cdr Bryer declared T'dapa to be dead, with hard work and increased efficiency being the order of the day, that was enough for certain imaginative types to arrange a suitable send off for said phrase.

under the command of Group Captain CT Walkington.

The establishment of a Maintenance Unit more or less set a precedent at Seletar, for this was to be maintained by the Japanese during their occupation of the base. After the war the practice continued, with Seletar carrying out most of the major servicing for aircraft in the Far East right up to the time of its closure as an RAF base.[33]

The presence of the maintenance facilities at Seletar before the war meant that a multitude of aircraft types were to be seen on the station at one time or another, and sometimes whole squadrons were detached there for long periods. When war was declared the station was host to Wirraways and Blenheims, in addition to the aircraft permanently based there: Singapore's, Sunderlands, Vildebeests, et al. In February of 1941, the first of Consolidated's Catalinas was to arrive from San Diego, USA, an as yet neutral country. This presented the problem of how the aircraft were to be delivered. In 205 Sqn's case this was resolved by giving ninety dollars and a temporary discharge from the service to each of selected aircrews. These airmen then sailed as civilians to Manilla, in the Philippines – to where the aircraft had been delivered – picked them up and flew them back to Seletar, accompanied by United States Navy crews, also suitably attired in civilian clothes. Surprisingly, everyone returned; a discharge from the Air Force at that time, temporary or not, must have been very tempting. These Catalinas were eventually to replace the Singapores of 205 Squadron, which were then handed over to 5 Squadron, RNZAF. Hudsons and Buffaloes were also to be seen at Seletar, as were some Albacores (the Swordfish replacement that failed). Other assorted types: a Gladiator and some Walrus aircraft, two of which were on the strength of 205 Squadron.

A flying boat contingent also pointed to a marine craft section – the air force's own sailors – with a wide diversity of vessels on hand; floating fuel bowsers, ammunition scows, lighters, pinnaces, fire tenders, and crew transport. Peter Masters recalls working at a radar site on an island to the east of Johore. He says, "the site was ideal for the radar, but notorious for malaria." Before long, Peter was stricken, and requiring immediate hospitalization, the marine craft section sent their secret weapon (and their pride and joy) to pick him up. Pinnace 105 was an experimental high speed crash rescue vessel powered by three Merlin engines. Although brutally fast, it was said to be somewhat of a failure; if all three engines were opened up at once they almost tore the boat apart, therefore only two were normally used. The return leg of this rescue mission proved to be a bit of a problem in that Seletar happened to be holding an after-dark exercise at the time, the station blacked out. With the channel markers switched off, the skipper was trying to get a fix by radio, but no one on shore would answer, everyone under the impression it was all part of the exercise. All turned out well in the end.

To accommodate all these machines, and the men who were to service them, required a host of new buildings, and, for convenience, the camp's division into two sections became more pronounced. "West Camp," as it became known, accommodated the TB squadrons and other land-based aircraft, while "East Camp" became home to No 151 Maintenance Unit (MU); it was also where the flying boat base, and its associated marine craft section, was located. On a camp this size, a bus service also became a necessity.

March 1939 saw the apparently troubled station magazine, *The Straitsman* (cost 40c; a not inconsiderable amount in those days), replaced by a new, free, quarterly version entitled, *Apa Khabar* (which roughly translates as "What News?"), the editorial of which related the following story:

> *A brand-new AC2, just posted to 205 Squadron, was taken by dinghy for his first visit to a Short Singapore, out at its mooring. Passing beneath the wing, with very little overhead clearance, he was heard to remark, 'Gosh! We wouldn't have made it at high tide!'*

But between its covers there was also an item labelled "Stop Press." This made special mention of the need for new facilities on the base, going on to reveal: We are pleased to report that the building programme in the near future will include many amenities for the long suffering "tenants." The following are excerpts from it:

A new NAAFI grocery store is being built and is well under way on the right-hand side of the road leading from the Guardroom to the Families' Club, just beyond the Works and Buildings garage.

Plans have been drawn and construction will begin in the very near future on the new swimming pool. The sum approved to be expended on it is £8000. Its site will be approximately 50 yards within the coconut grove just beyond the Wireless Transmitting Station.

A new children's school, with accommodation for 150 children, is being built near the golf course. Construction work commenced on 20th February.

A sum of £160 has also been approved for a children's playground, and work will commence at once.

The NAAFI store opened its doors in June, but it was to be eight months before the school was ready for occupation, just prior to the swimming pool opening. In September 1940, a new station Church was dedicated by the Reverend BC Roberts, Bishop of Singapore.

Huts and tents also began to appear outside Seletar's boundaries. Initially intended for the evacuation of the coolie population in the event of aerial bombardment, this area became an emergency transit camp for new arrivals, there not being enough accommodation available on the station itself. Tents apart, there were eight huts, each sixty feet long by eighteen feet wide. They had a central passageway and a double-tiered platform on either side, the lower for kit, the upper for sleeping. There were no other beds, but mattresses were supplied on the top platform. New arrivals could expect to stay here for one or two days before moving onto the camp proper.

Even then they were unlikely to see any immediate improvement, for tents and huts were also springing up all over the station. Not only for Air Force personnel, but for members of the other services too, and civilians, such was the rate of expansion. Two companies of the 2/15th Punjabs were accommodated in such fashion when they arrived at Seletar in February 1941.

This swelling of the population must have imposed a strain on the regular camp personnel, which is probably what prompted one JAH Russell (possibly a medic) to pen the following piece of poetic prose, which also was published in Vol 1, No1; that first edition of *Aka Khabar.*

• • • • • • • • • • •

The Distressing Tale of Wilberforce White

Sad is the story of Wilberforce White, whose knees were both pale and a pitiful sight. He worked in Sick Quarters and frequently wrought us hot foments, in which he took fiendish delight. But Wilberforce White was glum indeed, until from his troubles his conscience he freed, in a curious way, which I really must say, was hardly the treatment the doctor decreed. His fate was discovered at first, so they say, by the man in the Watch Hut who rang up one day, to tell Wilberforce, that flying, of course, had been on for an hour and was now in full sway.

But to his surprise, no reply could he get from the Sick Quarters 'phone. Never a moan, or "line engaged" tone; not even a click, a squeak, or a groan. The man in the Watch Hut smartly informed the Guard Room, and shortly the Sick

Bay was stormed by a large posse of Jagas – some slim, some obese – led by a Corporal of Service Police. In the grey light of the early morn, just as the trumpeter blew on his horn, for Wilberforce

White they started to look. They searched every cranny, searched every nook, verandahs and wards, rooms meant for boards, while the Corporal made copious notes in his book. They found jugs and mugs, dangerous drugs, rattan chairs and coconut rugs. But none of the Bobbies could shed a light on the strange disappearance of Wilberforce White.

Soon there came news from the slipway direction, a Flight Sergeant making an early inspection, discovered with loathing a pile of wet clothing which he took to the Orderly Room of his section. In the left sock they discovered a note, for Wilberforce White took the trouble to quote how lonely he was, and how sad and forsaken, and why this particular step he had taken.

My life (he had written) was dismal and grim, nothing but ear drops and Mist Expect Stim, men in the toils of multiple boils and pitiful persons bereft of a limb. Bumps and lumps and aching stumps, and swollen necks suggestive of mumps. Colds in the nose and Singapore toes, were but a few of my cares and woes. Pale persons pining from general debility, families expecting the best of civility, sisters and brothers (some worse than others) all to be treated with utter tranquillity. Following each Sergeants' Mess celebration, regular clients (in some trepidation) came up for doses in high concentration of something to lessen their cranial gyration. Doing their drills, drinking their fills, flying their kites over Johore's hills, paling at gills, making their wills; pleading on bended knee for some pills.

By the time you've translated this letter disjoint, I'll be well on my way, around Punggol Point.

There should be a moral to this little ditty, but what it may be I can't think – what a pity! But you may as well all just keep in sight, the terrible doom of Wilberforce White.

● ● ● ● ● ● ● ● ● ● ●

The civilian population had begun to expand back in March, 1939, when volunteers began to be trained in Operations Room procedures, and within a year civilians were being instructed in different aspects of service life. Subsequently, when the Special Technical Corps was formed, they were required to wear uniform. Unfortunately, methods of recruitment were occasionally less than honest. Because of his ability to speak both Chinese and Malay, a Scottish local enlistee was duly appointed recruiting officer. And although immediately successful, he had to be replaced when it was discovered that the incentive being offered was to assure all new recruits that they would be promoted to sergeant within five months. His successor apparently suffered more than a few awkward moments trying to explain the position once the five months were up! Even worse was the embarrassment caused by the escapades of another early volunteer, a Pilot Officer. He persisted in touring Malaya dressed up as a Group Captain.

This Special Technical Corps – mainly a mixture of Chinese, Indians, and Malays, generally served the Air Force well, and were held in high regard. When the time came for the RAF to leave Singapore, these Specials were given the option of shedding their uniforms and remaining behind, or of serving overseas. About one hundred decided to continue in service with the RAF, but all were ultimately captured in Batavia. Such was their loyalty, it is said they refused the Japanese offer of release, having to be marched out of prison camp at the point of a bayonet. But at war's end over ninety of them marched back with their new wives and families, ready to report for duty!

One vessel occasionally to be seen berthed at Seletar jetty, or anchored out by the flying boats, had nothing whatsoever to do with the marine craft section. This was the RAF Auxiliary, *Tung Song* (known for a time as the *Anne*).[34] It had been chartered from the Singapore Straits Steamship Company at the end of 1939, and was used to run supplies – fuel, ammunition, etc – to outlying areas such as Gan, in the Maldives, ie: emergency landing grounds for use by 205 Squadron's flying boats, and suchlike. It also ran down to Indonesia, and across to Ceylon. Manned by Straits Steamship officers and crew, she also carried an RAF contingent on board, and it was the RAF who controlled its operations. Now painted grey, and flying the RAF ensign, from August 1941 she was commanded by P/O Broadhurst. The ship was fitted with RAF radio equipment, and was armed with Vickers machine guns. Probably the last operational unit of the RAF's Far East Command in March 1942, the *Tung Song* carried over two hundred evacuees – mainly personnel of 205 and 211 Sqns – from Tjilatjap, Java, to Freemantle, Australia. 211 was a Blenheim squadron, originally destined for Sembawang, but eventually operating out of Palembang. [A detailed story of the *Tung Song's* RAF service is told in the recent publication, *So Long, Singapore*; details in Further reading, page 213.]

One 205 Sqn escapee aboard the *Tung Song*, Robert Hampson, in a letter to Len Parry, dated May 1997, describes a little of his life when first posted to Seletar, in 1939, and fond memories of his time with 100 Sqn.

"I joined 100 Squadron, where I spent the next 2½ years and made many good friendships. It was a joy to fly in the old Vildebeest, pure Biggles.... Then came the big change. 205 (Catalinas) needed extra, experienced aircrew, 100 Sqn – re-equipping with Aussie-built Beauforts, with a good sprinkling of Aussie crews – had surplus, and I found myself transferred. I missed the close relationship of the two-manned (sometimes three) Vildebeest, though I did enjoy the comfort of the 'Cat.' I made mates with a fair number of 205 bods, but spent nearly all my off duty hours back with my old mates of 100 Sqn." Robert signs off with the Latin phrases, *Pertana di Malaya* (First in Malaya – the 205 Sqn motto) and the, one supposes, self-composed, *Per Ardua au Seletar* (through hardship at Seletar.)[35]

Young RAF officers found married life in the service to be extremely difficult. Few of them were old enough to receive a marriage allowance, and although they were allowed to live off base, they were still expected to pay for quarters in the Officers' Mess. Marriage was generally frowned upon, although the mask of military discipline could be shed now and again. Neville Shorrick, in his book, *Lion in the Sky*, tells the story of one

such officer. Recalling the time he applied to get married, he tells of how he was ordered to report to his Commanding Officer. 'I stood to attention with my hat on for a full twenty minutes while he tried to talk me out of it. Eventually, seeing the futility of it, he said, 'I suppose nothing I say will make you change your mind, you bloody fool?'

'No sir,' I replied.

'All right then, take this and get out.' He handed me a cheque which paid for our two weeks honeymoon!'

Before war was actually declared, the pace of life at Seletar had already quickened, due in part to the build-up of excitement at the prospect of war, and to the type of man serving – many having entered the Air Force during, or as a result of, the economic slump of the early thirties. One party of men decided to embark on a moral crusade in Singapore town, and were surprised to find that the reaction to their setting fire to a brothel was not at all well received! There were high jinks in the Officers' Mess, too. On one occasion the Station Commander was said to have been kept engaged after a dining-in-night by what he thought were a group of dedicated young officers. Their friends, meantime, were building a brick wall around his car, using quick-drying cement. By the time he was able to extricate himself from proceedings in the Mess, the cement had bonded. He recovered his vehicle next morning, after Works and Buildings personnel had managed to extricate it. Another time, a horse was led into the ante room of the Mess, where it was chloroformed. It apparently took a lot of men to remove it!

But all such escapades came to an end with the declaration of war. This had an almost immediate sobering effect, largely as a result of the restrictions it caused to be imposed. Among them; censorship of the press from September 1st, and the compulsory wearing of uniform outside the camp, introduced three days later.

It seems that even back in 1939 everyone expected any attack to come from the north, this was borne out by a story told me by Ray Mader, at the time a Wop/AG with 100 Sqn.

"It was a Sunday evening, September 3rd 1939, and we were at the Astra cinema when the lights came up and it was announced that all of 'B' Flight, 100 Sqn, and 'A' and 'B' flights of 36 Sqn should report to the hangars immediately. Once there we were informed that we would be leaving first thing in the morning for an undisclosed destination, for an undisclosed period; three aircraft from each flight. Sealed orders were issued prior to take-off and we were not allowed to open them until airborne. Once opened they instructed us to fly to Alor Star, northern Malaya. Once there, we did nothing except standby, then, fifteen days later it was all cancelled and we returned to Seletar. False alarm, or exercise? We never found out."

At Seletar, machine guns and guard posts were mounted at various points around the station, and Sikhs were detailed to patrol the revetments in the bomb dumps – then known as Z MU. For a time, this innovation was to create problems for the Orderly Officer, one of who's duties was to check the security of these storage areas. It seems the Sikh guards had been given strict orders on maintaining this security, so it was not unusual for the Orderly Officer to hear a wild cry, and find a Sikh leaping down on him, loaded rifle and bayonet to hand! Something similar to what befell an officer during the author's spell at Seletar, in the late fifties:

By 1958, Singapore was still officially in the war zone, even though it had long since been declared "white" – as opposed to "black" for operational areas in Malaya; now an independent State. Testimony to the war – or "Emergency," as this particular war was known[36] – lay in the dog tags with which we were issued, and required to wear: name, rank, serial number. Further evidence was provided by the exercises which were occasionally foisted upon us.

I recall one such where an SAS troop were the attacking force, the idea being for them to enter the hangar and symbolically blow up our aircraft; still the Sunderland, although now the Mk 5. We, of course, would prevent just such a thing happening, so we were informed. A game, really, to check on security, but it was a game which kept us up all night.

I was patrolling alongside Squadron HQ when I caught a movement out of the corner of my eye; a shadowy figure attempting to sneak past along the storm drain.

Gotcha, you bugger, thinks I. 'Halt! Who goes there?' I challenged, as required – yes, still the same old procedure. I made a production of cocking the weapon I held, an ominous sound that echoed in the night. That alone was almost guaranteed to stop anyone in their tracks, as it did this joker.

Back through the darkness came the authorized reply; some password or other.

'Advance and be recognized,' I called, sticking to the script, even though I wasn't too sure about the scenario. It might be a game to us, but from tales doing the rounds, those SAS guys played rough. To them, the game was always deadly serious. Fine, so far as my country's enemies were concerned, not too pleasant a thought for such as me, in this kind of situation. For although in reality we were on the same side, tonight, we were technically not. So I wasn't going to him, that was for sure. If he was who I thought he was, nasty things could await me. No thanks, he could come to me, out here in the light where I could see. And where I had a mate to back me up.

Advance someone, or thing, did, emerging from out of the murk and gloom, heading in the general direction of the business end of my rifle. Gradually, almost as if by parthenogenesis, a figure took shape. A figure dressed as an RAF officer, Flight Lieutenant no less. Yes, well... Maybe, maybe not?

'Could I see some identity, sir, if you don't mind.' I didn't ask so much as order, enjoyed doing so. I felt I was quite within my rights in such a situation. Especially as I was at the advantageous end of a weapon, which I pointed threateningly. It was the usual, an ancient Lee Enfield. Unloaded, of course – they weren't taking too many chances. But would he know that?

When he handed me his ID, I realized he would. It was a card: photo, name, rank. Official observer. OK, due etiquette, he now got a salute, for he had his rights, too. He'd been testing me, which made me feel quite chuffed, even though he had been easy to spot. Should have known the SAS wouldn't have been so careless, or compliant. Still, it was enough to keep me on my toes. No one else tried it on that night, I can almost guarantee. Almost? Well, yes. You see, when we entered the locked hangar next morning we found it to be a bit of a mess. A bit good these lads. Paint was everywhere. "SAS were here", and other such messages, plastered across walls and floor. Took some cleaning off, that.

But back to the Seletar of 1941, where minefields had now been laid off the coast, much to the distress of the local fishermen who, in innocence or ignorance, were said to have lost a surprising number of boats in a very short time.

With war now declared, aircraft were placed on a two hour state of readiness, and operational training was intensified. The two TB squadrons, still flying the Vildebeest, had by now become extremely proficient in torpedo bombing. Nevertheless, they were extremely relieved to hear that

in August, 1940, the Chiefs of Staff had declared their aircraft to be obsolete, the planned replacement being the Bristol Beaufort. Despite good intentions, a year later both 36 and 100 Squadrons found themselves pitted against modern ships and Zero fighters from an open cockpit, with a speed of less than one hundred mph, and a radius of action of only one hundred and eighty nautical miles.

The position of the Royal Air Force as a whole was grim, but in Singapore it was desperate. As of July, 1940, the total strength comprised of eighty-eight mainly obsolescent aircraft, and on October 16th, the Chiefs of Staff approved a tactical appreciation of the situation in Malaya which called for five hundred and sixty-six front-line aircraft. Unfortunately, with resources limited, the defence of Britain had to be given the highest priority. Requirements in the Middle East were increasing, and the subsequent invasion of Russia by the Germans meant that still more British aircraft were having to be diverted to help the Russians.

A compromise figure of three hundred and thirty-six aircraft was accepted, but when these reinforcements did eventually begin to arrive they included not a single modern fighter; little help in alleviating a critical situation.

By the time Japan struck, in December, 1941, RAF strength in Malaya was still less than half the revised figures; one hundred and fifty-eight operational aircraft, and a few light planes of the Volunteer Air Force.

Did this lack of preparation result from the fact that, in London, the powers that be, despite evidence to the contrary, refused to believe that the Japanese air forces could be remotely comparable to ours. Even the Commander-in-Chief, Far East, Sir Robert Brooke-Popham, was to later write, *"The strength of the Japanese Air Force came as a complete surprise – in quality, performance, mobility and experience of its personnel."*

With 205 Squadron now converting to the Catalina, the Singapore III being phased out, there is little wonder this poem was to be found on the back of the 'Programme of Doings' at the Squadron Dance. This bash was held at the Roof Garden of the Adelphi Hotel on September 27th 1941 – "a very posh do" I was reliably informed. The poem was attributed to no one.

• • • • • • • • • •

"There was something about those old boats which made them special," says Len Parry, a Cpl instrument repairer with 205 Squadron. "Hard to explain really, with their old-fashioned cockpit with all the fittings and switches in brass. Each boat had a coolie allocated to it full time, just to clean the brass work. The open gun positions, front, back, and one in the middle, had swivel scarfe rings, with a single gun on each, and those huge wings were really something to see. Years later, when I found out the Singapore III's we had given to the RNZAF were scuttled in Fiji harbour, because they were of no further use to them, I confess I nearly cried.

"Compared to war-torn Britain, with its rationing, blackouts, the war going badly," Len explains, "life at Seletar, in peace-time con-

ODE TO THE OLDEST INHABITANTS

Stroll down to the pier one day,
And gaze out o'er the creek,
You'll see them riding at anchor,
I confess they don't look sleek.

They've done a wizard job o' work,
And still are game for more,
Don't think they're growing barnacles,
They've hours in by the score.

Years ago the natives
Gazed on them with awe,
Now the airmen do the same,
Being shaken to the core.

For these old craft can take it,
Of that there is no doubt,
For when there is a panic on,
They call these ancients out.

They charge along the water,
And stagger to the skies,
To carry out their duty,
No matter where it lies.

The pilot's log books tell a tale,
of many journeys flown,
From Kuching, Kuantan, Sarawak,
They always get back home.

In all the publications,
You'll never catch a sight,
Or even any reference ,
To this old warrior kite.

But maybe in a year or so,
When the time is ripe,
The ministry will mention them,
And the world will say, "New type?"

ditions, with plenty of food, was still fairly easy-going. Work from 07:30 to 12:30, a spot of lunch and then "heads down" until 16:00. Down to the pool for a swim, or maybe watch a football match, dinner, then a jar or two in the NAAFI. Excitement was when the mail arrived, usually three months old. There were the odd occasions when some poor soul would receive a 'Dear John' letter from his sweetheart back home, saying it was all finished between them. Squadron tradition at the time was for the letter to be pinned on the notice board and the girl's photo to be hung on a piece of wire in the gents urinal. Everyone was then invited to perform over the poor girl, who eventually became very soggy and finally disappeared down the plug hole to great cheers from the assembled guests. The evening that followed would be a very beery one indeed with Tiger at threepence (2½p) a pint, and a bottle of whisky at nine shillings (45p)."

So what of the officers? In January, 1938, P/O Newall, a 60 Sqn pilot on detachment from India to Seletar, stated in a letter to his parents: "This is a huge station, with a mess that reminds me of a Hotel Splendide. There is hot and cold in all rooms and all mod cons."

P/O Basil Gotto – a pilot with 100 Squadron, more or less confirmed that the officers lived a similar, if rather more upmarket lifestyle, to the airmen. He says that pre-war life at Seletar was "very pleasant, especially so in the case of GD (aircrew) officers, who were seen to be rather exclusive. The normal working day was 8 am until noon, after which, unless there was night flying, one was usually free – disregarding the occasional special duty; assistant officer of the day, etc.

"One usually had a drink before lunch and a siesta after. Then it was usually tennis, squash or some team game. Later, if one was in funds, one could go downtown to the 'Worlds,' or some of us had civilian friends to visit. I had a car, so was quite popular!

On Sunday mornings the Singapore swimming club was confined to men, and we played liar dice before curry tiffin, then lay in the lounge chairs until 3 pm when wives and the children were admitted, shattering our peace."

Things began to change in October 1941, when Japanese Forces began moving into French Indo-China. And by the end of November, some seven hundred aircraft were reported to be based there. Meanwhile, the Japanese invasion fleet carrying Lieutenant-General Tomoyuki Yamashita's troops had set sail, and by the morning of December 6th, 1941, it had rounded Cape Cambodia. Standing by in close support was a force which outnumbered the RAF by a ratio of almost four to one; six hundred and seventeen modern aircraft of the Japanese Army and Navy.

Thus the scene was set, the contestants lined up. The Royal Air Force with its ill-balanced squadrons of veteran aircraft, and the Japanese Forces, ready to fight for a swift and conclusive victory in the air. At Seletar, the main British air base in the Far East, the years of preparation and waiting were over, the moment of truth was nigh. Following years of peace, Seletar's aircraft were about to be committed to fighting, a situation in which they would remain for a majority of the next 25 years.

FAMILIAR FACES AROUND THE CAMP

He'd shine your shoes, make the bed, sweep up, take the laundry, & generally pamper you, all for around a dollar a week. Multiply that dollar by the number of persons per floor & there was no wonder he would also loan you money at a considerable rate of interest!
John Smith

Long time policeman Mehar Singh was in charge of the Guardroom before the war. He also tutored in Malay, and acted interpreter during the Japanese war trials.   *Ken McLean*

A familiar sight & sound around Seletar's barrack blocks. Sew, sew would, for a small fee, darn socks, fix buttons & carry out most sewing repairs.   *Ken McLean*

Known as 'Maingate Mary' this lady was a female searcher at the guardroom during the 1950s.

Ron Willkinson

CHAPTER SEVEN

Prelude To Disaster:
The Importance of Air Power

"...the Japanese are caught in a trap of their own making... Neither by land nor sea nor in the air do they have even a glimmer of a chance of victory."

  The Malayan Tribune, December 3rd 1941.

● ● ● ● ● ● ● ● ● ● ●

The days of wine and roses came to an abrupt end at Royal Air Force Seletar on December 6th, 1941, when the Operations Record Book (F540) for 205 Squadron recorded: *Seletar-6.12.41-0841 No.1 degree of Readiness assumed*. This meant that the RAF squadrons were to be ready to go into action at four hours notice. This was acted upon when a report was received from patrolling Hudsons of 1 Sqn RAAF, that Japanese convoys had been spotted some eighty miles south-east of Cambodia. At 11:20 that same day, in some secrecy, a Catalina of 205 Squadron, coded FV-S, was dispatched to search for, and then to shadow the convoy. This was to be followed at 17:30 that evening, by a relief aircraft, W8417, FV-W, captained by W/O William E. Webb. (Most contemporary reports record F/O Pat Bedell as being the captain of this aircraft, but this was not so. The misconception was probably based on the fact that, with F/O Bedell being the ranking officer aboard, he was assumed to be the captain; his position was in fact that of co-pilot.)

Singapore slept peacefully, unaware of these events, but the operations room at Seletar was a hive of activity. Senior officers, having been informed of what was unfolding up north, awaited news which could set in motion actions which had been long prepared: Operation Matador, a defence plan that called for the occupation of a part of Siam (Thailand) – not exactly a neutral country, but supposedly so. This was delayed by both politics, and the need to get American agreement, by which time it was too late. Politics; being "too late"; clashes of personality; incompetence in high places: scenarios that, in retrospect, seemed to occur all too frequently during the following weeks.

A message was received from the first Catalina to say the Japanese had not been located, the aircraft landing back at Seletar at 00:30 on December 7th. (All times referring to the incident up to this point are taken from the log kept by P/O CH Keon-Cohen – 205 Sqn's Operations Officer – and are therefore in GMT. From this point we revert to local time.)

Of the relief aircraft, nothing more was heard. After a time, even though there had been no signal to the effect that the aircraft was being attacked, the Squadron Commander could only assume that contact with the enemy fleet had been made, and the aircraft shot down. But, misled by a report that the Catalina had been contacted on an incorrect frequency, hope continued to prevail until the aircraft's endurance had to be regarded as an impossibility. This unwelcome situation occurred at 14:45 hours, but it was not until much later that anxiety gave way to hopeless despair: the aircraft had rightly to be assumed lost. However, this was only confirmed after the Japanese surrender, in 1945, when documents relating to the incident were made available and translated.

The Japanese convoys had apparently been sailing northwards along the Cambodian coast, accompanied by a strong fighter escort. At about 07:50, a Catalina appeared to spot them from a position a few miles north-west of Pulau Penjang. (In the report, the Catalina was wrongly identified as a Sunderland; pretty poor a/c recognition!) When it dived to take a closer look it was jumped by at least four fighters, and, suddenly aware of the danger, it made a desperate attempt to shake off its pursuers. Suddenly there was a huge explosion, and the Catalina disintegrated in mid-air, almost taking one of the fighters with it. The actual destruction of a flying boat was logged as 08:00 local time.

Thus, to W/O Webb and his 205 Squadron crew, went the unfortunate distinction of not only becoming Seletar's first wartime casualties, his was also the first aircraft to be shot down in the Pacific War. Information on the presence of this Japanese convoy was transmitted to both London and Washington, the information being received in Hawaii a full sixteen hours before the attack on Pearl Harbour. It had been assessed as not affecting Hawaii!

Naturally, the people at Seletar who were involved were worried by the non-appearance of their Catalina. For 205 Sqn personnel it was, "sadness and anger at the loss of friends you had known for quite some time," but for the majority, life went on as normal. Indeed, throughout December and January, most airmen recall little change worth writing about in their letters home. They did mention the daily bombings, of course, but one has to assume these people were observers rather than targets; those out on the airfield had plenty to keep them occupied.

Sunday December 7th,1941, and Singapore was a city ablaze with light, bustling with activity, filled with people seemingly determined to enjoy themselves; in fact, Singapore was normal. The streets were still busy at midnight on December 8th, when the first moves of war in the Pacific occurred, the Japanese storming the beaches above Kota Bahru, on Malaya's north-east coast. Seventy minutes later would come the strike on

RAF strength on December 7th 1941

Aircraft	Unit	Location	On line	U/s	Totals
Vildebeest	No.36 Sqn	Gong Kedah/Seletar	15	3	
Vildebeest	No.100 Sqn	Seletar	16	2	36
Hudson	No.1 Sqn RAAF	Kota Bahru	8	6	
Hudson	No.8 Sqn RAAF	Kuantan	8	5	
Hudson	MU		2	2	31
Catalina	No.205 Sqn	Seletar	3	2	5
Blenheim I	No.27 Sqn	Sungei Patani	8	4	
Blenheim I	No.60 Sqn	Kuantan	9	4	
Blenheim I	No.62 Sqn	Alor Star	12	1	
Blenheim I	MU			5	43
Blenheim 5	No.34 Sqn	Alor Star	21	2	
Blenheim 5	MU			1	24
Buffalo	No.243 Sqn	Kallang/Kota Bahru	11	12	
Buffalo	No.453 Sqn	Sembawang	19	5	
Buffalo	No.488 Sqn	Kallang	14	3	
Buffalo	No.21 Sqn RAAF	Sungei Patani	23		
Buffalo	MU		12	27	126
Totals			**181**	**84**	**265**

Pearl Harbour, across the ocean, although the difference in time zones saw this attack on America being recorded as the start of the Pacific War. As can been seen, the Japanese declared war by the dropping of bombs. Singapore was to suffer its first air raid at around 04:00; sixty-one civilians being killed, one hundred and thirty-three injured.

Seletar also was subjected to its first aerial bombardment on this day, various domestic buildings being hit resulting in two deaths. Eleven other bombs hit the airfield, six of them failing to explode. Cpl Eric Cooper, who was in the barrack block that was hit, describes the raid in his book, *Tomorrow You Die*, as follows:

'There was a terrific explosion, immediately followed by a great rumbling of falling masonry, with brick and concrete splitting and falling everywhere. I was fortunate that I was partially screened from the blast and falling debris... my bed was in a corner of the billet. However, above everything there was a great pall of dust which seemed to signify the end of the world was nigh. Suddenly, there was a cry, a terrible wailing moan, an indescribable sound... A quick role call revealed two sergeants failing to answer... all we could find were bits of clothing and personal kit... As far as I know, these were the first casualties at RAF Seletar.'

A Malayan airman gave his version of the same raid:

'At approximately 4.15 am, there were several thunderous explosions. Most of us were out of our beds the next instant.... The pom-pom next to "F" block, where we were billeted, started sending tracer bullets into the air and searchlight beams stretched into the sky..... There was a big panic as those on the top and first floors started running for the stairs shouting "Germans, Germans." All eyes were turned towards the sky.'....

Later, an "Order of the Day" was issued. Signed by Air Chief Marshal Sir Robert Brooke-Popham, Commander-in-Chief, Far East, and Vice Admiral G Layton, Commander-in-Chief, China, it was read out in the Mess at Seletar to the Station Commander, Group Captain H.M.K. Brown, along with some fifty other officers.

The order began:
Japan's action today gives the signal for the Empire's Naval, Army and Air Forces, and those of their Allies, to go into action with a common aim and common ideals.

It went on to state:
We are ready. We have had plenty of warning and our preparations are made and tested ... We are confident. Our defences are strong and our weapons efficient. Whatever our race and whether we are now in our native land or have come thousands of miles, we have one aim and one only. It is to defend these shores ... While from the civilian population, Malay, Chinese, Indian or Burmese, we expect that patience, endurance and serenity which is the great virtue of the East and will go far to assist the fighting men to gain final and complete victory.

The point of such a declaration must surely have been an appeal to all races to resist a common enemy, for the RAF personnel at Seletar were well aware of the fact that they were about to go to war using inferior equipment. And what irked them most, was the fact that, as a consequence, they would be hard put to live-up to the expectations many local people had of them.

The net result of this raid was that ground defences were strengthened, trenches were dug all over the camp, buildings and roads were painted black. This was also about the time that a new unit came into being at Seletar. X Party, under the command of Sqn/Ldr O.S. Gregson, became unofficially known as Gregson's Grenadiers: a contingent of airmen that were being trained for the role of airfield defence. It is said that Sqn/Ldr Gregson, an inspirational leader, personally instructed the party in bayonet practice, and was often to be seen charging around amongst the rubber trees, rifle and bayonet to hand. Although taken prisoner by the Japanese, Sqn/Ldr Gregson (by now a Wg/Cdr) survived the war, eventually settling in West Australia.

The effect on morale of this raid was said to be almost negligible. Most seemed to look upon it as an excitable incident which had broken the monotony, and few seemed to doubt that, should push come to shove, Britain would come out on top. These thoughts were to be quickly dispelled during the raids to come.

Meanwhile, with 205 Squadron carrying out reconnaissance sorties, seven Vildebeests of 36 Squadron – on standby at Gong Kedah, Northern Malaya – went into action against the Japanese fleet at Kota Bahru, joining other British aircraft in an offensive against ships and landing craft. Upon retuning to Gong Kedah, they reported that a number of landing craft, plus a ship carrying tanks, had been sunk.

Peter Masters, by now a W/Op with the squadron, says: 'There is no doubting the Japs took very heavy casualties making this landing at Kota Bahru. They used strings of local boats towed by armoured power barges, and because these boats were packed with troops and very vulnerable, our aircraft caused heavy damage. The lads I spoke to were full of praise for the RAAF chaps in their Hudsons. Because the strip was so close to the point of the landings it was almost like Circuits and Bumps, with a quick re-arm in between.'

The squadron took off again at 06:27, into the teeth of a heavy storm. Refuelled, and re-armed with torpedoes, their orders were to deliver a concerted attack on the invasion fleet, but with conditions rapidly deteriorating, and with almost zero visibility, two aircraft lost touch with the main formation and proceeded on their own. The other five Vildebeests, led by their Squadron Commander, Sqn/Ldr Witney, failed to sight the convoy until 07:30, when they launched into an immediate attack on a Japanese cruiser. By this time the storm was so fierce that it proved impossible to synchronize their efforts, only four torpedoes being dropped – without positive result.

Battered by the elements, all seven aircraft managed to return safely to Kota Bahru; where in July 1940, 100 Sqn had been detached to open up the new station. Heavy fighting was taking place along the coast, and three Vildebeests received immediate orders to take off again to attack barges and strafe the beaches. But by 16:00, hours, the enemy had reached the airfield boundary, and 36 Squadron were ordered to take off for Kuantan, one hundred and fifty air miles to the south-east. All seven aircraft survived to fight another day.

Inexperienced ground-crews joined in with elements of the 11th Indian Division of the British Army to put up an almost fanatical defence of the airfield at Kota Bahru, buying time whilst the aircraft withdrew. An aircraftsman described what happened, in this, his first taste of action.

'We fought with rifles and tommy guns from billet to billet. The Japanese would be in one place, we in another, and the range was 25 yards. Very soon all the aircraft which had not got away were a burnt mass of twisted metal, and still the Japs came on.'

The heroic ground crews managed to hold out until, under cover of the monsoon rains, and with nothing left to defend, they were able to slip away to safety. They were taken by road down to Kuala Lipis, and from there back to Singapore by rail.

Come war's end, Japanese prisoners under interrogation were able to testify to other acts of heroism at Kota Bahru; one of the most poignant being that of a Blenheim pilot. With his aircraft hit, and in flames, the pilot, managing to maintain some control as it plunged towards the ground, was able to guide it into a Japanese landing craft, accounting for the vessel and all its occupants.

Back at Seletar, the relative peace was shattered when a Hudson of No.8 Sqn RAAF crashed onto the airfield whilst attempting to land. It had been hit and damaged when attacking a well-armed launch.

The only unit yet to see action was 100 Sqn. Nine of their Vildebeest's, plus two from 36 Sqn, had been ordered to stand by, ready to make a torpedo attack on the Japanese fleet. But by the time they arrived at Kuantan, and had been armed and refuelled, it was all too late, the enemy had already secured a beachhead at Kota Bahru, and the town had fallen.

December 9th was the day the first raid was launched from RAF Tengah, six 34 Squadron Blenheims departing, three of them crewed by personnel from 60 Squadron. When their fighter escort failed to show up at the rendezvous, the bombers proceeded to the target alone. At Singora they were first subjected to a tremendous anti-aircraft barrage, followed by a prolonged attack by thirty plus fighters. Despite these odds, they succeeded in bombing the airfield; albeit at the cost of half their aircraft.

A second raid on the same target was planned for later that day, though this failed to materialize. Even as the Blenheims of No's 34 and 62 Squadrons were lining up for take-off from Butterworth, the Japanese mounted a raid on the airfield, destroying or disabling all the machines on the ground. Sqn/Ldr Arthur Stewart King Scarf, being first off, was already airborne, so he decided to carry on alone. Although subjected to attack by enemy fighters over Singora, he managed to carry out his bombing run. Then, on the run for home, his aircraft was riddled, Sqn/Ldr Scarf, having been hit in the back and left arm, was severely wounded. Becoming increasingly weak through loss of blood he, assisted by his navigator, somehow managed to keep the battered machine airborne and return to Alor Star. The aircraft was seen to approach from the north, then, on the crosswind leg of a high circuit, it dipped suddenly. With a supreme effort, Scarf, taking control back from his navigator managed to recover the situation, putting the Blenheim down in a paddy field close to the hospital without injury to the rest of the crew. In need of a blood transfusion, Sqn/Ldr Scarf was immediately transferred to the hospital at which his wife was a nurse, but, tragically, he succumbed to his injuries two hours later.

Sqn/Ldr Scarf was awarded the Victoria Cross "For outstanding gallantry and devotion to duty," the first to be won in the Pacific war. (At RAF Tengah, his deeds were commemorated by the naming of a barrack block in his honour. The VC won by Sqn/Ldr Scarf is on public display at the RAF Museum, Hendon.)

Meanwhile, Seletar was experiencing problems of her own; a high-level bombing raid around noon had destroyed four Hudsons and a Vildebeest on the ground, as well as causing extensive damage elsewhere on the station. Then, at 22:00 hours, a report was received from Army Intelligence that the enemy were now landing at Beserah, just north of Kuantan, giving them a foothold halfway down Malaya's east coast, barely 200 miles north of Singapore.

With the telephone line to Kuantan dead, it was decided to send a strike force from Seletar and Sembawang. Six Vildebeests of 36 Sqn had recently returned from Kuantan, and these, along with three Hudsons of 62 Sqn, were briefed for a night attack, although the operation was once again delayed by the weather – this time with disastrous consequences. At 02:00 hours, as the Vildebeests began to get airborne, Sqn/Ldr Witney's aircraft, well into its take-off run, collided with the taxiing aircraft of Flying Officer Langley. Peter Masters observed the event, and described what he saw.

'It was a dark night and the camp was observing a strict black-out. There were widely-spaced gooseneck flares marking the runway, but nothing to indicate a taxying lane. We heard the CO's aircraft begin its run and saw the flames of its exhausts. He looked to be almost airborne when a shadowy shape moved at a slow rate from the direction of the bomb dump, and at right angles to the CO's aircraft. There was a thunderous explosion and the CO's aircraft sped on as a ball of fire, the bombs exploding, killing all the crew. F/O Langley's aircraft took fire, its ruptured fuel tank – situated in the centre section of the upper wing – pouring burning fuel on the two-man crew. Enveloped in flames, F/O Langley managed to scramble out, but it was a little time before he was grabbed by some ground staff, and he, too, subsequently died of his injuries. The W/OP, Sgt Philpot, got out on fire and rolled over and over in the damp grass, and although badly burned he was eventually sent home on a hospital ship.'

A.J.C. (Dick) Fowden, a medic assigned to the garages which at the time formed the emergency SSQ, also recalled the incident. 'I had seen badly burned patients before,' he says, 'but these were the worst. I never heard until much later what happened to these men as I was posted from Seletar the next day.'[37]

The four remaining aircraft took off and set course for Beserah. After further delays, the Hudsons finally departed Sembawang two hours later.

When the Vildebeests arrived on station all that was to be seen were four small ships. The Hudsons failed to locate anything either. And with the arrival of dawn, with no shipping at all being visible, it became evident that the reported sightings of the previous day had been false. These reports were also to play havoc with the movements of the British fleet, which was at present sailing off the east coast of Malaya.

Against professional advice from the Admiralty, Mr Churchill decided to send a deterrent force out to help in the defence of Singapore. This fleet – known as Force Z – under the command of Admiral Sir Tom Phillips, departed the UK in October 1941. It comprised of what was then available: the brand new, King George V class battleship, *Prince of Wales*, and the ancient cruiser, *Repulse*. Escorted by four destroyers, the fleet arrived in Singapore on December 2nd, 1941. Their accompanying aircraft carrier *Indomitable* had been unavoidably delayed, dry-docked in Norfolk, Virginia, after running aground; prelude to a major disaster.

'This was just the thing to boost our morale,' stated a Seletar-based airman who was witness to the arrival of these capital ships. He, along with several friends were apparently strolling by the shore when the *Prince of Wales* and the *Repulse* passed through the Straits on their way to the naval base, a scene that was much heralded in the local press.

The elation was not to last for long however. By December 10th both vessels lay on the bottom of the South China Sea, off Kuantan, diverted to the area on the strength of a false report. With their escort carrier still delayed, they had sailed without air cover, into an area infested with Japanese aircraft. Admiral Phillips, who went down with his ship, was of the irreversible opinion that the danger to ships from air power was wildly exaggerated. Even Sir Arthur Harris, with whom he had once worked, had warned him, 'Tom, never get out from under the air umbrella, if you do, you'll be for it.'

Admiral Phillips, having ignored this advice, apparently chose to go down with the *Prince of Wales*, reports stating he made no effort to abandon the vessel when he could so easily have done so.

And so, in an action lasting little over an hour the enemy had almost totally eliminated our naval forces in the area. With the evening bulletins already being dominated by news of withdrawals in North Malaya, the sudden announcement of the loss of the *Prince of Wales* and the *Repulse* was nothing short of devastating.

As an aside to the loss of these ships, Dick Fowden says that from then on, airmen going into Singapore for an evening out – especially to the Union Jack Club – were deliberately sought out by navy personnel. Blaming the RAF for the loss of their ships and men, they were prepared to fight any air force personnel they could find.

During the first three days of war the Japanese had gained an unprecedented ascendency, virtually driving the Royal Air Force out of the skies and airfields of northern Malaya, the Japanese Army Air Force flying around three hundred strike missions against our bases up there. Only fifty out of the one hundred and ten aircraft which had been stationed in northern Malaya remained operational, and of these, only ten were still located in the area, concentrated at Butterworth, on the West coast. Butterworth seemed safe for a while – at least from an overland attack from Kota Bahru – effectively protected from the east coast by virtue of one hundred and fifty miles of inhospitable jungle-covered mountains, and a lack of roads. Naturally, it was vulnerable to attack from the air.

It seems quite possible that at least some of the credit for the Japanese success could be laid at the feet of an Irishman named Heinan. As an

'Whispering Death' – a pair of Beaufighters over the Malayan jungle.   *Bill Richardson*

Army Captain, he came to Seletar about six months before the war on an air/ground liaison course; he was later caught at Butterworth with wireless sets and other spying kit in his possession.

Seletar's torpedo bomber squadrons, having not yet seen action, were still largely intact. With the decision having been taken that the aircraft were far too vulnerable to risk on daylight missions up north, the Vildebeests had been held in reserve to deal with any sudden emergency, such as a seaborne assault on Singapore. They were therefore forced into an uneasy five weeks of waiting, although some anti-submarine patrols were flown, and over a period of five days – December 12-17th. And they did manage to recover a large number of torpedos from the base at Kuantan. This aside, the men of 100 Squadron felt they had not yet played a part in the war. On top of which, their long-promised conversion to Bristol's Beaufort – claimed to be the fastest medium bomber in the world, at the time – failed to materialize.

Crews, led by their CO, Sqn/Ldr McKern, had been despatched to Australia to pick up some Beauforts, and the type did arrive on December 6th, much to the joy of the squadron, only for their hopes to be dashed just days later. A misunderstanding had led to these Australian-

built aircraft being supplied minus defensive armament of any kind, and upon arrival in Singapore, the RAF, quite rightly, refused to accept them. The unwanted aircraft were therefore returned from whence they came, being absorbed into the RAAF. The lumbering Vildebeest's days were not yet up.

Quietly and efficiently the flying boats of 205 Squadron continued to patrol the seas; six reconditioned Singapores still lending support to the Catalinas, until, on December 13th, the last two Singapores were handed over to the Royal New Zealand Air Force. Other Catalinas, on loan from the Dutch, were flown to Seletar from Surabaya and brought into use, and by December 15th squadron strength was up to seven, albeit, three of which were unserviceable. In addition to the Catalinas, 205 also possessed two Supermarine Walrus amphibians, transferred to them from the Fleet Air Arm. 36 Squadron had thirteen Vildebeest III's on strength, plus five Fairey Albacores – these again, transferred across from the FAA. Now bereft of the five Beauforts which had, theoretically, belonged to them – albeit briefly – 100 Squadron were back to their Vildebeests: seventeen MkIII's – two of them unserviceable – and a single MK1. The aircraft may have been obsolete, but perhaps the Japanese should have paid heed the motto which adorned 100 Squadron's badge: "Never stir up a hornet's nest."

With all of these aircraft being based at Seletar – a large part of Singapore's surviving air power – it was important that every effort was made to prevent them being destroyed on the ground. With this in mind they were dispersed to all corners of the airfield: along the road round the perimeter fence; out on the way to the main gate; on the golf course; and by the Officers' Mess.

Families were being moved away from the station, their quarters required to house essential personnel and equipment. Most of these families found themselves evacuated to Woodbridge Hospital, a mental institute on the Yio Chu Kang Road. Ground crews were split into four groups: the first – those vital to the efficiency of the squadrons, retained use of their barrack blocks; the second – a sufficient number of men able to arm and get the aircraft airborne at short notice, lived in tents under the rubber trees lining the golf course. The main body were housed in a transit camp outside Seletar, whilst Maintenance Flight – which dealt only with major overhauls, and were thus never needed in a hurry, were billeted in a cinema out at Paya Lebar, five miles away. Just prior to Christmas, 1941, the Ling Nan School, along Orchard Road, was taken over and used to accommodate two hundred airmen.

'There was a very real danger of being bombed in the main blocks,' Peter Masters commented. 'I lived on the second floor, and a Japanese aircraft, with landing lights ablaze, flew across – looking just like a Catalina on finals – and let go a cluster of anti-personnel bombs. These killed the few lads on the ground floor and five others having a drink of lemonade on the veranda of the NAAFI, opposite.'

Well aware of the fact that, as the situation deteriorated, discipline might suffer, the Station Commander, Grp/Cpt Brown, paid particular attention to the needs of the station, keeping everything more or less under control. But, so the story goes, deciding to hold a full scale parade for all personnel, he inadvertently created the very situation he had been trying to avoid; part of the proceedings ending in chaos, even if it is credited with causing some hilarity. This is what is purported to have happened:

Led by Wing Commander Burgess, 205 Squadron arrived at the airfield, where the parade was to be held. At the conclusion of the march past, all squadrons set off back to their individual areas, 205 led by their Wing Commander and his Adjutant.

The squadron was divided into two flights, the first led by Flt/Lt Atkinson, the second by Flt/Lt Stilling. And as they neared the end of their hot and tiring trek, Wg/Cdr Burgess gave a command which apparently no one heard very clearly.

Flt/Lt Atkinson is said to have interpreted the command as "left wheel," which he did, taking his flight along a road which led between various buildings. Flt/Lt Stilling, on the other hand, took it to be "halt," his flight doing so. In complete and blissful ignorance of what had happened behind, Wg/Cdr Burgess marched solemnly ahead, accompanied only by his Adjutant and the 2 I/C. Needless to say, the sight of the three officers disappearing into the distance took quite a while to live down.

Such treasured moments were now becoming all too rare, for the invasion of Borneo had begun, and the Catalinas were required to patrol around the clock. The aircraft had been attacked frequently, but all had survived. The situation was to change dramatically on Christmas Day.

Two Catalinas were airborne, one flown by Sqn/Ldr Jardine, the other by Flt/Lt Atkinson. They were on patrol over the South China Sea when suddenly, well outside the range of the Catalina's guns, Flt/Lt Atkinson's aircraft was attacked by a Japanese, twin-engined, armed reconnaissance plane. Cannon and machine-gun fire hit the Catalina's port wing. After an action lasting some minutes, fire broke out, forcing the flying boat down, two hundred miles east of Kuantan, where the aircraft exploded. The second Catalina checked the exact position and signalled it in. It was too rough for them to land and pick up survivors, and no launches were immediately available, but the Dutch sent a destroyer to help out. Meanwhile, another

Catalina had sighted wreckage, managing to drop a dinghy and supplies. Badly burnt, cut and suffering from shock, the survivors spent that night at sea, eventually being picked up by a submarine on Boxing Day. They were found to be in extremely good spirits, thanks largely to the efforts of Flt/Lt Atkinson. This action resulted in the award of two DFCs

Christmas Day on the station was extremely quiet. Parties at the Officers' and Sergeants' Messes were cancelled due to the imposition of normal working hours. The airmen fared better, there being an unusually large number of officers and NCOs on hand to serve Christmas lunch, as is traditional. This party was reported to have been a very happy affair, with plenty of beer flowing for those few airmen not needed for essential duties; for everyone else it was a clear choice between warm lemonade or water.

According to Peter Masters, the officers and NCOs serving lunch would not have had their work cut out! 'We had a tin of bully beef between every two lads, this in a shattered dining hall, with a few grim reminders up the side of the white tiles as to the fate of those caught there when the bombs fell. We did have a boxing match between 100 and 36 Squadrons. There was still Tiger beer to be had, and some of the lads rode station bikes off the diving board into the swimming pool.'

As the year drew to a close, impending misfortune was clearly evident. Hong Kong fell before Christmas, Borneo, shortly after, and in Malaya, British forces were being unceremoniously pushed back down the peninsula, towards Singapore. Aircraft reinforcements were an immediate priority, but only six Hudsons, three Catalinas and seven Blenheims had reached Malaya by Christmas Day. Starting December 29th, Japanese aircraft began to attack Singapore in a great show of strength. RAF Tengah bore the brunt of the first of this new series of raids, its runway badly cratered, with three Blenheims being rendered hors de combat. This signalled the start of a period when the ground staff at all four of Singapore's airfields – RAF Seletar and Tengah, FAA Sembawang, and the civil airport at Kallang – struggled night and day to keep the runways open and the aircraft flying. No praise could be too high for their efforts. One of the many stories from that time concerned the occasion when fire broke out in the bush around Tengah, threatening the remaining stocks of fuel and ammunition. Undaunted by the obvious danger, a bulldozer driver succeeded in using his machine to create a fire break between the burning bushes and the dumps. In a lighter vein is the story of how spotters, up on one of the water towers, were said to have laughingly ripped up their clothing to plug the bullet holes, thus protecting the vital water supply. [Though they probably laughed later, it is difficult to believe they'd be doing so at the time, with bullets whistling about their ears.]

In addition to the almost ceaseless low-key attacks, Seletar was to suffer five high-intensity attacks during January of 1942. Most accounts refer to formations of twenty-seven high-flying aircraft sweeping down from Malaya (three squadrons of nine aircraft), and of the bombing being very accurate, the formation appearing to release their bombs upon a signal from the leader. Extensive damage was inflicted during this period; hangars, workshops, and the Headquarters building all suffered by varying degrees, but because of that decision to disperse vital equipment and aircraft around the station, the damage caused was of little strategic importance. Even so, throughout the month of January, five aircraft were destroyed on the ground or in the water, twelve servicemen and two local labourers being killed.

After the third such raid it was decided to reduce the number of personnel working in the administration building, which was located fairly centrally. Most of the staff were withdrawn into Singapore town, though Unit Headquarters was transferred to a Warrant Officer's quarter, on the far side of the camp. This proved to be a rather fortuitous move, for during the next raid the original Headquarters building was hit a number of times. One bomb scored a direct hit on the hutted extension, completely gutting the building, equipment and records being destroyed.

Back home, during the Battle of Britain, it is said that Londoners fell into the habit of listening to "Lord Haw Haw" on the wireless, until his voice began to fade. Only then would they take to the Andersen shelters in their gardens; that fading voice a sure sign that an air raid was imminent. Likewise, Singapore's residents soon developed a similar routine; reading the signals.

Charles McCormac – who was stationed at Seletar – states in his book, *You'll Die in Singapore*:

> *Soon, visits from the Japanese bombers began to come with monotonous regularity. At first, they concentrated on the aerodrome, using small, anti-personnel bombs, perhaps because they were anxious not to spoil a prize they knew would soon be theirs. Later, Singapore town and harbour came in for their share of bombing, but usually the aircraft made a point of attacking Seletar on their return journey. It was all done with repetitive timing: every morning at 09:50 hours, every afternoon at 15:00 hours. Twenty-seven bombers flying in perfect formation.... 09:50 hours, 15:00 hours.... day after day.*[38]

Eventually, everyone would anticipate the arrival of the enemy. Night raids were not nearly so accurate, possibly because of the searchlights. But by watching the searchlights, Seletar's residents were still able to judge just how close the danger was.

From the early days of the war, effective early warning of Japanese air raids was given by a radar station which had been established at Mersing, on the east coast, about eighty miles north of Singapore. But, coming under threat from the unexpectedly swift Japanese advance, this station was hastily dismantled and removed. Reliance for warning of impending attack was now limited to visual identification, and much thought had obviously been given to the siting of Seletar's look-out post, so as to ensure maximum field of vision. Rising from the shore beside the creek, the tall, spindly tower was constructed from lashed-together bamboo, topped by a small eyrie. It was connected to loudspeakers, strategically sited at various places around the camp. The task of manning this vital post seemed to have been entrusted to a single man, his idiosyncratic Glaswegian voice alone being heard over the air. Matching its dialectal singularity was the remarkable composure it was said to display. Even during the attack by enemy fighters which sank some of 205 Squadron's Catalinas, peppering the tower itself with some fusillades, the imperturbable voice maintained its running commentary. Being endowed with courage, its owner also seemed to be blessed with good fortune, for he continued to function in his eyrie at least until the last of Seletar's surviving aircraft left for Palembang.

James McEwan (at the time, intelligence officer for No's 36 and 100 Squadrons), describes in his book, *The Remorseless Road*,[39] what he heard from his shelter during his first experience of a raid.

'I've picked them up,' the voice announced. 'They're coming in from the Causeway. I think there are twenty-seven of them. They're flying at about twenty-five thousand feet, in three viks. They seem to be making for Sembawang.' Pause. 'Correction. They've passed Sembawang. It must be Seletar now.' Another pause. 'They're closing in on the perimeter. Soon they'll be overhead. Take cover! *Take cover!* Bombs away!' came the voice in final admonition from the loudspeakers. '*Bombs... away!*'

People's recollections of those days often make amusing reading. An NCO with 205 Squadron recalled that: 'Seletar, in my memory, will always be the Sergeants' Mess during a night air raid. The siren would go, the old Far East types would make for the air-raid shelters, the ex UK types would collect all the beer from the evacuated tables and have a throughly enjoyable night!' Whereas Basil Gotto – who later committed to paper his recollections during this time [RAF Hendon, Aviation Records Department document B1758] – recalls always being well prepared. "I used to arrange my clothes for a quick getaway. As soon as the sirens went, I could put my legs straight into my trousers and flying boots, and my shirt was handy. On my way downstairs, my gas-mask was hanging, with attached to it, a tin hat, mackintosh and a cushion."

The shelters were reported as being not very ambitious; simple trenches, half-covered with corrugated iron[40] and earth, and designed to accommodate six. The floor was of granite chips, and they were said to be very uncomfortable, hence the need of a cushion, one supposes.

P/O Gotto also tells of a fellow pilot who was in the shower when the sirens sounded, arriving in the trench wearing only his tin hat. He says he had also grabbed a towel, but, being white, he thought it too conspicuous, so threw it away. He went on to say, "Our nights were getting so disturbed that all aircrews were given permission to live out, so long as they were within five miles. As the station was miles from anywhere, this did not offer much scope. Some went to Paya Lebar, which was only just within range. 36 Squadron opted for the Singapore United Club, some of us took one of the doctors' houses at the Lunatic Asylum." (Woodbridge Hospital.)

Many families still lived on the island, but between raids they somehow still managed to enjoy most of the facilities they had come to expect in peacetime. One person particularly concerned with family welfare was Seletar's famous Padre, the Reverend Alan Giles. His fortitude and consideration gave many the necessary strength to face the trials imposed on them. But Alan Giles, as well as being a dedicated man of God, was also gifted with great presence of mind. It is said that on one occasion, enemy aircraft arrived overhead just as he was about to begin a christening, the proud young officer and his wife already walking up the aisle. Leaping forward, so the story goes, Padre Giles snatched the baby from the arms of the startled couple and shouted, 'The Father, the Son, the Holy Ghost, and get the hell out of here as soon as you can,' justifiably claiming an all-time record for a christening.

The accuracy of the Japanese bombing was by now causing increasing concern, and by January 1st it was officially accepted that lights were being used to guide the bombers onto their targets. Almost certainly correct, for it was about this time that Vildebeest pilots reported seeing lights in the Straits, and on the north-east side of the island, as related to me by Peter Masters.

'On the 5th of Jan, in an air of "great secrecy," Flt/Sgt Allison, pilot, with me as W/Op, took off at night and flew over an island in the Straits, thirty or forty miles from base. After circling three or four times we were rewarded by compact fires on the ground in the formation of a "T", pointing towards Singapore. Naturally, we never heard what transpired.'

Everyone was immediately warned to be on the look-out for collaborators. 'We were furious to think that people were actually helping those so and so's,' said an officer whose wife was living off the Tampines Road, a few miles from Seletar. 'So one night when I managed to get home, and my wife told me that a house up the road wasn't observing the black-out regulations, I saw red. I stormed round to see for myself, and sure enough the house was ablaze with light. Every window was open and every light was on. The occupant turned out to be Dutch, and when I told him to turn his lights off, he told me to go to hell, and that it wasn't his war. I drew my gun and said I'd shoot him if he didn't do as I said – and I would have, too! I also put him under arrest and marched him off to the police station.'

One less to worry about, although it did little to ease the burden of worry. The situation was about to become desperate.

CHAPTER EIGHT

The End Is Nigh: The Battle Lost

"There were in Malaya no transport aircraft, no long-range bombers, no dive-bombers, no army co-operation aircraft, no special photo-reconnaissance aircraft. To sum up there was in fact no really effective striking force in Malaya .... Nevertheless, there was throughout the fighting services a firm resolve to do the best with the limited means at our disposal ...."
(from *The War in Malaya* by Lt Gen A.E. Percival, General Officer Commanding Malaya, 1941-1942.)

• • • • • • • • • •

By the beginning of January 1942, Seletar had lost many of its aircraft. Catalinas were now having to be used in roles for which they had not been specifically designed, bombing raids in particular, and the Vildebeest squadrons were at last being allowed on major operations. With a Catalina carrying 16 x 250lb bombs beneath the wings, and a full fuel load, the take-off was said to have been something to behold. On full boost the twin Pratt and Whitney engines screaming their heads off, it could be a couple of miles before they became airborne. In such a condition, 205 Squadron's Catalinas attacked Gong Kedah on January 7th, and on the 9th, four aircraft carried out a raid on the railway yards and storage areas at Singora, over the border in Siam, where the Japanese were using the railway. Three of the aircraft successfully located the target, disposing of their loads on the marshalling yards and starting a number of fires. All the aircraft returned safely to Seletar after a flight of almost twelve hours. A similar operation the following night resulted in the loss of one aircraft.

January 9th was when the Vildebeests also began mounting operations. That night, twelve aircraft of 36 Squadron – having been fitted with long-range tanks, and carrying between them a bomb load of nine thousand pounds – set out to blitz the airfield at Ipoh. Amidst heavy flack they swept in to the attack, their bombs starting fires which were visible many miles away. One Vildebeest, unable to locate the airfield, bombed instead a column of armoured vehicles. There were no major casualties from this raid, although one aircraft was forced to land at Kuala Lumpur due to a shortage of fuel. The squadron could also claim a successful attack on some enemy barges off Muar – less than one hundred miles to the north west – again without loss, but their main task had been to drop food and water to some troops who had been cut off by the advancing tide of the Japanese offensive.

By now the stock of the Royal Air Force, Far East, was extremely low. They were unjustly being held to blame for not being able to contain the enemy in the air. Soldiers were rarely afforded air cover, therefore felt very bitter when their friends were mown down, defenceless from unimpeded attacks by Japanese aircraft. The Army, it seemed, felt they were having to fight alone, as a result, relationships between various arms of the services were somewhat strained for a time. Many of Seletar's "old hands" have referred to incidents which took place between servicemen, but the Vildebeests, despite their shortcomings, provided evidence that an air force of some kind did still exist. That this was appreciated was demonstrated to P/O Gotto one evening at the hotel in Singapore. He says a complete stranger approached him and said, 'I understand you fly a Vildebeest. Allow me to buy you a drink.' Later, an army officer he was introduced to, told him, 'Your Vildebeests are the only RAF aircraft we ever see near the front line. If any of your chaps can come over to our Mess one night, we'll have a party.'

In his book, *Lion in the Sky*, Neville Shorrick states:

> *"This was about the time when someone began to notice that the number of aircraft returning from a sortie did not always tally with the number of Vildebeests that had been sent out, there invariably being one aircraft too many. And it was quickly realized that some rather audacious, yet enterprising Japanese pilot was taking advantage of the situation; carrying out some useful reconnaissance. Naturally, it was agreed that this would have to be stopped, so one day a Vildebeest was sent up to carry out circuits and bumps. Soon it was observed that a second aircraft had joined the manoeuvres so, as planned, the Vildebeest suddenly landed. This left the Japanese aircraft in a rather conspicuous position, and it was quickly shot down.*

[A rather unlikely scenario, I would have thought, given the obvious differences between a Zero – or any other Japanese aircraft – and a Vildebeest. But perhaps this was the incident referred to by James McEwan in *The Remorseless Road* in which he mentions a daring act on the part of a Japanese airman.]:

> *Tagging on unnoticed at the tail of a returning and unsuspecting flight of Hurricanes, this infiltrator, his deception aided by the glowing twilight, managed to approach the aerodrome. Then, at the last moment peeling off from the flight, he swooped down over the (Officers') Mess and released a bomb. Grazing the roof harmlessly, it plunged into the Sergeants' Mess beyond, causing many casualties and extensive damage.*

● ● ● ● ● ● ● ● ● ●

It was a battle-scarred convoy that steamed into Singapore harbour on January 13th, 1942, having just run the gauntlet of a Japanese air attack. The convoy had been saved from destruction only by the intervention of a fierce tropical storm, it seemed. But amid great relief that it *had* survived, work began on unloading its precious cargo: fifty-one crated Hurricanes, along with twenty-four not yet acclimatized, therefore vulnerable, pilots, upon whom Singapore's residents would now be pinning their hopes of survival. The aircraft, part of a shipment originally destined for the Middle East, had been diverted, some to Burma, the remainder to Singapore.

Having successfully survived one hazzard, the crated aircraft were very soon to be faced by another, one which could well have ended in disaster. The aircraft had been dispatched from the port area in two separate consignments, but as the first arrived at Seletar a senior officer ordered them to go and disperse amongst the trees. Slowly, the vehicles managed to turn around and head back, only to come up against the second convoy. The meeting point, a narrow road with deep monsoon ditches on either side, allowed little room for the articulated vehicles to manoeuvre. The ensuing traffic jam presented a tempting target which no raider could possibly miss, had not two factors combined to save the situation. First, it rained heavily that night, right through to 08:00 hours; that same Act of God which had saved the ships bringing them to Singapore provided just as good cover for the road convoys. Secondly, was the presence of mind of the convoy commanders and the dedication of their men. In appalling conditions they laboured all night to manhandle the heavy crates to safety.

In less than forty-eight hours the first Hurricane was airborne, on a test flight. By January 17th, the hollow-eyed and haggard crews, having worked all hours under impossible conditions, had twenty-one aircraft operational; a near-miracle.

A message was received from the Chief of Air Staff later that day: "Congratulations on getting No.232 Squadron into action so quickly. This is magnificent work."

It said much for the continued devotion and gallantry of the men who managed to keep those Hurricanes flying, and the runways of Seletar, Tengah, and Kallang in some sort of repair.

January 17th, 1942. Although no bombs fell on Seletar this day, moored at their buoys in the Straits, four flying boats proved too attractive a target for two enemy fighters. Mistakenly taken to be Hurricanes, they suddenly appeared over Punggol Point. Then, guns in the leading edges of their wings blinking fire, they attacked the Catalinas of 205 Squadron, setting fire to two and sinking them, as well as badly damaging the other two. Sergeant Arch, who was on board his aircraft at the time, opened the side blister and engaged the fighters with a machine gun, continuing firing even as the burning flying boat went down. Sgt Arch, along with an LAC, died in the engagement.

Now there were only three serviceable Catalinas left, but other aircraft on the station were operational, and the position on January 18th, was as follows:

No.36 Squadron	4 Albacores
	10 Vildebeests
No.100 Squadron	15 Vildebeests
No.205 Squadron	3 Catalinas
No.232 (F) Squadron	21 Hurricanes

No. 232 Squadron had been organized into three flights, under the command of Sqn/Ldr L.N. Landels. "A" and "B" flights remained at Seletar, while "C" flight operated from Kallang under Flt/Lt P.M. Cooper-Slipper. On January 20th, just over a week after their arrival, the squadron were fully operational. There were two raids on Singapore that day, and although the Hurricanes destroyed a Zero and three bombers, it was at the cost of three of their own aircraft. Worse still, two pilots were killed, including the Squadron Commander, and a third, Pilot Officer Williams, was seriously injured.

Next day an attack was launched on the island by around a hundred enemy aircraft. 232 once again rose to meet the challenge, claiming four of the enemy destroyed, and one probable. Two Hurricanes were lost, and one damaged.

January 22nd, saw the fiercest air combat situation yet take place in the skies above Singapore, two waves of heavy bombers, along with their fighter escort, launching a heavy raid from twenty-two thousand feet. 232 were quickly airborne to engage them, and the battle raged on. When at last it was all over it became clear that the RAF had been heavily hit. Five Hurricanes and four Buffaloes were lost, with three more pilots killed; these included the commander of "A" flight, Flt/Lt H.A. Farthing. The Japanese had lost six Navy type 96 bombers, and a Zero, with two more probables. But the Japanese could easily absorb such losses.

It was becoming clear that too much hope had been placed in the ability of the Hurricanes; they had no tropical modifications, and their performance was well down. Superior to the Zero above twenty thousand feet, at lower altitudes the Japanese fighter was quicker and more manoeuvrable. What's more, the Hurricanes were almost always heavily outnumbered. It is said that the bombers were rarely to be seen being attacked by the RAF fighters, but this was probably because the Hurricanes were busily engaging the Japanese fighters before they could close on the bombers.

Lucky to survive the fray was an Australian named John Gorton; one of those pilots transferred from 135 Squadron, in India, to fly with 232 at Seletar.

After being forced to crash-land his crippled Hurricane on the petrol-tank studded Pulau Samboe (just off Singapore), he received serious facial injuries: 'My face got rather mixed up with the instrument panel, with lasting effects upon my beauty,' was how he described it later. The people on the island cared for him, eventually returning him to Singapore from where he was evacuated, only for the ship he was on to be torpedoed by the Japanese.

Clinging to a life-raft with around twenty other survivors, John Gorton was eventually rescued by an Australian corvette, but that was not to be the end of his personal ordeals. Returning to combat, he was again shot down, this time descending on a plantation on an island in the Timor Sea, where he survived for days on turtle eggs, and fish.

Discharged from the Royal Australian Air Force in 1944, with the rank of Flight Lieutenant, Gorton entered politics, eventually to become Minister for the Navy. On January 10th, 1968, John Gorton succeeded Mr Harold Holt as Prime Minister of Australia.

While the "Battle of Singapore" was taking place, Seletar's strike force was hitting the enemy airfields as hard as was possible. On the night of January 20th, for instance, twelve aircraft of 36 Squadron joined forces with seven 34 Squadron Blenheims from Tengah, for an attack on Kuala Lumpur. At the same time, eleven Vildebeests of 100 Squadron, along with six Hudsons, hit Kuantan. The results were extremely good. 34 Squadron claimed that twenty-five Japanese aircraft were destroyed on the ground at Kuala Lumpur, and that "the enemy was taken completely by surprise." At Kuantan the count was "at least six aircraft damaged or destroyed." The cost to the bomber force was just one Blenheim, although a second crashed when attempting to land back at Tengah.

The Fleet Air Arm was also flying from Seletar, and although small in numbers, they did co-operate in many operations. One such took place during the afternoon of January 23rd, a dual-wave combined attack on enemy communications south of Muar, using Seletar-based Commonwealth Wirraways (an Australian-built development of the Harvard), Fairey Albacores, and Blackburn Sharks – a right mixed bag! The following night, aided by the light of parachute flares, Vildebeests and Albacores successfully destroyed the vital railway bridge at Labis.

It was around this time that the order was given for all of the RAF's chemical warfare supplies in Singapore to be destroyed. With the decision made in 1940 to supply Singapore with chemical weapons, a Mr Le Ferve (given the honorary rank of Wing Commander), was sent to Seletar late that year as the RAF's chemical warfare adviser. His job was to make arrangements for the handling and storage of these weapons – Batu Caves, Kuala Lumpur; Batak Quarry, Singapore; Seletar and Tengah. Ahead of the Japanese advance, and to guard against a stray bomb finding one of the storage dumps at Seletar, all had recently been transferred to lighters, floating off Singapore. Now it was decided they should be destroyed, to prevent them falling into enemy hands. This operation was fraught with problems, but eventually all stocks were successfully disposed of at sea.

● ● ● ● ● ● ● ● ● ●

THE "ENDAU RAID"

The Japanese moved rapidly. Gaining ground on all fronts, they were now preparing for an operation which could finally gain them control over the whole of the Malayan Peninsular. On January 22nd, an invasion fleet departed Saigon; two cruisers plus a dozen destroyers provided escort for two ten thousand ton merchant ships. Carrying the 18th Division, this fleet reached Singora at midnight on January 25th. Undetected, and now escorted by units of the 12th Air Brigade, based at Kuantan, they departed Singora and headed southwards. It was not until 07:45 hours on the 26th that the convoy was spotted, two Hudsons logging the position as being twenty miles north-east of Endau, on the northern border of the State of Johore. News of this was received by Air Headquarters, Singapore, at 09:20 hours.

The situation was grave, for a successful landing so far south would inevitably lead to a link-up with Japanese forces on the west coast, thus cutting off large numbers of British Army Units. This in turn would mean that the battle for Malaya was lost.

It was decided that the convoy must be stopped at all costs, and that as there were few suitable allied aircraft available, the main burden of the attack would have to be borne by the outdated Vildebeest; a drastic decision born out of necessity. A cruising speed of ninety-nine mph pointed to the lumbering, obsolete torpedo bombers being sitting ducks for the Japanese fighters, the very reason they had up to now been mainly restricted to night-time sorties, allowing them to approach the target under cover of darkness, as had taken place the previous night. A strong force of Vildebeests had been covering the evacuation by sea of a battalion of Australian troops, trapped up near Batu Pahat, barely eighty miles to the north-west. Two more Vildebeests had successfully dropped medical supplies, enabling yet more troops to join their comrades. This operation had earned both squadrons congratulations from Air Headquarters. Now the tired crews, flying inappropriate aircraft, were ordered out once more.

The first aircraft, twelve Vildebeests, took off in the early afternoon of the 26th. Ten were from 100 Squadron, two from 36 Squadron. They were accompanied by nine Sembawang-based RAAF Hudsons, and a mixed fighter escort of Buffaloes and Hurricanes. Unfortunately, the distance to the target from Seletar when combined with the very slow speed of the Vildebeests, made protection for them a complicated and almost hopeless problem.

Over the target the force encountered heavy fighter and ack-ack opposition, yet despite this, one of the merchant vessels received two direct hits. A cruiser was also hit, as was another merchant vessel. What the aircrews were not to know, was that the Japanese troops had disembarked some four and a half hours earlier, and were now well established on the beach. The British fighters did manage to shoot down between seven and nine enemy aircraft, but losses amongst the British force were extremely heavy: five Vildebeests from 100 Squadron were lost, and two of the crew of a Hudson were killed.

Undeterred, a second wave took off later that afternoon. This force consisted of nine Vilde-beests (mainly 36 Squadron), led by a flight of three Albacores. A small, mixed fighter escort was provided by four Buffaloes and eight Hurricanes, but conditions were against them from the start. Cloud cover was available to shield their approach, but so it was to the Japanese, a large patch of cumulus just beyond the target concealing a number of Navy 0's (Zeros) and Army 97s. Swooping down, the Japanese fighters quickly accounted for five of the Vildebeests, all the Albacores, and one Hurricane, for a personal loss of four fighters. Eight hits were claimed by the few remaining British bombers.

Both No's 36 and 100 Squadrons had suffered irrevocable losses in these actions, with their respective commanders, Squadron Leaders RFC Markham, and JTB Rowland being killed. It had been a suicidal raid, as the crews of the Vilde-beests had known. Despite promises of only operating night sorties, the approach of a large enemy fleet had forced the Air Staff's hand. The Air Officer Commanding, in congratulating the survivors, also told them they would never again be put in that situation.

Against overwhelming odds, the fighter squadrons had fought as well as they were able. A particularly outstanding performance was that achieved by Sergeant Pilot Ronald Dovel, whose Hurricane had shot down four Japanese fighters; two in each of two sorties over a two and a half hour period. At least two of these had been Zeros. A Hurricane pilot shot down during the second sweep, Sergeant JPF Fleming, had accounted for a fighter before his aircraft went down in enemy-held territory. All hope of his survival had been abandoned by the squadron, but after six days he triumphantly turned up at Seletar, ready to resume battle.

Another incident reported by Peter Masters relates to an Albacore which, after landing, taxied directly to flying control, where the "Blood Wagon" was located.

'It was nothing short of a miracle that the pilot, Flt/Sgt Peck, had managed to land at all, for one of his legs was just a bloody mess below the knee. They wrenched the door open to find a large hole in the cabin, through which, we all concluded, the Nav and W/Op had been blown out of. Happily, a few days later they turned up. After bailing out, and setting off on a dangerous journey, they had been lucky enough to stumble across an Aussie forward patrol.'

It seemed as though nothing could halt the relentless Japanese conquest, and it was totally disheartening for those at Seletar to learn the sacrifices made at Endau had been in vain. A Japanese report, in summing up the operation, had stated: 'Nearly all the remaining enemy air force which had been hiding until now, was destroyed.'

Timing apart, one of the major reasons for the failure at Endau had to be attributed to the lack of adequate fighter cover.

Hurricanes from Tengah had been detailed for the raid, the plan being for them to rendez-vous with six Blenheims of 34 Squadron, but in an incredible oversight, it was discovered that the ground crews – by now, long gone for some much-needed sleep – had not been detailed to pre-flight the aircraft, and when the aircrews arrived they did not have as much as a screw-driver between them. A desperate attempt was made to rectify the situation, but by the time enough groundcrew had been rounded up it was far too late, take-off and rendezvous times had come and gone, and the Blenheims had been forced to return to Java.

But Endau was not yet finished, for, as a direct result of the above, it was to bring about a final tragedy. The Station Commander of RAF Tengah, Group Captain "Poppa" Watts, was ordered to report to Headquarters the following day, to explain the debacle over the failure of his Hurricanes. It was the final straw.[41] He was in the Mess having a drink with some of his crews when the fatal signal was handed to him. With an air of resignation he finished his drink, bade every-one goodnight, and went quietly to his room where he shot himself.

Amazingly, it seemed no lessons had been learnt, hence the following account related by Terence Kelly – a pilot with 258 Squadron – in his book, *Hurricane Over The Jungle*. This incident occurring a few days later.

Fifteen Hurricanes of No. 258 Squadron had flown in to Seletar – via Java – from the aircraft carrier *Indomitable* (the late-arriving vessel that was originally supposed to have provided air cover for the *Prince of Wales* and *Repulse*). Unfortunately, these aircraft had arrived without ground crews, and with their guns still packed in grease! As Sgt Kelly tells it, *'This was unbeknown to us. Had we met up with any Japanese, or even tried trial bursts, we would probably have blown the wings off! Or so they said.'*

In an effort to make the aircraft operational, Seletar's existing, overworked armourers, fitters and riggers worked to rectify the situation – although, again according to Sgt Kelly, Pilot Officer Bruce McAlister and himself had to force the groundcrew, by means of drawn pistols, to keep working during the period the morning raid was supposedly due. As it happened, there was no raid that morning. The Hurricanes departed for Tengah the following day, a flight of four or five miles. Despite the short distance, some of the aircraft encountered the enemy, P/O McAlister being killed. This must have come as a bit of a shock to airmen who, during their briefing aboard *Indomitable* had partially been led to believe that the Japanese flew "feeble wooden biplanes." After all, before the war, the word "Japanese" was considered an adjective for "rubbish." Another official briefing was said to have described Japanese aircraft as, "being made of cardboard, so if you do find yourself in trouble, you just dive away and their wings will fall off." It also stated that, "their pilots are practically blind; unless wearing three pairs of spectacles they can't see anything at all." Not very helpful!

Almost immediately, the aircraft were ordered to withdraw to Palembang, though Sgt Kelly's aircraft, being unserviceable, remained at Tengah. He says: 'The station was like a morgue, the messes empty, billiard room deserted, the bar a silent place. It was a very solitary feeling being the last pilot of a squadron on an empty airfield, chivvying unwilling ground staff to put my aircraft right.

'On the evening of February 2nd the gloom was suddenly lifted when, totally unexpectedly, the balance of 258 Squadron returned to Tengah on a mission to escort Blenheims and Lockheed Hudsons on a dawn, up-country raid on the airfield at Kluang. The strident roar of aircraft engines after the unnerving silence was a joy.

'But it was to be short-lived.

'The following morning we went out to our aircraft, my own serviceable at last, only to find them with their gun panels removed, the guns unarmed, and no ground staff in sight. There had been, one gathered, contrary orders given, although no one knew by whom. Nothing could be done in time. The Hudsons, due to bomb first were already on their way, the Blenheims, due to attack at first light, after ground strafing by their attendant Hurricanes, were already airborne. So the bombers went alone, and the Japanese were waiting for them. It was a disaster. Most of the Hurricanes returned to Palembang.'

Seletar was taking a severe battering by now, with air raids twice a day, usually at 10.00am and 3.00pm, always with twenty-seven twin engined bombers in vee formation at between twelve and fifteen thousand feet. They had no opposition and the ack-ack guns got nowhere near them. Eventually they brought Zero fighter escorts with them and these came down strafing everything they could find.

On January 29th, with the end almost in sight, ninety Japanese bombers, along with their fighter escort, inflicted heavy raids on Seletar and Sembawang. Damage to buildings and installations was considerable, and with the Japanese now so close to Singapore, the decision was made to withdraw all aircraft from the island; although this was later reviewed, and some of the fighters remained for a few more days.

All that remained of 36 Squadron were five Vildebeests and two Albacores, plus two more Vildebeests that had been used for radar calibrations (K6391 and K6393). 100 Squadron fared marginally better, fielding eight aircraft. All departed for Kemayoran[42] at 04:30 on January 31st, fully loaded with torpedoes. The ground crews followed two days later aboard the SS *Perak*, bound for Palembang (Sumatra), eventually to rejoin their aircraft in Java.

As far as Seletar was concerned, its long association with 36 and 100 Squadrons, and the Vildebeest, was at an end, but it wasn't yet the end of the Vildebeest. February 8th, 1942, saw the remaining aircraft regrouping as one squadron, No.36, now commanded by one of the old 36 Squadron pilots – Sqn/Ldr JT Wilkins. It wasn't to be a long association, for by March 6th, only two aircraft remained operational, and many of the aircrew, including Sqn/Ldr Wilkins, had been killed. When the Dutch decided to surrender Java, the order was given to destroy these aircraft. But two of the pilots, Flt/Lt Allanson and F/O Lamb, proposed that each machine be manned by a crew of four (as opposed to the usual three), and be used in an attempt to escape by flying along the Sumatran coast to the extent of their range before being ditched.

The plan then called for the crew members – names to be drawn out of a hat – to make their own way by sea, either to Burma or Ceylon. This ambitious plan would appear to have contained more than a slight element of wishful thinking, given that the nearest landfall was fifteen hundred miles distant! There again, when your back is against the wall....

Whatever, the project was given official sanction, with the stipulation that bombs must be carried, with a target being attacked on the way!

Given the all-up weight – four crew, full fuel, five hundred pounds of bombs – the take-off promised to be rather hazardous, to say the least! This it proved to be, but, setting off at 01:45 hours on March 8th, they just made it, brushing the tree-tops on lift off. But success became failure when, several hours later, both aircraft were ditched off the coast of West Sumatra. One crew made it ashore, being taken prisoner almost immediately, but surviving the war. For some obscure reason, the second aircraft was ditched some miles offshore, all crew members surviving the ditching, but only one making it ashore. He too survived the war.

Peter Masters, recalling his, and the squadron's departure from Seletar, reveals just how critical things were.

'The Japs were now within mortar range of Johore, on the far side of the Straits, when I flew my last calibration with the flight Commander. I then did a short familiarization flight with a New Zealand pilot, Sgt Parker, who had just arrived, and had never flown a Vildebeest before. On the 31st of January we were all warned to stand by for a take off just before dawn, I suppose to avoid the mortar fire. The ground crews had fitted torpedoes to all the aircraft. This meant that Sgt Parker was about to take off with a fully loaded aircraft, in the dark, with only 30 minutes experience on type. We flew in formations of three, and at dawn came down to just over the tree tops to avoid detection. We all landed safely at P2 – a secret airstrip in the Indonesian jungle.' After refuelling, apparently a story in itself, they flew on to Batavia civil airport, as Peter says, 'To land in the middle of a heavy storm, with so much rain that old K6391 made a wake like a speedboat. I severed my last link with Singapore when I switched off my radio.'

Next day these aircraft were also flown to Kemayoran, which he describes as, 'a very poor quality strip cut out of the jungle.'

He says the aircraft were by this time in very poor condition, with no ground crew and no tools to repair them. The RAF Auxiliary, *Aquarius*, loaded with spares and tools had departed Seletar for Java sometime before, but it had been sunk by a Japanese submarine en route.

At Batavia docks, the NCO aircrew helped in the loading of transports, which included a consignment of Scotch Whisky. He suspects this was 'a precaution against the Japs finding it and running amok.' Peter eventually found himself aboard the ship *Orchades*, ending up, after further adventures, in Colombo, where, 'the reception had been very chilly, to put it mildly.'

Back in Java, the remaining squadron members were ordered to surrender by the Dutch Army Headquarters, eventually being confined as prisoners-of-war at Kalidjati, north of Bandung, Java.

Air Vice-Marshal Sir Paul Maltby, KBE CB DSO AFC, writing of No's 36 and 100 Squadrons after the fall of Singapore stated, 'These two squadrons attacked enemy landings at Endau, covered as it was by numerous Zero fighters, whereas our own escort was unavoidably small. They pressed home their attacks in obsolete Vildebeest torpedo bombers[43] regardless of the casualties, amongst whom I regret to report were the Commanding Officers of both squadrons. After being reorganized as a composite squadron in Java, and, after having patched up their old aircraft once again, they pressed home attacks against enemy convoys which were invading that island, this time at night, again suffering many casualties and the loss of their Commanding Officer, Sqn/Ldr Wilkins. Such Gallant conduct speaks for itself.'

Three Catalinas of No.205, Seletar's first squadron, pulled out at the same time as the Vildebeests, with a forth later joining them at a base on the southern tip of Sumatra. Eventually, most of the squadron personnel were successfully evacuated to Ceylon and Australia, as were some of their aircraft, the last two eventually being sunk in Broome harbour during an attack by Japanese Naval aircraft on March 3rd, 1942. A total of around twenty-three aircraft of various nationalities was destroyed in that raid, including two Empire flying boats. It appears that the sole surviving Catalina was one that flew from Java to Ceylon, where it became part of a re-formed 205 Squadron, taking part in the heroic defence of that island.

Air raids also resulted in casualties among the families, so they were being repatriated as fast as possible. Some were lost at sea, and a number were captured and placed in prison camps, but the majority escaped to either Australia or England, and some of their stories often made as exciting reading as did the exploits of their husbands.

Take the case as detailed in *Lion in the Sky*: This tells the story of a Mrs Ada Tupholme, Canadian wife of 100 'Squadron member Flt/ Lt John Tupholme. She had married him in Singapore, giving birth to their son, Michael, eighteen months later. With the outbreak of war, she, in common with a number of wives, helped with the Red Cross and St John's Ambulance.

About two weeks prior to Singapore's surrender, she was hustled aboard the American troopship, *Wakefield*. She describes what happened.

'All I had were the clothes I stood up in, which in that heat was a particular ordeal. With a four month old baby it seemed almost impossible, but somehow we managed to cope. Then the *Wakefield* dropped us off at Colombo, Ceylon, where we were left on the dockside for hours.

'Then we were herded to and confined in an Australian hospital, where every meal was a horrible stew. We were eventually taken to Durban in the *Reina Del Pacifa*, which was packed with civilian men, women and children, including a large number of Seletar families. Also on board were survivors from the *Repulse* and *Prince of Wales*, as well as men from the other two Services. We got to Durban with its lights and happy people – it was like a new world. Then we went via Cape Town, up the Atlantic to Liverpool. My first impressions of England were the chimneys – there seemed to be millions and millions of them.

'Like many other wives I officially became a widow, was told that my husband was missing presumed killed. For eighteen months I was given a pension of just over ten pounds a month. Then one day in Oxford Street I met Padre O'Connor, who used to be the Roman Catholic Padre at Seletar. He said he believed John was a prisoner-of-war in Java. A month later I received a card from my husband, and then I went on half pay!'

The fact that her husband had been promoted to Squadron Leader shortly before going into prison camp was to add a neat little footnote to this story. As was usual among officers, he had banked in London, getting to know one of the clerks quite well before the war. Upon repatriation, when checking on the state of his account, the same clerk greeted him as though having seen him only the previous day. He then found himself being ushered into the Manager's office, who said, 'I hope you don't object, sir, but we took your money and invested it.'

His pre-war deposit of six pounds ten shillings now amounted to three and a half years pay, plus some very profitable investments! [But what if those investments had turned sour, one wonders?]

• • • • • • • • • •

By the end of January an air of defeat hung over Singapore. Practically all the civilian employees had deserted Seletar, for conditions had become intolerable. Those that remained proved themselves to be most faithful servants of the Crown, the extent of this loyalty being displayed a variety of ways. Oft-quoted examples concern the barmen at both the Officers' Mess and yacht club, both of whom took it in their minds to conceal their club's silver from the Japanese. With the return of the British, after the war, they proudly returned this treasure and resumed their jobs as if nothing had happened. Possibly this was a trait among the Colony's barmen, for the same thing happened down town, at the world-famous Raffles Hotel. Here, the staff buried the hotel silver – including their famed Beef Trolley – beneath the lawn of the equally famous Palm Court. It remained undiscovered for the three years of occupation, during which time the hotel became known as the Syonan Ryokan – Light of the South Hotel. Senior Japanese officers for whom the hotel was appointed quarters probably strolled over the spot many times.

Another person who had it in mind to safeguard some silverware was Seletar's Padre Giles, and a history of the period would be incomplete without a mention of this. The story had its beginnings on April 1st, 1940, the day the Reverend Alan Giles conducted the wedding ceremony of Mr and Mrs BG. Taylor in St Andrew's Cathedral. As a mark of appreciation, the Taylors presented Padre Giles with a beautifully engraved lectern bible, for use in the chapel at Seletar. During the evacuation, Padre Giles took both the bible and the Communion silver with him to Java, although he was eventually forced to abandon the silver. This was placed in a hermetically sealed box and buried in the grounds of a hospital, soon to be prisoner-of-war camp, about fifteen miles from Bandung. The bible remained in Padre Giles possession – most of the time – wherever he went, and it was to become a source of inspiration to thousands of prisoners. 'Whenever the Japs spotted it, it was confiscated,' Padre Giles said. 'Each time, however, the men managed to steal it back.' The padre says that on two of the occasions when it was confiscated, he managed to talk the Japanese into giving him a receipt. 'I suppose if we sent these in, with a claim for two new lectern bibles, we might get them,' he was said to have joked after the war.

The war ended with Padre Giles still in possession of his bible, and he did manage to recover most of his buried treasure, still in good condition. The silver and Bible were returned to Seletar, and remained in the Church to the end of the RAF's tenancy, though the bible, after many years use, was laid up in 1963. Suitably inscribed, it was cased, and placed on display, its story there for all to see.

The night of January 31st was quiet, the moon full. Retreating Australian, British and Indian troops crossed over the Causeway to Singapore, the Argylls defending the bridge-head during the operation. At 07:30 hours next morning, February 1st, two pipers played the Argylls across, the skirling notes of their pipes echoing defiance. Engineers then blew a thirty-foot gap in the roadway, a futile act by which it was hoped to halt the Japanese advance. Singapore had effectively announced her severance with the imperial past.

One would now have imagined this to be a city preparing for the worst. But judging by the entertainments pages in the *Straits Times* of Saturday, January 31st, that was far from the case. The military may have been worried, the expatriate community were apparently not. The Cathay cinema was still featuring four shows daily and the Sea View Hotel was featuring a concert by the Rellers Band on the Sunday. The most exclusive hotel on the island, Raffles, was still staging dinner dances, whilst Robinsons offered morning and afternoon teas almost to the end. Yet others were playing safe. The New

World cabaret was "closed until further notice," both the Great and Happy Worlds having already closed their doors. People were also being urged to "Give blood and save an air raid victim," whilst the British & Malaya Trustee & Executor Co were apparently in little doubt the as to severity of the situation; they were advising people to "make a will."

The withdrawal of British aircraft continued apace, until only a token force remained, yet that small band of extremely brave pilots, the Volunteer Air Force, operating mainly from Seletar, continued to fly their tiny, vulnerable Moths, providing support for the Army and assisting in the search for any downed aircrew. General Percival paid tribute to their efforts in his book, *The War in Malaya*.

In particular, Flight Lieutenant Dane, a resident of Malaya and a member of the Malayan Volunteer Air Force, was untiring and quite fearless in the efforts he made. In fact, the whole of this Volunteer Air Force, flying a miscellaneous collection of club aircraft, was at this time doing most gallant work. Operating from a temporary landing ground on Singapore Island, these frail and defenceless aircraft were carrying out daily reconnaissance patrols and generally managing to get back.

A large number of Seletar's servicemen, including Group Captain Walkington, OC 151 Maintenance Unit (MU), five other officers and one hundred and nine of his men, were instructed to board the SS Perak. This vessel departed Singapore at 07:30 on February 2nd for Sumatra. The ground crews of 36 and 100 Squadrons, along with the torpedo sections, were also aboard. The boilers were stoked by volunteers from the squadrons, its machine guns manned by 151 MU personnel. No escape, this, for most of these people were destined to spend the next three and a half years in prison camps.

Seletar's sole surviving squadron was 232 – its pilots and aircraft the remnants of 258, 232 and 488 Squadrons – but the air defence of Singapore ended on February 9th, 1942, the day the squadron flew its last missions from the island. Now operating out of Kallang – the runways at Seletar and Tengah no longer in a fit state to use – these eight remaining serviceable Hurricanes were the remnants of British air power in Malaya. But the battle put up by these fighters was against such odds that their efforts must be compared with the most epic achievements of the service. Led by Squadron Leader "Ricky" Wright, promoted from acting Flight Lieutenant barely a week earlier, Sqn/Ldr Llewellyn having been killed when, departing Tengah – he flew into the boom of a crane shortly after take-off – all eight Hurricanes took off at first light to engage a force of no less than eighty-four enemy aircraft, approaching from Johore. A measure of surprise was achieved, the squadron being credited with two enemy aircraft destroyed, four probables, and ten damaged. They flew once more that afternoon, and again later when, in response to the Army's call for help, four Hurricanes managed to take-off. Using the cover afforded by the smoke now rising from the naval base, they successfully drove off a large number of dive bombers which were harassing the troops.

When visiting the squadron that evening, Air Vice-Marshal Maltby, declared the position to be hopeless, and therefore ordered the last eight hurricanes to be evacuated. They were anyway in a deplorable state. In the words of Sqn/Ldr Wright, 'patched and held together by wire.' It showed, one bursting into flames a few miles from the airfield at Palembang, Sumatra. The pilot was fortunate in being able to bail out, landing safely. From Palembang, the remaining aircraft continued offensive missions and air defence sorties over Singapore and Malaya, but in reality the air battle for Singapore had ended.

The Hurricanes had arrived too late and in too few numbers to change the course of events, yet in the short time they had operated, they had accounted for around one hundred enemy fighters and bombers against the loss of forty-five Hurricanes. At one stage even the Japanese Staff Officers noted with concern the "temporary change in the air position."

Seletar's days were now drawing to a close. An eyewitness described the scene "on or about" February 7th thus: 'It had indeed taken a tremendous hammering. Day by day huge formations of Japanese bombers had come over and bombed it. The craters were the biggest I ever saw on Singapore. Hardly a building stood intact, most were blackened skeletons. The field itself was pitted with bomb holes. It was littered with some half dozen burnt out Hurricanes, Buffaloes, and Blenheims. In some of the less damaged hangars near the shore, were aeroplane engines in crates, and miscellaneous equipment. The place was deserted except for British soldiers down on the foreshore. They had three or four machine guns, not many, which had been placed among some rocks. There were coils of barbed wire down by the water's edge. Yachts with engines were moored offshore, others were pulled up on the beach under mat sheds. We drove round the field, past all those burned out buildings, out of the gate and then home. I could not help feeling that afternoon that we were witness to one of the supreme tragedies of war.'

But the place had not been deserted, for a party of 151 MU personnel under the command of Wg/Cdr Saw remained at Seletar until February 10th, and between thirty and forty men from No.1 Repair and Salvage Unit, under Sqn/Ldr Christie, were there until at least the 11th.

Due to the danger of being shelled from across the Straits, it became impossible to work on the aerodrome during daylight. Nevertheless, repair work was still carried out in among the rubber plantations outside the perimeter fence, a couple of 258 Squadron Hurricanes having been patched up in these appalling conditions by February 10th. They were flown out to the Dutch Indies, via Kallang, on the 11th.

When remarking on this episode, Flight Lieutenant Donahue, the last pilot to leave Singapore safely, stated that, 'Two of the boys had been detailed the night before to get up early and be driven to Seletar, to bring back a couple of damaged Hurricanes that had been fixed up so they would fly. They turned up before breakfast, having done their job, and told of a creepy trip going over there along the blacked out road, and being stopped and examined frequently at the point of a bayonet, never sure if they'd run into any enemy trap until they could see who it was who'd stopped them. They said the aerodrome had been captured the afternoon before, but that our troops had retaken it in the evening. They were preparing to blow up the field as soon as the boys had taken off.'

Flt/Lt Arthur Donahue, pilot of that last aircraft, was an American who, anxious to be in the war, had crossed the Atlantic to join the RAF. He had been the first of his countrymen to take part in combat with the Royal Air Force, and was one of only a handful of Americans to fly in the Battle of Britain. Subsequently awarded the DFC in March 1942, he was killed in action that September. He left behind some fascinating photographs, along with a manuscript that detailed the RAF's last, pre-war days in Singapore. The work was later published as a book entitled *Last Flight From Singapore*.

Once those Hurricanes and the MU personnel had departed, so the Repair and Salvage Unit got busy, though in a reversal of what it was they had been trained to do. Using five hundred pound bombs, they did as much damage as possible, after which they distributed aircraft parts all over the landing strip. The generating station and petrol installations were also destroyed. And on the night of the 11th, the last men from Seletar embarked for the trip to the Dutch East Indies. Arriving in Java three days later, they too were destined to spend the rest of the war in prison camps. A lot of valuable equipment – machine tools, aircraft engines and spares – was loaded onto ships which were then scuttled on the way over.

With the departure of the last aircraft, General Percival ordered the AOC, Air Vice-Marshal Pulford, to leave Singapore, but it was not until February 13th, that, satisfied his duty was done, he set sail in a "Fairmile" launch. Also aboard were Rear Admiral Spooner, another seven officers and thirty-five other ranks. Unfortunately the vessel was attacked from the air and damaged, having to be run aground on an island of the Seven Brothers group, one hundred miles north of Banka Island. The party remained at large for two months, but with the island being malarial, unhealthy, and having little food, and with the party possessing few stores, no medicines, and no doctor, eighteen of them were to die, including the two senior officers. The survivors, by now in a terrible state, were eventually forced to give themselves up; one more tragic chapter enacted.

It is still not clear how and when Seletar was finally captured, but it is widely understood that the Japanese took over the empty and desolate airfield at noon on February 14th, a day before the official fall of Singapore.

Perhaps the words of AG Donahue in *Last Flight From Singapore* give us an insight into those final moments:

> 'My final memory of Singapore, as it appeared to me looking back for the last time, is of a bright green little country, resting on the edge of the bluest sea I have ever seen, lovely in the morning sunlight except when the dark mantle of smoke ran across its middle and beyond, covering and darkening the city on the seashore. The city itself, with huge leaping red fires in its north and south parts, appeared to rest on the floor of a vast cavern formed by the sinister curtains of black smoke which rose from beyond, and towered over it, prophetically, like a great overhanging cloak of doom.'

Within weeks, Japan – an insular, feudal nation, which less than a century ago had relied upon bow, arrow, and divine intervention for defence – had swept all before it. It now had a navy second to none, along with a seemingly invincible army.

CHAPTER NINE

Seretar Hikojo:
Japanese Interlude

"When we entered Singapore we were surprised to see that the aerodromes, harbour, and city had not been destroyed by the enemy. Seizing a junior enemy officer we questioned him. 'Why did you not destroy Singapore?' we asked. 'Because we will return again,' he replied. Again we asked, 'Don't you believe Britain is beaten in this war?' He replied, We may be defeated ninety-nine times, but in the final round we will be all right – we will win that.' This one junior officer prisoner of war spoke with the voice and the belief of the whole Anglo-Saxon nation."

(p.280, *Singapore: The Japanese Version,*
by Colonel Masanobu Tsuji.)

● ● ● ● ● ● ● ● ● ● ●

With the arrival of the Japanese, most of Singapore's airfields – including the naval base at Sembawang – were taken over by the army, but Seletar (now known as "Seretar Hikojo") was destined to come under the command of the navy.

If this airfield was considered not to have been destroyed it is difficult to imagine the Japanese interpretation of the word; their aircraft, being denied the use of Seletar for almost a month, were obliged to operate from Sembawang.

A mere a handful of Japanese arrived at Seletar on February 14th, 1942, but, being an experienced detachment of No.10 Naval Base Unit, they came well prepared to make Seletar fully operational. Reinforcements in the form of the 101st Maintenance and Supply Unit arrived the following day to begin restoration of the airfield.

The landing ground was littered with wreckage of the numerous aircraft which had been broken up and scattered around any area that was free from bomb damage. Holes would need filling before the ground could again be levelled, and, lacking anything but shovels pointed to this being tedious, back-breaking work.

Despite the magnitude of the task facing them, first impressions were said to be very favourable. 'It was a splendid airport,' said Corporal Shiratori Tomizo, a member of the 101st. 'I had seen many other places, but Seletar must surely have been the best in South East Asia. We were all thrilled to think that Japan could defeat a country that had built such an outstanding airport.' First Lieutenant Motsuhara Konagaya, who took the ground contingent of No.40 Naval Air Unit to Seletar on February 25th, was equally impressed.

'I found Seletar to be an extremely nice airport,' he is reported to have stated. 'I was also impressed by the highly sophisticated way in which the petrol stores and other strategically important places had been camouflaged.'[44]

The Officer Commanding No.40 Naval Air Unit, Captain Yoshio Furuta, arrived the day after his ground party, and from that time on Seletar was jointly commanded by two Naval Officers, with a rank equivalent to that of Group Captain. The second officer, Captain Hideo Sawai, was in charge of the maintenance unit.

Three hundred men from the 101st were allotted the task of restoring the airfield. Billeted at Sembawang, they were driven back and forth each day, their drivers also being required to help out with the clearing and filling. Even so, it was March 8th before the first Japanese aircraft were able to land; two type 97 torpedo bombers which were required for patrol work in the Burma campaign.

A widespread search was instigated for civilian employees who had previously worked at Seletar, most having departed long before the Japanese arrived, afraid of what may lie in store.

Despite the inhumanities such as occurred at Singapore's Alexandra Hospital, where the invaders slaughtered orderlies, doctors and their patients, many nationalists at first believed the propaganda which said the Japanese were really the liberators of South-East Asia. But the Chinese knew different. They had already heard of the atrocities inflicted on their kind by the new conquerors. All waited anxiously for events to unfold.

Chinese fears proved to be justified, although all races suffered to some extent. Under the guise of anti-communism – but, in reality, because of their anti-Japanese leanings – it was the Chinese purge, known as "Sook Ching" which was most severe. For some months the Japanese unleashed a reign of terror, at the end of which they had completely lost all hope of gaining the support of the local community.

Seletar's workers reacted in various ways. Some escaped to the mainland where they dispersed into the jungle to join what was to become known as the Malayan Peoples Anti Japanese Army, some effectively disappeared, but the majority remained in their homes, panic-stricken. The latter, eventually had little choice but to return to the station and work for the enemy, for, as one man explained: 'Inevitably, the Japanese discovered where I was living, having apparently been told by other ex-Seletar workers. They told me I had to return to the station to work for them, threatening to behead me if I didn't. And who could refuse as persuasive an argument as that?'

Another civilian forced to work for the Japanese was Charles Richards. Mr CP. Richards BEM, who first arrived on the station in 1931, was associated with Seletar for many years. Awarded the BEM in 1949 – the first major award of any kind given to a civilian employed by the Far East Air Force (FEAF) – he was to remain at Seletar until 1970, less than a year before the RAF left for good.

A few employees found themselves being allocated new posts, but generally the same people were in the same places, doing more or less the same work they had always done. And, working for the Japanese, they were probably treated better than most other inhabitants on the island. As one survivor recalled: 'On the whole the treatment was not so bad, and the Japanese did not shoot or behead any of us. There were slappings and beatings, but this was the normal method of punishment among the Japanese themselves. A junior rank disobeying a senior rank would be punished by being slapped.'

Things were a little different in the city, historical evidence shows that shortly after their arrival, the Japanese beheaded a number of looters, displaying their bodies at salient points in the town as a warning to further transgressors.

Seletar-based personnel seemed to have two things in their favour: Firstly, the Kempeitai (Secret Police) – who were particularly barbaric – were not allowed on the station, discipline there being largely enforced by the naval authorities. Secondly, naval airmen tended to be of a superior class, and were thus far more humane than the soldiers who terrorized the rest of the population. In fact, many Japanese at Seletar were said to be appalled by the way their compatriots were behaving, but as Singapore – now renamed Syonan (Light of the South), its clocks synchronized to match Tokyo time – was controlled by the Army, they were powerless to act. It is true to say that although the relationship between Seletar's civilian and service population was never cordial, many officers did gain the respect of their workers. It is even reported that, on more than one occasion, naval officers were known to have successfully intervened with the Kempeitai on behalf of their civilian staff.

But even at Seletar, working conditions were very hard. In return for a standard daily wage of one dollar twenty cents (less than thirty pence), civilians were expected to work from 07:00 through to 16:30, six days a week. Their wages were paid in Japanese substitute currency. Almost worthless, and scornfully referred to locally as "banana dollars" (the ten dollar note featuring a banana tree). The money had no backing whatever, and people soon lost all confidence in it. But civilians working for the Japanese service authorities were granted certain practical privileges which were denied to the rest of the community. For the first six months the food ration was set at two pounds of tapioca per day, and a pound of rice a week. Seletar personnel received an additional amount of rice, plus two pounds of sugar; sufficient to avoid starvation, but many people suffered badly from malnutrition.

Because of the weakness of the currency, many people became deeply involved in black market activities, including the Japanese themselves. As one Seletar employee recalled, 'Nearly everyone operated in the black market. I remember one occasion that I purchased a watch from a Japanese sailor for a small quantity of rice. I exchanged the watch for a bicycle and resold the bicycle to another sailor for double the quantity of rice, making a one hundred per cent profit. I was then able to quote my own price for the rice in Singapore.'

The biggest problems facing the population were shortages of food and medicines, the latter available only at hospitals, where treatment was anyway limited, preference being given to the Japanese forces. It was estimated that around three quarters of the population suffered from beri-beri, malaria, tropical ulcers, or general malnutrition.

About twenty lorries were required to bring workers to the base each day for a large number of civilians continued to live outside the camp, where conditions became extremely unpleasant. From *Lion in the Sky* comes the story told by Kamachi Veresami. Only eleven years old in 1943, when she lived in Seletarville, she retained vivid memories of what conditions were like.

'We lived one family to a room and we shared a bathroom with eight other families. Water was restricted to two periods a day, 3am to 6am in the morning, and 1pm to 2pm in the afternoon. But the water was dirty and mosquitoes were rampant. There were many accidents due to overcrowding. In the year we were there I saw my sister and two brothers die of malaria and malnutrition.'

Strict rules were imposed, even at Seletar – where naval discipline was nowhere near as severe as the army's – and these needed to be observed, failure to do so would lead to swift punishment. Civilians were required to bow to the guards when entering or leaving the camp, and if they had to pass into a restricted area they first had to dismount their bike and bow to the sentry on duty.[45]

Initially it seemed nothing short of a miracle could halt the Japanese conquest of Asia, their military strategy having been brilliantly executed. The original plan, calling for capture of the Philippines, Malaya, Siam, the Dutch East Indies and Burma was almost complete, and it was intended that these countries should form the greater East Asia Co-Prosperity sphere, with Singapore the focus of military power. But 1942 saw the Japanese becoming overly ambitious, their projected area of conquest being expanded to encompass India, the Nicobar Islands, Papua New Guinea and the Solomons. With Singapore no longer being of front-line importance. And since it was now assumed there was no possibility of allied air strikes, little was done to strengthen defences on the island.

At Seletar, the Japanese enjoyed a far higher standard of accommodation than they had experienced at military bases back home. All officers lived in Seletar's palatial Mess, apart from those of No.101 Maintenance Unit who shared the three large bungalows situated nearby. The men used the same barrack blocks and married quarters once occupied by the British. They even used the same beds and mosquito nets. But as soon as it became obvious that

Japanese industry was metal starved, the iron bedsteads were shipped off to Japan, the men now sleeping on wooden boards placed on the floor.

During the early days of occupation, food supplies could be imported from the homeland. Fish was available locally, but, due to the possibility of food poisoning, it could not be served in the accustomed manner – raw. The main complaint was with the meat. Shipped in from Siam, we are told this was generally unsuitable for the preparation of Japanese specialities. By this one assumes that Sukiyaki is likely to have been reduced from the status of a national dish, to something approaching a national disaster.

By 1944, standards had deteriorated considerably. With convoys now unable to get through with any amount of regularity, local purchase became the order of the day: papaya, worm-eaten rice and such. And though the quality was extremely poor, the quantities required were generally available. But both officers and men were eventually reduced to bartering with the locals, exchanging tobacco and such for bananas and fish.

As wives and families were not allowed to travel from Japan, special arrangements were set up to meet the men's needs. The few Japanese who had managed to find local girlfriends were allowed to reside outside camp; typically in small, native-style attap bashas. The needs of the rest of the camp were served by a brothel which had been set up about fifteen minutes walk away; near the junction of Jalan Kayu and the Yio Chu Kang Road. Girls were imported from Japan, and worked to a strict timetable; as far as working hours went, one assumes! Certain hours were allotted during the day, two separate sessions, one for non commissioned officers, the other for – to use an American term – enlisted men. The evenings were strictly set aside for officers – though, one supposes, not necessarily gentlemen.

More sophisticated "houses" were set up by the enterprising locals in Singapore. Staffed by Chinese girls, these too were mainly frequented by the officers.

On the camp itself, entertainment of a more formal nature was frequently organized. Shows were brought in from downtown Singapore, with films being imported from Japan. During the early days of occupation, when the convoys were travelling virtually unmolested, Japanese touring shows would visit the station every two months or so. These were eagerly awaited, assuaging, as they did, a great deal of the homesickness felt by many of the men. How much so became evident when, in 1943, a group of men travelled from Seletar to the naval base to witness the arrival from Japan of a large number of female dancers. Unfortunately, a case of cholera had been reported on board the ship bringing them, and as a result, no one was being allowed to disembark. Word spread, and soon hundreds of sailors began to gather at the dockside. Shortly thereafter, a number of medical officials were seen to board the vessel and, much to the delight of the watching men, the girls were lined up and inoculated on the spot, then allowed ashore. 'That turned out to be the most dramatic moment of my entire stay in Singapore,' one sailor was said to have stated when recalling the event!

Servicemen worked normal hours for six days a week, unless on special duty. Sunday, an off day, was normally spent in town, although, for their own protection, certain areas were restricted. A Mr Yoshitoko Takahashi, who was training at Seletar in 1944, is said to have been of the opinion that the Japanese were more feared than trusted by the local residents. [I wonder why!] Officers were warned never to walk down alleys, and some areas were totally out of bounds. The regulations for other ranks were even more stringent. They were restricted to an area around the Cathay Hotel, but were not allowed to frequent any of the bars. They were however allowed to visit special brothels which, apart from their normal services, were also licensed to sell beer.

Seletar's population varied greatly; anywhere from the four to five hundred initial occupying force, to as high as three thousand. But at the time of surrender there were only fifteen hundred personnel on the base. Similarly, the types of aircraft were always subject to change, and numbers were often augmented by visiting squadrons. One junior officer recalls there being over a hundred and eighty planes using Seletar at one point, but as official records for the entire period were eventually destroyed, no verification was possible.

The shortcomings of Seletar's grass strip became clearly apparent in June 1942, when 753 Mobile Wing visited the base, bringing with them over sixty aircraft. As a direct result, a meeting was held where it was quickly decided that a concrete runway should be built. Captain Furuta, one of Seletar's joint commanders, had hoped for a runway of five thousand feet, but just three thousand feet of actual concrete was laid, an additional section of hardened ground providing an undershoot/overshoot area at the seaward end. This was achieved by laying and rolling flat thousands of small stones; the entire, labour-intensive construction was hand-built – that is, with only shovels and the bare hands of Allied POW's. Taking a month to complete, it was aligned 03 – 21.

Seletar's 40th Air Unit was initially charged with responsibility for patrolling an area of the South China Sea bounded by French Indo-China, Borneo, and Malaya – escorting convoys and carrying out anti-submarine patrols – but during the battle of the Indian Ocean this was quickly extended to include the Straits of Malacca.

936 Air Unit was formed on November 1st 1942, incorporating the 40th Air Unit with its "Kate" 12 and Navy 97 carrier attack aircraft, plus "Val" 22 and Navy 99 bombers. One flight of this new unit was immediately detached to reinforce Army Air units covering the Indian Ocean area. Then, early in the new year, the bombers were transferred, too. The only element of 936 to remain at Seletar was the reconnaissance unit, which included a number of Zero seaplanes.

Numerous elements were by now staging through the base, including the 12th and 13th Training Units for carrier-borne and land-based crews respectively, along with squadrons belong-

ing to the carrier fleets. Additional ground crews were brought in to cope with the increased workload, and there was also a change in command. Captain Natsuo Muda assumed control of No.101 MU, and two months later, Captain Furuta was replaced by Captain Seizo Konishi.

But the tide of war was rapidly changing, and the Japanese found their resources were being stretched to the limit. Two events occurred in September 1943 drawing Singaporeans' attention to the changing balance of power. On the 8th of that month, an Italian merchant vessel was berthed in Singapore when news broke of Italy's unconditional surrender to the Allies. The ship immediately slipped anchor and departed under cover of darkness. Seletar's seaplanes, having been alerted, carried out a thorough but fruitless search of the area; it seems the Italians had escaped by way of the Cocos Islands.

An even more dramatic occurrence took place two weeks later. In that same harbour a small group of British and Australians were to carry out one of the greatest sea raids of the war. Operation "Jaywick" was led by Major Ivan Lyon MBE DSO, of the Gordon Highlanders, Lt DMN Davidson DSO RNVR, and Lt R.C. Page DSO AIF. They had started out from Australia, then, once in the area they transferred to a number of small canoes, and utilizing the cover offered by various islands, successfully managed to evade detection by the Japanese Navy, ending up close to Singapore. On the night of September 26/27th, they slipped into the harbour and mined seven ships, including the ten thousand ton tanker, *Suikoku Maru*. Many people witnessed the incredible sight of mines detonating and ships exploding. The *Suikoku Maru* was said to have lifted bodily out of the water before disintegrating in a huge ball of flame. The Japanese were of course immediately goaded into furious action, with all available boats and planes being ordered to conduct an extensive search of the area. Seletar's seaplanes took to the air at first light. Advised by the Japanese Naval Command to look out for submarines, they naturally searched the stretches of water most likely to be used by such vessels. And while this sweeping search was taking place to the west, the canoes were sneaking away to the east. Only later in the day did the search area extend east and south, by which time the canoes were well on their way to rendezvous with their vessel, *The Krait*. After a forty-seven day epic effort, the party arrived safely at an American base.

Japanese pride had suffered a terrible blow from which it was never able to recover, although enhanced security did succeed in foiling a similar raid a year later. Meantime, a shortage of raw materials back home forced the Japanese to increase the export of metal from their conquered territories. In Singapore this began with the removal of all the lamp standards, thus plunging the island into total darkness. Iron railings, gates, iron bars, and all other metal structures were systematically plundered. As previously mentioned, Seletar's metal bed frames were long gone, attention now being focussed on the hangars. The Japanese began dismantling these towards the end of the war, so as to facilitate removal of the metal girders.

By the end of 1943, many of Seletar's two thousand Japanese inhabitants were reduced to living in tents. The increase in numbers was in part caused by the arrival at Seletar of the Second Field Air Force, under its Commander-in-Chief, Rear Admiral Takatsungu Shirojima. A large carrier fleet – now at the naval base dockyard – had brought one hundred and thirty-seven aircraft with them; seventy-four Zeros, thirty-six type 99 bombers, and twenty-seven type 97 fighter bombers. During their intended three months stay the crews were to undergo intensive training in landing, air to air combat, and dive-bombing. But, with Japan not able to afford the luxury of having a large fleet docked in Singapore when they were desperately needed elsewhere, the ships and the Second Field Air Force were ordered to move out on December 10th.

A Sergeant Naeshiro recalls an episode at this time which showed just how confused the Japanese were becoming. 'It took place while I was working in the Communications Centre at the Naval base. Fifty Zeros from Seletar were ordered to fly to Sumatra to support our forces up in the Andaman Islands. They were well on their way when they were ordered back to Singapore, and then rerouted through Java to assist in the Solomon Islands area. Upon landing in Java they were to receive a telegram from the Commander-in-Chief, querying their intentions. Despite this, and a warning that the weather was deteriorating, their Commanding Officer decided to continue on. Attempting to keep together, they soon found themselves in the middle of a typhoon, and over a third of the planes were lost. Battered by the elements, the remainder survived, only to come up against the United States' Forces.'

Allied naval operations had decimated the enemy's convoy system to such an extent that Japan was experiencing an acute shortage of essential supplies and fuel, so to ease the situation they decided to place greater emphasis on air transportation, and to build up training facilities at airfields located close to the oil producing areas.

Seletar now assumed an important role as a training station. A base in Japan would send about one tenth of its pilots to Seletar, where they received instruction in flying and airmanship, and in anti-submarine warfare and the use of radar. On completion of the course they would return to Japan and instruct other pilots. At least, that was the stated intention.

On February 14th, 1944, the 1st Air Flotilla's flying unit – which the following day became known as the 601st Air Unit – arrived at Seletar for training, bringing one hundred and thirty aircraft with them; a strength which, even taking account of losses, actually increased to one hundred and thirty-seven operational aircraft by the time the Unit was required to leave the base. Senior officers were concerned that many of the crews were still inexperienced, as it had not been possible to complete the full training programme. But, the strategic situation having become quite desperate, they could delay no longer; they departed for the carriers, *Hokaku*, *Shokaku*, and the *Zuikaku* on May 5th.

In April, 1944, the Japanese had been forced to withdraw a fleet of over fifty vessels from their base at Truk, in the Caroline Islands. This was directly attributable to recent Allied successes; the Americans, having captured the nearby Marshall Islands were now massing to strike at the Marianas – a vital chain of islands which extended north to within striking distance of the Japanese mainland. The Japanese had decided to meet the challenge by bringing together a large part of their fleet.

But for the Japanese, disaster followed disaster. June saw an action which became known to the Americans as "The Marianas Turkey Shoot." In just two days Vice-Admiral Marc Mischner's Task Force 58 claimed four hundred and eighty Japanese aircraft, and almost the same number of pilots, along with the carriers *Taiho*, *Shokaku* and *Hiryo*. The Americans had won a great battle; one of the turning points of the Pacific War. A large percentage of the Japanese fleet was destroyed or badly damaged, and virtually all the aircraft which had been at Seletar for training with the 601st Air Unit were lost.

The Japanese, by now resigned to their fate, were determined to make the Allies pay dearly. The pilot training programme was accelerated, more units continuing to arrive at Seletar. In mid March it was the 381st Air Unit, to be joined in September by the Zeros of the 11th Air Unit. The two units amalgamated in December, the Zeros returning to Japan.

Sqn/Ldr Neville Shorrick, Education Officer at Seletar in the 1960's, uncovered the following interesting story when conducting interviews in Japan for his book, *Lion in the Sky*.

A minor mystery arose in September 1944, when Captain Furuta returned from Japan to replace Captain Konishi as Commanding Officer. Official records, such as they are, state that Captain Konishi was ordered back to Japan, only to die in a sea battle when his ship was sunk. Captain Furuta, who had been a naval cadet with Konishi, and knew him well, tells a different story. 'Captain Konishi was commanding a patrol boat unit around the Japanese coast,' he stated. 'What happened, was that he got off a ship in Yokohama and almost immediately afterwards was killed in a car accident!'

Whatever the reason, Captain Konishi's death – though not the circumstances – soon became a talking point at Seletar, and some local employees, prone to superstitions, believed he had been murdered on the station. Even their version was reshaped by time, and in later years one would hear stories about the ghost of a Japanese "General" occasionally seen to be stalking around the camp. Captain Konishi would probably have been amused by his elevation in rank as well as spirit, but it is doubtful he would have appreciated the change of service. Seletar remained a naval unit throughout the entire occupation, the Army at no time being based there.[46]

So as to protect fleet movements off North Borneo, a majority of 936 Air Units' aircraft – the first to be based at Seletar – were detached to Brunei in October 1944. Days later is when the Americans chose to attack Singapore, a very heavy raid being staged by B-29's. Captain Furuta was said to have claimed that around one hundred and fifty aircraft flew over the island on October 13th, and that all available fighters were sent up to intercept them. Although admitting to extensive airfield damage, he said there had been no Japanese losses either in the air or on the ground. This does not tie in with official records, which state that Seletar suffered a serious raid by thirty B-29's on the morning of November 5th, with the runway being hit, and a number of aircraft from both the 11th and 13th Air Units being destroyed or damaged. The remaining seaplanes of the 936 Air Unit were reported as being able to fly out before the raid actually started.

Another six raids were carried out by Allied air forces during the early part of 1945. This had the Japanese worried, for the cream of Seletar's aircraft were now back in Japan, those which remained being of little practical value. This was borne out by the fact that American and British aircraft reported little or no aerial resistance, the Japanese being driven to the most desperate forms of bluff.

'Towards the end of the war our aircraft were thin on the ground,' a Japanese airman was reported as saying. 'Whenever we thought the enemy was coming, wireless operators would be sent to various high points around the island: Mandai, Changi, Kranji, and Bukit Timah. We would relay messages to hundreds of illusory Japanese pilots in the hope that the enemy would pick up our signals and think there were more aircraft in Singapore than there actually were.'

Now, hopeful of maintaining their position, the Japanese were driven to suicidal lengths, literally! This period saw the introduction of the units known as *Kamikaze* or Divine Wind (after a typhoon which saved Japan from a Mongol invasion in the year 1281). There had been previous instances of pilots deliberately flying their aircraft into the target, but usually only when the pilot was mortally wounded, or his aircraft fatally stricken. This new tactic took the American's by surprise; one escort carrier was sunk and four others damaged during the first deployment of these aircraft.

Meantime, another new weapon was being installed in Seletar's reconnaissance aircraft. Known as the Magnetic Anomaly Detector (MAD),[47] this instrument had been used very effectively in anti-submarine warfare during the previous year, but only now was it being introduced to the Singapore area. Said to have an effective range of between one hundred and fifty and two hundred and fifty metres only, and that at a height of ten to fifteen metres, depending on the pilot's skill! [Maybe MAD applied to the pilot's mental state also.] Nevertheless, it was claimed that aircraft using the system accounted for at least seven submarines in the South Sea area alone.

With the main fleet being recalled to Japan in February 1945, the Army assumed responsibility for all forces remaining in the Singapore area – which of course included Seletar. By April, the area was virtually cut off from Japan, becoming an independent theatre responsible for its own defences. Although some three hundred front-line aircraft still remained in South East Asia, most of these had also disappeared by June; ordered back to Japan to play their part in the defence of the homeland. The area could still boast of almost one thousand aircraft, but two thirds of these were trainers. Of the rest, many required major repairs for which there was a shortage of parts. A thousand pilots were on hand to fly these aircraft, though the majority were only trainees. Given this state of affairs, the Southern Army decided to conserve what little strength it had until Singapore or Malaya was actually attacked.

In actual fact, plans for the invasion of Malaya (Operation "Zipper") – with initial landings set for Port Swettenham and Penang – were already scheduled to take place before the events at Hiroshima and Nagasaki brought the war to an abrupt end. It has been admitted by the Japanese that had this operation gone ahead, they would not have been ready, and their air operations would probably have been nowhere near as effective as had those of the much smaller, similarly-placed British force back in 1941-42.

With so many troops and equipment already on the move, Operation 'Zipper' effectively became Exercise 'Zipper', the end coming without a drop of blood shed on Malayan soil.

With the surrender, Captain Furuta was ordered to place all his aircraft out in the open, in good order. He was also instructed, as were other Japanese senior officers, to retain control of his men until the Allies arrived to take command – orders which were generally adhered to. The seaplanes were quickly beached and their propellers removed, the airframes being lined up on the airfield with the rest of the aircraft – Zero fighters, twin-engined bombers, and the trainers. But there were difficulties, a number of sailors and warrant officers fleeing immediately they learned of the outcome of the war. Admiral Fukudome referred to this aspect of the surrender when he was interrogated by the Allies. 'About three hundred men were involved,' he admitted. 'Some apparently tried to turn pirate and were themselves killed by native pirates. Some were killed by bandits, but most of the survivors have returned to Singapore.'

Seletar was officially handed over to the British by Captain Furuta, who was himself, along with other officers, then taken to Malacca where they remained prisoners-of-war until September 20th, 1946.

It seems appropriate to end the story of the Japanese occupation with a small footnote on Captain Furuta, the longest serving Japanese commander of Seletar. By 1966 he was a retired Rear Admiral, living a quiet life in the suburbs of Tokyo, and when interviewed by Sqn/Ldr Neville Shorrick, he stated that he had always regretted the War against the British, and pointed out that the Japanese Navy had been modelled along British lines. 'I enjoyed my stay in Singapore, and am only sorry I could not have served there in happier circumstances,' he said.

Referring to the Malayan War, the Admiral added, 'In 1941, our first aim was to knock out your air force. Only then could we bring in the army. If you had had more modern fighter squadrons, it would have been impossible to land in Singapore and we may not have won.'

The Japanese had gone on to win that battle, but in the end they had lost the War. Seletar was once more a British base, and in the uneasy years ahead it was to achieve its greatest triumphs as a flying station, as was Tengah. Changi, too, was to see massive expansion, for it had now been transferred to the RAF.

Painting discovered on an office wall in the flying boat hangar after the war. It depicts sinking of the battleship Prince of Wales. *Japanese text reads, "Display of Fighting Spirit."* **Public Records Office**

Japanese Navy Mitsubishi F1M2 "Pete" seaplane on the dump at Seletar, its float no doubt already earmarked for some future project. **Malcolm Lancaster**

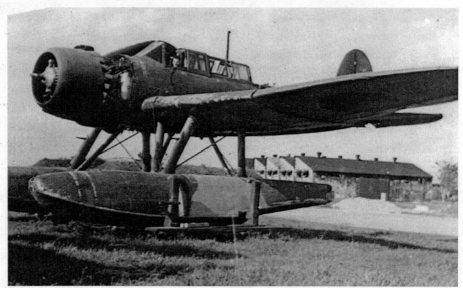

Japanese floatplane - Aichi A13A1 "Jake" reconnaissance aircraft - beached & propellers removed as required by the terms of surrender. **Malcolm Lancaster**

Another aircraft abandoned at Seletar. Yokosuka MXY-7 model 11 Ohka (Cherry Blossom) "Baka". This rocket-powered aircraft carrying a 2600lb warhead was carried to within 50mls of the target area slung beneath a G4M bomber. Not a machine you would willingly strap to your back unless you had a death wish! **Malcolm Lancaster**

CHAPTER TEN

Contrary To Expectations: From War to the Netherlands East Indies

August 1945, and "Operation Zipper" was about to commence. With seven infantry divisions and an armoured brigade, battleships, cruisers and destroyers, along with over five hundred aircraft of the FAA and RAF, it was planned to be the largest all-British combined operation of the war. But with the announcement of the Japanese surrender on the 14th of the month, it seemed Malaya had now only to await liberation by the Allies. However, this abrupt cessation of hostilities seemed to come as something of a surprise to those Allies; plans for the eventuality of peace having not yet been formulated. The landings went ahead as scheduled, with over ten thousand men going ashore at Port Swettenham on September 9th, with similar events being re-enacted in Penang and Singapore. In fact, it was very nearly the privilege of the Royal Air Force to be first of the British services to return to Singapore, they being preceded only by two army officers, one a Lt Wishard, who had parachuted in on August 30th, to organise a supply drop for the POW's.

The RAF made their unscheduled arrival the following day, a Mosquito aircraft of 684 Squadron, crewed by Flt/Lt C.G. Andrews and W/O Painter, making an emergency landing at Kallang. Extracts from Flt/Lt Andrews' official report of the incident make interesting reading:

On August 31st I took off from Cocos at 0610 hrs to carry out a sortie in the Singapore area. The purpose was to obtain large scale vertical photographs of Kallang airfield to assist in the execution of a special mission to be carried out at a later date. Approximately one hour from the target area I descended from my cruising height of 20,000 ft. Upon reaching about 5,000 ft, some twenty minutes from the target, I noticed my starboard engine drop revs from 2,300 to 2,200. I endeavoured to re-synchronise, but found that full movement of the pitch control made no difference whatsoever.

An inspection of the pitch control linkage in the cockpit revealed all to be intact there, meaning there was a failure in the linkage of the engine mounted controls, or of the attachment to the constant speed unit. Twice before I had experienced a similar fault and I felt confident that the cause of the trouble would not be difficult to locate, and perhaps even possible to repair with limited facilities. With revs now down to 1,900 – the limit of the fully coarse position – our situation was rather difficult.

I could not get sufficient power from the starboard engine to allow me to climb to a safe height for a return to base; I had to negotiate the Sumatra mountains, high frontal cloud and bad weather. Added to this was the fact that the low revs were not sufficient to allow the generator to charge the batteries. This meant the radio aids were dangerously limited, if not useless. With these points in mind, and taking account of the present military situation in Malaya, I made the decision, not without qualms, to land at Kallang, touching down at 10.20 hrs and taxiing to the old airport buildings, where great excitement was taking place amongst the Japanese. After a little trouble, I gathered that it was their intention for me to park on the other side of the field. This I proceeded to do and was marshalled to the parking area by Jap ground staff equipped with flags. My navigator and I got out and endeavoured to inform the Japs that our aircraft was u/s, a matter which was extremely difficult until an interpreter arrived. He spoke quite good English and this eased the communication difficulties. He was shortly followed by a Jap Air Force officer accompanied by several 'hangers on' and later by a Jap Staff Officer from Singapore, all in full uniform and armed.

My early fears were beginning to disperse with the consistent courtesy shown to us, and a desire of the Japs to meet all my wishes. I stressed the point that my unit would be worrying about my welfare, and would be out searching for me in the area next day. To my amazement they immediately offered to broadcast over the Singapore radio my whereabouts, and the reason for my being there. I was asked if it was my intention to take off that day, to which I replied that it was if the trouble could be located and repaired in time. I then asked for a tool kit which was eventually produced, with an apology for the delay due to the fact that they had been instructed to evacuate the area the following day and the tools had been packed. However, with tools, and the assistance of three Jap ground staff, my navigator and I removed the engine cowlings and carried out an inspection, the cause of the trouble being located fairly easily.

The wheel operated by the pitch teleflex control had fallen off the actuating spindle of the Constant Speed Unit. The locking nut had apparently fractured and allowed the retaining nut to screw right off. I asked if a suitable nut could be produced, but the only one that would fit was a normal mild steel hexagon nut, not castellated; locking it was going to be difficult. As time was getting short for a return to base, I decided that work should continue the following day. This information was given to the interpreter who said that accommodation would be arranged for us at Raffles Hotel. I declined, however, upon learning that we could contact an army officer who had parachuted into Changi the previous day. During these few hours we were with the Japs, they were at all times respectful and obedient to my wishes. Their entire attitude was that of eating humble pie and displaying a wish to please, even if it was not too genuine.

The only question of military importance which was asked of me was the top speed of my aircraft. My reply was to the effect that I did not know as I had never tried it flat out. Just prior to leaving the airfield, a Liberator flew over, which I presume noticed the Mosquito on the ground, for it made several passes over the field. I endeavoured to attract attention but it flew off, leaving me unaware of the extent of their observations.

We were then transported to the POW camp at Changi where I contacted Lt. Wishard. He organised accommodation for us and a guard for the aircraft. The guards were, funnily enough, Japanese, and were threatened with their lives if anything happened to the aircraft. At Changi we were introduced to Wg/Cdr Wills-Sandford, senior Air Force Officer in the prison camp, and he arranged for an engineering officer, a fitter and a rigger, to carry out the work on the aircraft. The remainder of the day and evening we spent with the POWs – the first real outside contact they had had for three and a half years – an amazing experience for all of us.[48]

Next morning we left the gaol with Flt/Lt Sturrock, a fitter, a rigger, a Major Wild – who acted as interpreter – and a Jap officer as a hostage. We proceeded to Kallang where the fitter and the rigger under Flt/Lt Sturrock made a careful inspection of the aircraft. The fitter replaced the CSU control and managed to lock the retaining nut to the satisfaction of Flt/Lt Sturrock. While they were working on the aircraft, Mosquito "E" appeared overhead and flew low several times across the field.

I gave the crew the all clear sign and shortly afterwards the aircraft landed. We were indeed relieved to meet the crew, Sqn/Ldr Newman and Fl/Off Burns, and learned that they had heard of our whereabouts from the Jap radio and the

Liberator. Sqn/Ldr Newman had expected R/T communication with me while flying overhead, but as my batteries were fairly low I dared not use them for fear of not being able to start my engines. Sqn/Ldr Newman and I inspected the runway with a view to ascertaining its capabilities, reaching the decision that it was suitable for heavy aircraft of Liberator standard. Lunch was supplied by the Japs.

They also supplied us with about 130 gallons of fuel for each aircraft of what was reputed to be 100 octane. I had this put in the empty bomb bay tank, to use independently, if needed, in case the octane rating was lower than claimed. We took off at 12.50 hours and set course for base. I used the Jap fuel en route at low cruising power, and it operated satisfactorily. Touch down at Cocos base was 16.20 hours.

• • • • • • • • • •

Sqn/Ldr KJ Newman's official report reiterates these facts:

At 06.20 hours on 1st September, I took off in Mosquito 'E' for a PR sortie, and to search for Flt/Lt Andrews, who had not returned from his sortie the previous day. Probable position of aircraft 'J' was known from reports intercepted from Jap controlled radio in Singapore, which stated that a twin engined aircraft force-landed at Kallang airfield at approximately 12.00 hours on 31st August 1945. Also a report from a 356 Squadron Liberator crew stated seeing a Mosquito at Kallang airfield on the same afternoon. I arrived overhead Kallang at 10.00 hours, sighting a PR. Mosquito on the grass. I circled several times, very low, during which time I tried to contact the aircraft on VHF without success. I saw what I thought to be Europeans working on the aircraft, and other Europeans in company with Flt/Lt Andrews, from whom I received the OK signal, and decided to land to determine (i) the cause of forced landing (ii) the extent of damage, if any, and (iii) what steps had been taken to make the aircraft serviceable.

On enquiry after landing, I found that an engineering officer, a fitter and a rigger from the POW camp were on the job. After a chat with Flt/Lt Andrews, I learned that temporary repairs were being carried out, and that in the opinion of Flt/Lt Sturrock, the aircraft would be serviceable for the return trip to base. Within fifteen minutes of my landing a Jap staff car appeared, complete with Staff Major and stooge. I was introduced, amid much bowing and saluting etc, by Major Wild from the POW camp, who acted as interpreter. The Major proved to be most helpful during my stay. The Japs were very polite and could not do enough for us. Refuelling was carried out by the Jap ground staff.

I inspected the runway with Flt/Lt Andrews and decided that, as it was concrete and appeared in good condition, it was suitable for heavy aircraft, the length being 1860 yards by 50 yards. A Jap interpreter informed me that they were evacuating both Kallang and Changi areas and airfields, as they were for the use of the British. He also informed me that Changi airfield was approximately 2,500 by 100 yards but was not surfaced and would be of use to heavy aircraft only during fair weather. I took off at 12.50 hours and landed back at base at 16.20 hours, after an uneventful trip. As the cloud base was very low, no photos were taken.

• • • • • • • • • •

On Sept 5th, 1945, 2896 Sqn RAF Regiment arrived in Singapore, and within a few days, one of their number, Cpl Allan Jenkins, was to lower the Japanese flag which had flown over Seletar since 1942. Cpl Jenkins was later to be accorded the honour of striking the RAF colours once more. On that momentous occasion, along with the new Station Commander, Grp/Cpt G Francis DSO DFC, the salute was taken by representatives of the army and navy. The enforced presence of Japanese Vice-Admiral Kogure was also a feature of this ceremony, he too being required to salute the flag.[49]

The first RAF aircraft to make a return to Seletar were flying boats, as befitted this station. Six Sunderlands arrived on detachment from Koggala, Ceylon on September 10th. Five of these aircraft belonged to 209 Squadron (whose badge featured a falling red eagle – commemora-

Cpl Jenkins strikes the RAF colours over Seletar. The CO, Grp/Cpt Francis DSO DFC is accompanied by representatives from the Army & Navy, along with Japanese Vice-Admiral Kogure, who was obliged to salute. **Imperial War Museum, Ref CF726**

ting the shooting down by this squadron of "Red Baron" von Richthofen by Captain A.R. Brown, April 21st, 1918). The sixth Sunderland was, appropriately enough, an aircraft from Seletar's original squadron, 205.

Colin Brewer was among the first airmen to return to Seletar, and his story is one of "take care of yourself." Colin, along with the rest of his group, were briefed by an army officer before departing Ceylon, and his advice was for them to purchase some camouflaged clothing rather than spending their money on "wine and women." When the men told him they didn't mind fighting, but it was a bit much to expect them to buy their own uniforms, his reply was: "Well, it's your life, and in those sun-bleached clothes the Japs will pick you off like flies." In the event, the atomic bomb saved them from putting this advice to the test. But Colin was told years later by a Mountbatten aid that the expected casualties for their group had been estimated as seventy to eighty percent!

"On arrival at Seletar," Colin says, "we were just dumped, and no one seemed to know what was happening for the first couple of days. We had to locate for ourselves somewhere to sleep, and something to eat. We did manage to find some boxes of American 'K' rations, don't know who they were meant for, or how old they were, but we ate them. As regards somewhere to sleep, we were again fortunate. A local rolled up with a truck full of tents, and he enquired where a certain army unit was located. Being dressed only in shorts we said, right here. We unloaded the tents and scribbled Captain Smith, or some such, and that was us fixed up. A few days later we were moved into the blocks, but they were a complete shambles, took ages to make them reasonably habitable. All this was before the Japs at Seletar had officially surrendered. This happened shortly after a white painted aircraft arrived with the surrender party."

For the first few days, 209 Squadron more or less took over Seletar, supported by the Catalina's of an Australian squadron, which arrived shortly afterwards. A great deal of hard work was required, for their aircraft had a prominent part to play in the forthcoming victory celebrations, due in two days.

On the morning of September 12th 1945, three years and nine months since the first bombs fell on Singapore, Field Marshal Count Terauchi – Supreme Commander Japanese Expeditionary Forces, Southern Regions, surrendered the six hundred and fifty thousand men under his command to the Supreme Commander South East Asia, Admiral Lord Mountbatten, although for some inexplicable reason, Count Terauchi himself wasn't present at the official signing, the Japanese being represented by General Itagaki. Shortly after the ceremony, Lord Mountbatten, along with his Naval, Army, and Air Force Commanders-in-Chief, plus representatives from the various Allied powers, watched the surrender flypast. Led by Grp/Cpt Francis in the first of the six Sunderlands, it was a display of great majesty; an indication that the Royal Air Force once again ruled these skies.

Although the Sunderland detachment was soon to return to Ceylon, it wasn't long before Seletar was re-occupied by a squadron on a permanent basis, Sunderlands of 230 Squadron now fulfilling the maritime role, with 17 Squadron's Spitfires arriving from Burma, via Tengah. These were commanded by Battle of Britain ace, Sqn/Ldr "Ginger" Lacey, but were destined to depart for Japan before too long.

The station was found to be in a very sorry state indeed, over three years of neglect being well evident. Shoulder-high grass on the once beautiful golf course would present a challenge to any groundsman, never mind golfer, and the many lawns had almost reverted to jungle. Monsoon drains were choked with the kind of stagnant water in which mosquitoes thrive, and the swimming pool showed signs of obvious use – as a dump for old aircraft engines and suchlike! The electricity supply was totally unreliable, subsequent inspection revealing it to have been maintained by the crudest of methods imaginable: nails replaced fuses, and wires conducting thousands of volts were bare of insulation. All the radio masts were on the ground.

A 230 Squadron crew-member's first thoughts: 'A brief inspection of the station showed Seletar to have been well maintained operationally, but the appearance was shabby, recreational facilities and accommodation having been neglected. We were surprised at the number of aircraft on site, certainly many more than intelligence reports had indicated. However, there was a great deal of unserviceability evident. Most had their propellers removed, in accordance with the terms of the surrender, but quite a few looked to be operational. It is difficult to remember, but I estimated there to be approximately one hundred aircraft of various types: single engined monoplane, floatplane fighters; single engined biplane, floatplane fighters; Zeros; twin engined bombers and transports. All water-borne aircraft had been beached, and were either in the hangars or on the hard-standing outside the hangars.

'The hangars were fairly well stocked with spares, but I regret to say that within a short time

the orderliness of them was disturbed by British personnel seeking "souvenirs." Grass on the playing fields and non-operational areas had been allowed to grow wild and become infested with snakes. Airmen's dormitories were filthy and contained no beds. The wooden platforms on which the Japanese slept had been laid on the floors. These were also evident in the public rooms of the Sergeants' and Officers' Messes.'

It didn't take long for the locally employed civilians to start reporting back, many of them having served at Seletar both before and during the war. They, along with the additional labour force of several hundred Japanese and Korean prisoners, began clearing up the mess. These POW's – perhaps to circumvent Geneva Convention rules on prisoners-of-war being made to work – now became officially known as "Japanese surrendered personnel." Organised into working parties under command of their own officers, these JSP were given the priority task of cutting the grass and killing the snakes. The swimming pool was drained and cleaned out. Monsoon drains were cleared, mosquitoes largely eradicated. With so much activity taking place it wasn't long before the station was again looking spick and span.

One of Seletar's post war blocks under construction in 1946. **Malcolm Lancaster**

A time of expansion. Another shot of one of Seletar's post war blocks under construction.   **Malcolm Lancaster**

The Japanese were reported to have worked much harder than had been the case with Allied prisoners in similar situations, the difference being, that no matter what state the Allied prisoners were in, they still tended to fight the war by whatever means possible. Now, there was no longer a war left to fight.

Some of these Japanese remained at Seletar for up to two years, and seemed to show little resentment at having lost the war. The few instances of violence which did occur immediately after the war, were quickly stamped out by Lord Mountbatten. He issued strict instructions that the Japanese were to be treated fairly, but made to work hard. It was also laid down that they must be made to realize they were a defeated army, and as such, were to salute all Allied servicemen, irrespective of rank.

When the island was first re-occupied, the Royal Air Force based its transport operations at Kallang, using mainly Dakotas and Yorks. But the runway, unable to cope with the increased traffic, soon began to wilt under the strain, showing signs of breaking up. So, with the rest of Singapore's airfields being unsuitable for heavy aircraft, the burden of air transportation rested with Seletar's flying boats.

The Short Sunderland ranks among the truly great aircraft of all time. They had served with honour throughout the war, in all theatres, often carrying out tasks for which they had not been designed. Production ceased in October 1945, after a run of almost eighteen years; factories at Rochester, Belfast, Dumbarton and Windermere turning out a total of seven hundred and forty-nine, of all marks. But with the requirement for the Catalinas to be returned to the United States at the end of the war – having been supplied under the "lease-lend" scheme – the Sunderland was destined to remain one of the principal aircraft in the Royal Air Force for another fourteen years, again, often assigned a role for which they had not been designed, but which they carried out admirably.

Their first major task was to transport food and medical supplies to the sick and starving throughout the Far East, Allied internees and prisoners-of-war being their primary objectives. But there were occasions when their assistance was more widely needed. An instance of this occurred early on, during the so-called "rice famine."

Production of this staple commodity had been badly hit during Japanese occupation of the major producing countries, bringing about an acute shortage. By the time the Allies returned, the situation had become so desperate that a huge operation had to be mounted to save people from further suffering. In this, the Sunderland squadrons played a principal part, their aircraft participating in "rice runs" for many weeks. Their efforts earned great praise for the aircraft and their crews. Not only were they often to fly in appalling weather conditions, they also had to land on dangerous and sometimes uncharted waters.

On completion of the last "rice run," the following letter was received from the authorities at Kuantan:

> *The Sunderlands put up a magnificent show, landing on a river which had not been charted for years. I cannot tell you how much we appreciate the help the Royal Air Force has been to us. It is not only that you helped out a hospital and saved a considerable population from a period of semi-starvation, but that a huge and isolated district, in which two European officers have been our sole representatives since before the Japanese surrender, has had a daily view of the flag.*

With shipping being in desperately short supply, the next task faced by Seletar's Sunderlands was that of repatriation of the POW's. Men were airlifted from Japan to Koggala, the flying boat base sited in the south of Ceylon. Flights were also made to all the major ports in the Far East, with hundreds of passengers being ferried around. During October 1945, Sunderlands carried four hundred and fifty-seven British ex-prisoners-of-war from Singapore to Koggala and Madras. At times the weather was appalling, with heavy storms and blinding rain, but still the Sunderlands flew.

Many of the passengers on these trips were in a terrible state, emotionally as well as physically. A 240 Squadron pilot recalled that one man had beri-beri, and knew he was being "carried home to die." On another trip the passengers were civilians, and while they all insisted on shaking hands with the crew, most of them were in tears. 'Evacuating British prisoners-of-war was the most satisfying job I have ever undertaken,' said another pilot. 'But it was not the sort of work I would recommend to anyone who was at all sensitive.'

Construction of the latter day Seletarville; a great improvement on the pre-war 'basha'-type stilted affairs (to be seen on the right).
Malcolm Lancaster

Jalan Kayu in 1948. Little more than the pre-war Kampong.   *Peter Nunn*

While the Sunderlands were virtually working round the clock to help the needy, the base at Seletar was being quickly built up. The nine hundred servicemen stationed there at the end of September had increased to over three thousand a month later, and this figure did not include the civilians and Japanese, which together added a further two thousand to the total. Dozens of small units were beginning to function. In addition to the Sunderland detachments of 209 and 230 Squadrons, there were the Mosquitos of 84, 89, and 110 Squadrons, plus 11 and 17 Squadrons with their Spitfires. It was late in 1945 that the CPIS – Central Photographic Intelligence Section, first arrived at Seletar. This unit (later known as JAPIC – Joint Air Photographic Intelligence Centre, and ending up as JARIC (FE) – Joint Air Reconnaissance Intelligence Centre, Far East) was initially housed in a building that was later to become the armoury; a far cry from the hallowed portals of the Hyderabad Palace, from where they had so recently moved. And with accommodation at Seletar being already stretched to bursting, CPIS were soon on the move again, this time to Tanglin. Returning to Seletar in early 1946, the unit were to operate from West Camp for the next twenty-four years.

Brief memories of some officers and airmen who arrived at Seletar shortly after the end of the war:

'The surface of the aerodrome, where it was not covered with buildings or tents, was, alternately, a red quagmire of laterite, or a jungle of Lalang grass.'

'In the distance, across the runway from the Officers' Mess, stood the gaunt skeletons of two huge hangars from which the roofs had been removed to be melted down for scrap by the Japanese. All that remained were the stark rows of sawn off girders, pointing accusingly to the heavens. Our aircraft stood out on the field, there being no shelter in the roofless hangars.'

'I was allocated jobs which ranged from servicing the radios on the Sunderlands out in the Straits, to helping clean out the swimming pool. The only accommodation was a concrete barrack block, stripped bare, but it provided a roof and living quarters which, in time, was fitted out with items scrounged from various sources.'

'After all my high hopes over the years of the magic of being posted to an operational squad-

ron, the chilly atmosphere here was like a slap in the face. The first cold shivers of a squadron with low morale ran down my spine.'

'Not having been detailed for a specific job, I spent time exploring remote parts of the airfield, taking care in case any booby traps had been set. I found none, an indication perhaps that the Japanese occupation had ended abruptly. This was borne out after finding a hut in which radio equipment was in the process of being serviced.'

'Aircraft were piled up in dumps. Japanese Bettys, seaplanes, Zeros, and some of our own. Just standing there, looking, I had a strange feeling that the last Japanese occupants were also watching.'

'It was distressing to see the POW's waiting for their turn to board the Dakotas for hospital or repatriation.'

• • • • • • • • • •

On Jan 28th 1946 a "Sally" (Type 17), crewed by members of the Japanese Air Force, arrived at Seletar from Kluang. This aircraft, once used by General Numata, was inspected by a Japanese ground crew, then air tested on Janury 30th.

And it was into this atmosphere that, in November 1945, Air Chief Marshal Sir Keith Park relocated HQ ACSEA – Air Command South East Asia – from its wartime location in Ceylon, to downtown Singapore; right into trouble.

It was early in 1946 that the word "Strike" – in its industrial guise – was introduced to the

RAF for the first time since its formation. Airmen who had cheerfully and resolutely endured the privations and discomforts brought about by the war, were now less inclined to tolerate such conditions. This situation, exploited by a well-organised, communist-leaning minority, caused unrest which spread from Mauripur to Ceylon, then back through India, and finally on to Singapore.

• • • • • • • • • •

The Strike

Due to a lack of troopships, repatriation to the UK was extremely slow, especially so in the case of airmen, thus Seletar was faced with an accommodation problem of grave proportions. This was partially solved by utilizing the former married quarters, but morale quickly began to deteriorate. Most airmen were serving on a "hostilities only" basis, and now that hostilities were presumed to be at an end, they wished to be demobilized. Disaffection at the speed with which this was taking place, along with stories filtering through concerning unrest at bases in India, was eventually to lead to the infamous "strike" situation. A major cause for concern appears to have centred around the fact that servicemen back home were being demobbed in their thousands, and the worry was that they would take all the plum jobs, though no doubt the living conditions and food at Seletar also played their part.

Once again, different people have different memories of how bad things actually were. One officer recalls: 'There was no food available at all fit for Europeans, consequently we had to use

Poor quality but significant photos of Air Vice Marshal Sir Keith Park addressing a meeting of the strikers in the flying boat hangar.   John E Grady

reconstituted dehydrated foods. [Exactly what most people in England were eating, if my memory serves me.] If one cared to venture into the village, or to Singapore, prices were outrageously high; a single egg and chips would cost ten shillings. But to offset this, one could get the same meal for two cigarettes.' [And there are also reports of a free issue of fifty cigarettes per week.]

A Warrant Officer pilot says, 'I will never forget those rusty tins of sardines,[50] and, if this is what the Sergeants' Mess had to put up with, what was it like for the airmen?'

Yet as one airman remembers it, 'The cookhouse curries of early 1946 were marvellous and always popular. We used to sail up to Changi and eat in the village. We did not find the egg and chips too expensive even on our meagre salary.' He went on to state that, 'I received many letters from my young wife and was well aware that the life I led in Singapore was a darned sight easier and better than the one she led in that UK winter of 1945/46: cold weather, food rationing, fuel shortages and power cuts.'

A great amount of black market trading and illicit dealing began to take place during this period, cigarettes, whisky and gin being bartered for cash, food or even items such as antique furniture etc. A more dangerous trend was recalled by Leading Aircraftman Day, a member of 17 Squadron. 'A lot of illicit stills were being run and some people went blind – including two on our squadron, who fortunately got their sight back. I was told others were less lucky.' [Sounds suspiciously like they were resorting to the use of that compass damping agent, methyl alcohol – deadly stuff, so we were informed during trade training.]

The civil and military police were eventually able to suppress the illicit booze situation, but the black market was not so easy to control. Everyone seemed to be caught up in this, senior officers down, especially aircrews travelling between countries.

By November, despite the renewed building programme which was already underway, the accommodation situation was becoming intolerable, two tented camps having to be established.

This situation went very much against the grain, especially amongst new arrivals who expected something much better now the war was over. It quickly became apparent that unless action was taken, the whole administrative machine was in danger of breaking down. The RAF police, firefighters, and other domestic services were seriously understaffed. The small catering staff were under an extremely heavy burden, being expected to feed over four thousand men from limited supplies. With around eleven hundred men now living under canvas, morale at Seletar was plumbing the depths.

Christmas somehow managed to revive the festive spirit, with parties being held all over the station, and one airman reported Christmas dinner as being 'excellent and most enjoyable, the officers serving us in time honoured fashion.' But that wasn't to last. The realities of their situation must have appeared particularly harsh in the weeks which followed that first post-war Christmas, and once again the grumbling became evident; ideal conditions for exploitation by left-wing biassed airmen. The situation was exacerbated when new arrivals from India told of similar discontent which was stirring over there. In fact, airmen in India had been using official telegraphic channels to send unofficial messages to all stations in the Middle and Far East, and very soon trouble was brewing at Seletar. Secret meetings were organised and preparations made towards taking positive action. Stories began to circulate of a sit-down strike by servicemen at Drigh Road, Karachi, and this was seized upon, disaffected elements instigating for similar moves to be taken at Seletar.

The situation was getting out of hand, and news filtered along the grapevine of a meeting to be held in the NAAFI on the evening of January 26th, 1946. The strike promoters were certainly not your normal barrack-room type lawyers, for they had planned their campaign well. The meeting was reported to have been well attended, and held in darkness, the instigators, their voices suitably disguised, skilfully managing to persuade all but the most loyal servicemen that strike action was the way forward. The debate ensued

The camp was so large it ran its own bus service out of necessity.   *Ron Wilkinson*

for some time before it was eventually decided to begin a general stoppage from 08:00 hours the following morning, this to continue until their demands were met.

Naturally, word filtered through to the Station Commander, and Grp/Cpt Francis addressed about three thousand men on the parade ground the following morning at 08:00 hours. Representatives, who were then allowed to voice their grievances, both real and imagined, refused to be swayed, insisting they should be afforded the opportunity of addressing themselves to the Commander-in-Chief personally.

This was agreed to, and duly set up. The following day saw the men gathered in the flying boat hangar, where they were addressed by Air Chief Marshal Sir Keith Park, CBE, the Allied Air Commander-in-Chief. Touching on the main subjects of dissatisfaction: the slow rate of repatriation, the unsuitable living conditions and the poor food, he carefully explained about the problem with troopships, or lack of, and that although it was beyond his power to make any promises on demobilization, he would act in cases of genuine individual hardship, and promised to inform the Air Council of the men's views on the matter. He also promised immediate action would be taken to provide full NAAFI facilities, and that every possible endeavour would be made to improve the standard of food. He said that steps were being taken to reduce the complement at Seletar, which in itself would

have an obvious effect on improving living standards generally.

The men were again allowed to air their grievances, emphasis being placed on the fact that, to do so would not prejudice their position. Despite this assurance, when one man was said to have stated, "Sir, with all due respect, you have used more red flannel in your speech than they use to make red flannel drawers," the police were seen to move in, but in such a crowd it was an easy matter for his mates to spirit him away. Nevertheless, the majority seemed to favour a return to work whilst the matters of release and repatriation were looked into. The general feeling appeared to be that, although they had probably gone too far, they had been effective in getting their point across, and at last some positive action was about to be taken. They had, moreover, made an important and immediate gain, that of an additional rest period each Saturday afternoon. With Wednesday afternoons and Sundays also being official rest periods, this brought their working hours into line with those in force in England.

A majority of the men returned to their duties after this parade, but many were said to have been threatened, some even assaulted by the few who seemed intent on milking the situation to its fullest. That night a another secret meeting was held, the strike promoters and their henchmen eventually proposing and drafting the following:

Since Air Chief Marshal Sir Keith Park apparently has insufficient authority to deal with the situation, we call upon the Supreme Commander, Admiral Mountbatten to meet the men and hear their demands. If he can do no more than pass the matter on to the British Government, then we will wait for a statement from the Government. Until such time as action is taken, the strike continues, and essential services such as food and medical supplies will be under the direction of the strikers themselves.

Next day the trouble had spread to Kallang, and efforts were being made to persuade the four hundred men stationed there to join the strike in support of their "comrades" at Seletar. But this was quickly sorted out, the trouble-makers being dealt with, the first arrests made.

At Seletar, steps were being taken to restore normal conditions. As the men were watching an "England vs Scotland" football match, organised amongst themselves, the Station Commander was said to have held a conference. Unit commanders were given their orders: First, the men were to be segregated in their barrack blocks. They were to be given details of the actions taken to remedy their grievances. Then they were to be given what must have been the most severe warning ever issued to Royal Air Force personnel. Informed that the British Government was taking an extremely serious view of their actions, they would be told that unless they returned to work by 14:00, the so-called strike would be regarded as a mutiny.[51] The orders were immediately carried out, and a parade that afternoon showed a full muster – the strike itself was over, the repercussions, apparently not. The Special Investigation Branch (SIB) now put in an appearance, groups of men being interrogated and then informed they were to be charged. But as nothing further came of this, it seems they were just trying to find out who exactly had been the instigators.

Most of the above details come from airmen recalling the situation many years later. This is mainly all that is available for, naturally, at the time, things were hushed up as much as possible; fairly easy to achieve back in those days of limited communication, and even now records of the event remain fairly elusive. Airmen were not allowed to keep diaries, though some apparently did; a risky practice, for had the SIB picked up anyone with some hastily scribbled notes on a piece of scrap paper, it certainly would not have been looked upon too favourably! The only verbatim report I have seen is from a junior officer at the time, and his experience paints a slightly different picture as to the possible cause – an apparent lack of interest shown by some officers towards the other ranks, viz:

'Funnelling out of Burma, masses of airmen were gradually ending up under canvas on the rain-swept, sticky laterite of Seletar waiting, in many cases, for a boat to take them home to dear old Blighty. Boats were few, information nonexistent, employment largely lacking, boredom rife...

'Approximately two weeks after my arrival I found myself designated "Orderly Officer," one of whose routine duties was, along with the Orderly Sergeant, to visit the Airmen's Mess at mealtimes, to solicit complaints....

'Procedures for lodging complaints are covered by King's Regulations and Air Ministry Orders, however, human nature being what it is, few airmen ever care to chance a complaint for fear of subsequent victimisation, thus, silence was what greeted us. This was in one of the two permanent messes and, appalled by the surly faces, I wondered what kind of reception we could expect in the temporary messes, under canvas. Sitting stripped to the waist at trestle tables, the usual silence followed. At the command, "Carry on" men started to move around again and I noticed that many were queuing up for their dehydrated vegetables and a leathery slice of water buffalo, then taking it straight outside and dumping it in the swill bins.

'The appalling futility of it all galvanised me into action. On several sheets of foolscap I wrote a long descriptive report of what I had seen, and handed it in with my normal report. Next day I was summoned to appear before the Wing Commander, and hardly had the door closed he was on his feet raging that I had insulted his catering officer, and that he proposed to make an example of me; I was to report to his quarters every evening at 9 o'clock for the next month. This ensured I did not get into Singapore to enjoy myself. This action was illegal and, had I any fight left in me I could, and should, have taken the matter higher. However, no mention having been made of the unfortunate airmen's problems at any stage, I quickly decided that the "old boy" network was in full and effective control, and was determined to stamp out any mutinous ambitions on the part of a junior officer.'

So ended what was almost certainly the one of the most shameful episodes in the history of the Royal Air Force. Every effort was made to clear the backlog of repatriations, and as soon as this became apparent, dissension faded to a point at which it became little more than an unpleasant memory. So possibly lack of communication *had* been the main cause. The upshot of it all was that Seletar's reasonably popular CO was replaced, and there were more than a few other postings out. A Cpl Norris Zimbalist – not a conscript – based at Kallang, had been caught red-handed inciting his mates to strike in support of those at Seletar, and faced a court martial. He was stripped of his aircrew status – which was said to have aggrieved him more than anything else – and sentenced to ten years, although, due to union power in England, and sympathisers who had since been returned home from Singapore and India and demobbed, he was released after serving only twenty-two months. Others that had been "found guilty," in somewhat *orchestrated* courts martial, had since been released.

It seems Seletar's strike leaders never were discovered. There again, although Seletar seemed to receive most of the publicity, the situation would appear to have been far more serious in India, where everything began. And how was it the Army and Navy were not greatly involved? Because in fact, despite assurances to the opposite emanating from Whitehall, it did appear that the Army and Navy were being subjected to far less repatriation delay than were the Air Force. (Official government policy at the time seems to have been that it was far cheaper to police the Empire with an Air Force, than with a large Army; thus the army was being run down, the Air Force effectively strengthened.)

Raffles Place in a far earlier era - 1929 - when rickshaws outnumbered the cars. This is where the Naafi later based their downtown HQ in the form of the Shackle Club. **Vernon JW Lee collection**

But Seletar was not yet out of the woods. The day after the airmen returned to work, the camp's civilian workforce staged a forty-eight hour copy-cat strike. This seemed to have been communist-inspired, the intention, to capitalize on the current unhappy situation. It was effective only in that certain administrative services were affected, but airmen were deployed on anti-intimidation patrols throughout the civilian lines, thus protecting those who didn't wish to be involved. Minor demonstrations were held outside the camp boundaries, with some men being prevented from reporting for work, but this was effectively curtailed by means of having the RAF Police patrolling outside the main gates.

It was during this time that 209 Sqn experienced a setback when Sunderland PP103 suffered a mishap during a night departure on a scheduled flight to Hong Kong. The pilot was attempting to put it back on the water after both starboard engines cut when the aircraft had reached a height of two hundred feet. It was later discovered that the flight engineer had inadvertently turned off the petrol cocks. Five crew and eight passengers died in the resulting crash; there were eight survivors.

During 1946/7, 81 Squadron's Mosquitos were detached from Seletar to Mingaladon to complete the photographic survey of Burma. Meantime, Seletar personnel were making full use of any Japanese aircraft which still lay around. There was said to be a good collection just over the Causeway at Tebrau – originally a Japanese naval airfield, now an RAF transit camp – lots of Zeros. Quite a few of these were actually airworthy, though it is reported that RAF pilots were barred from flying them, even though certain of the Japanese pilots were allowed to![52] The remaining Japanese aircraft at Seletar were being broken up, and lots of seaplane floats were converted for use as recreational boats; the slipway finding itself in demand other than for the launching and retrieval of flying boats.

Denis Rolph, at the time a Sgt wireless fitter with 209 Sqn says they first converted a scrap Sunderland float. They cut it down, kitted it out with the engine taken from an abandoned Japanese motor cycle, and fitted a home made propeller. Denis, along with Cpls Smith and Keith, would then zoom off around the coast to Changi, where the WAAFs were stationed. Their next project was even more ambitious. It involved the huge belly float off a Japanese "Ruth," to which they fitted a Japanese-copy Chevrolet truck engine. 'It looked the part,' says Denis, though I didn't see the finished result, being posted out to Koggala in the meantime.'

It also seems likely that Seletar is where the idea of the Pedalo first came into being, long before they were seen at those swish Mediterranean resorts. A Flt/Lt Wilson designed and built a pedal-powered, two-seater, plywood affair on a tubular frame. This he labelled an Aqua-byke, although it carried the name "Zinkabonk" on its bow. Not many people know that!

• • • • • • • • • •

Vicky – the Himalayan Black Bear
Throughout this period, there resided at Seletar a bear cub. Like most Himalayan Black Bears, this cub featured a white "V" on its chest, hence the name Vicky. Having been purchased by a group of 89 Squadron armourers in Calcutta – price, one hundred and fifty rupees – it was decided she would travel with them as unofficial mascot. On August 15th, 1945, the squadron ground crews boarded the M/V *Dunera*, bound for Malaya as part of Operation "Zipper." The crews found themselves dumped on the Malayan coast between Port Swettenham and Port Dickson, to travel by truck down to Seletar. Vicky was more fortunate, getting a lift in the Mosquito piloted by W/O Pearson, with W/O Shields as navigator.

Vicky was said to have settled in at Seletar much quicker than the airmen, but she was growing quite rapidly, and sometime after arrival she was caged in a purpose-built structure at the end of "G" block. This was satisfactory for a time, as she was often taken out for a stroll round the camp, which could occasionally be a little unnerving to the base's other residents. But as time went on, so Vicky grew larger and stronger, which effectively made the cage seem weaker

A favourite for the Saturday midnight show; the Capitol. Note the distinct lack of Japanese cars. **John Smith**

and smaller. One morning she was said to have broken out and marched into a barrack-room full of quietly dozing men; new arrivals at Seletar. A wild shriek soon alerted all the airmen to the situation, but they were too terrified to move. Vicky was said to have ambled across to an open locker and helped herself to a bag of sweets. A few minutes later one of the armourers entered, and, after some casual words in Vicky's ear, the pair ambled off.

Becoming too big and strong to handle, Vicky was placed aboard a Sunderland flying boat (PP106) in April 1946, and flown to England. When the aircraft arrived at Calshot in May, Vicky was received into the care of London Zoo. Housed in the Bear's Den, on Mappin Terraces, Vicky survived not long, unfortunately having to be put down in 1950, after she developed osteoarthritis.

Monkeys and dogs had, over the years, been favoured as pets amongst airmen in the Far East, a few of each often to be found around the barracks of the various camps. Monkeys were usually tethered to a "running line," the dogs free to roam, though they rarely seemed to wander too far from their owner's quarters unaccompanied.

It was in 1946 also, that service in Singapore officially regained its "accompanied tour" status, but as relatively few of those serving in the theatre during the pre-war period had been married, quarters were still an extremely rare commodity, although, here again, a building program was underway.

Amidst and despite of all this strife, Seletar's aircraft were still being worked extremely hard, for flying continued throughout the strike period, aircrews being responsible for loading their own aircraft, with the help of Japanese POW's. This is reported to have been generally successful, even though weight and balance may not always have been perfect!

In addition to the heavy transport commitment, the squadrons also became quickly embroiled in the struggle for independence taking place in the nearby Dutch East Indies.

Just days after the Japanese surrender, Indonesian nationalists, led a Dr Sukarno, issued a declaration of independence. In their opinion, the Dutch had forfeited their right to rule by failing to defend the country. Over the following weeks, while necessary preparations were being made to establish a workable system of government, insurgents were busily acquiring vast quantities of arms and ammunition from the Japanese. This led the Dutch to declare that Dr Sukarno and his associates were simply Japanese supported terrorists, and should be treated as the enemies of freedom.

Because of intense anti-Dutch propaganda in the country, it was decided that the first stage of the Allied occupation should be carried out by the British, their task being to liberate prisoners of war and to maintain order until the Dutch were able to take control. Seletar-based aircraft became involved almost immediately when on November 9th, Mosquitos of 84 and 110 Squadrons flew to Batavia to drop leaflets which demanded Indonesians to surrender any arms they had acquired.

The following morning, news arrived from the town of Surabaya that intense fighting had broken out, and that 60 Squadron's Thunderbolts had joined forces with the Mosquitos to launch bombing and strafing attacks in support of Allied ground troops. The message also stated that a Flying Officer Osborne, along with his Brigadier passenger, had both been killed. In circumstances which were never officially explained, the aircraft in which they had been due to travel apparently crashed whilst attempting to take off from Surabaya.

At this time, in addition to the constant comings and goings of the flying boats of four different squadrons – not all Seletar based – there were five Mosquito or Spitfire equipped squadrons operating from Seletar, most of which were to become actively involved. The Spitfires carried out widespread reconnaissance and leaflet-dropping sorties, the Mosquitos, along with Tengah-based Thunderbolts of 60 Sqn, intensified their bombing missions. The situation now deteriorated, the Indonesians demanding that the Allies should be driven into the sea. British and Indian forces were completely bewildered by this hostile reception, their sympathies largely favouring the Indonesian cause. This attitude was summed up by the Commanding Officer of 84 Squadron, who stated: 'The war in Java was received with mixed feelings. The question was asked, 'which side are we on, Dutch or Indonesian? Many supported the Indonesians. Everyone liked the idea of action, but wished they had a real enemy and a clear aim.'

The problem of a clear aim was shortly to be resolved, for, once stories of horrible atrocities being committed by some Indonesians began to filter through, attitudes changed immediately. One of the worst incidents occurred on November 23rd, when a Dakota carrying five British airmen and eighteen Indians had to make a forced landing in a paddy field near Batavia. The occupants were seen to emerge uninjured, but when later no trace of them could be found, it came to light that they had been taken to a local jail and murdered. Their mutilated bodies were later discovered in a nearby grave. The British answer to this tragic affair was to set fire to the village of Bekasi. And although Lord Mountbatten quickly ruled that retaliation must not be taken as a matter of principle, it was already too late, the damage had been done, antagonism increasing on both sides. The Royal Air Force in particular felt that their efforts now had a real purpose.

RAF planes carried out operations over Sumatra and Java until a truce was signed on November 14th, 1946. Within two weeks the Dutch had assumed all commitments, and the last British troops had departed. There were to be a further three years of bloodshed before the Dutch finally recognised Indonesian sovereignly, but never again did the British become involved; at least not until the Indonesians began to have designs on Malaysian territory, some twenty years later.

Strangely enough, although many people had been killed during the period of Allied control, the British were an unexpectedly popular army of occupation. Mr Sjahrir, a leading Indonesian politician, voiced the feelings of many of his countrymen when in a farewell statement he said, '...even in unfriendly contact or in conflict with us, we learned to appreciate and admire you. You introduced to our country by your personal qualities some attractive traits of Western culture – your politeness, kindness and dignified self-restraint.'

With the withdrawal of all British forces from Java and Sumatra, SEAC was disbanded and Air Command South East Asia (ACSEA) now became ACFE – Air Command Far East.

One of the most unusual units at Seletar during the post-war years was the Airborne Salvage Section of 390 MU. By the end of 1945, with three Maintenance Units now active on the station, it was soon realized that a flying element would be an invaluable part of the entire repair organization, three Dakotas were therefore assigned to 390 MU. Although primarily intended for the conveyance of spares, and the working parties who went out to repair damaged aircraft, these aircraft were soon engaged in the deliverance of vital cargoes to all points in the Far East. It would not be unusual for one of Seletar's Dakotas to be seen at the MU in Bombay, or up in Lahore, picking up items which were urgently required by our forces then engaged in keeping the peace in the Dutch East Indies. The record of this small flying unit was impressive: five hundred sorties covering three hundred thousand miles were flown during the short period of its life at Seletar, all without damage to any of its aircraft, or harm to passengers and crews.

Stories concerning the men who flew and serviced these aircraft became legend, for their aircraft were given many unusual tasks, some quite unpleasant. Corporal Forbes, who worked on 390 MU, explains. 'The most unpleasant job without doubt was servicing Dakotas which had been used for carrying donkeys and mules on the Burma campaign, and stank to high heaven. We knew the average Royal Air Force chap was supposed to be versatile – but this was a job none of us could have anticipated!' [As can well be imagined. Not only did they carry pack mules as freight, the mules occasionally formed part of the "air drop" cargo, the men being called upon to heave the terrified animals out the back on the end of a parachute!]

With the redevelopment of RAF Tengah, to the west, and the opening up of a new station to the east, in April 1946 – Changi's role transferring from that of Army base and prison-camp, to use by the RAF – Seletar ceased to be the focal point of air traffic on Singapore Island. Kallang had once again reverted to civilian use, becoming Singapore's international airport, but this period was also to see Changi develop into the Far East Air Force's major transport base.

The Japanese development of Changi as an airbase had not been ideal. Whereas the existing barracks were situated up on a hill, where they caught the refreshing breezes – the very reason the army had been reluctant to give up what was seen as the most desirable location in Singapore – the runway was laid out on marshy ground near Fairy Point. Upon taking over the base, the RAF had covered the strip with Pierced Steel Planking (PSP), the result showing only a marginal improvement, for whenever a heavy aircraft landed, a ripple of PSP was said to build up ahead of the wheels, much like the swell on the sea. This played havoc with the surface, repairs resulting in the strip being out of action for two days per week. But once the PSP was replaced by a concrete runway, in 1948, Changi became a much better option than Seletar as a transport base for the four-engined aircraft now in use. Tengah was the area's strike base, air defence and offensive support being the role of its Spitfires, Thunderbolts and Mosquitos. Seletar's magnificent facilities for flying boats could not be matched, it therefore retained these squadrons, plus any other flying units and detachments as could safely use the airfield's limited facilities. In fact, as will become evident, the station's original role, that of a flying boat base, was retained right through to the demise of the of the Sunderland; Seletar being the base from which these, the last of the RAF's flying boats, were to operate. The station was also destined to retain its other major role – that of being the main overhaul, repair, and supply base for the whole of the Far East.

It had been quickly appreciated that any plan to lay new runways at Seletar, quite apart from the expense, would have to involve the demolition of a large number of buildings, including their huge and somewhat prestigious Officers' Mess. In view of the difficulties with accommodation that were still prevalent, this line of thought could not even be considered. Another major factor in this decision was the fact that as Seletar's runway ended on the shores of the Straits, it could only be extended in one direction, and this was regarded as geologically unwise.

Right up to the end of their tenancy, Seletar's land-based squadrons continued to play a vital role in local affairs, with a large number of anti-piracy patrols being flown; Piracy having been a problem in the area from at least the early eighteen hundreds.

Pirates were reported to be active around the islands and marshes west of Lumut, on the Malayan coast west of Kuala Lumpur, and by the September of 1946, things had become so serious it was decided to make an all out effort to clear up the area. To Seletar's aircraft went the task of providing surveillance in support of the a brigade of the 7th Indian Division. Early one morning, ground troops made three simultaneous landings in the area, coming in from the sea, but strangely, nearly all the pirates had disappeared, the result being that only four prisoners and some small arms were taken. Not the resounding success one would have wished for, but the raid did, for a time, act as a deterrent.

84 Squadron's Mosquitos were also involved in an exercise in the same area the following day. Although not an anti-piracy exercise, this one could well have become even more embarrassing, had the people concerned been aware of the true facts at the time. Nine Mosquitos were detailed to formate with the Commander-in-Chief's Avro York over Port Swettenham, then escort him to Changi. They rendezvoused with a York at exactly the right time and place, duly escorting it to Singapore. Unbeknown to them, this particular aircraft was carrying a distinguished visitor from New Zealand, who naturally assumed the escort to have been laid on for his benefit. Upon discovering there were no less than five Yorks in the area at the appointed time, and

that his Mosquitos had inadvertently selected the wrong one, 84 Squadron's Officer Commanding used his initiative; he decided to hold off until the C-in-C's York had landed, then, just as the VIP was disembarking, led his formation overhead. The Commander-in-Chief, unaware that he was supposed to have been escorted, was apparently delighted to see such a welcoming committee. It is reported that there were a few red faces to be seen amongst the 84 Squadron pilots later that night, and for some time afterwards they seemed reluctant in volunteering their services whenever the subject of an escort was raised!

By the end of 1947, 81 Squadron had completed yet another aerial survey, this one encompassing Sarawak and British North Borneo – regarded locally as the most vital Royal Air Force commitment since the end of the war.[53] Completion of this survey was to see Seletar's last two land-based squadrons, No's 81 and 84, depart for Changi, and at the time it must have seemed that the end of an era was nigh. Not so. Within a few years Seletar would be home to more squadrons than ever before.

By June 1948, with the land-based squadrons having departed, the station had been reorganized as a complete Maintenance Unit. No.389 MU absorbed 314 MU, to become the Equipment Wing. Under the command of Grp/Cpt Northway OBE, this concerned itself with stores and supply. 390 MU, under Grp/Cpt RB Harrison, was the repair and maintenance unit, known as Technical Wing. The station CO was now Air Commodore GPH Carter OBE – the post having been upgraded when Air Commodore Vasse assumed command shortly after the strike in 1946.

The only squadron now based at Seletar was 209, with their Sunderlands, which had assumed the role of a lodger unit. But with a variety of aircraft requiring the services of the MU, along with the associated air tests, the airfield seemed as busy as ever. The station itself was still heavily populated, being staffed by almost two thousand servicemen and two and a half thousand civilians.

So ended one of the most difficult periods of Seletar's history. The POWs, internees and volunteer reservists had been repatriated and demobilized, the Japanese had returned from whence they came, leaving behind many reminders of their stay.

A lot of work went into the attempt at removing all traces of Japanese occupation. Even the French Navy – a small detachment of whom were at the time based at Seletar – were encouraged to remove some of the few remaining serviceable aircraft; these were apparently later used in Indo-China. Other, less sophisticated items, did survive; the Japanese safe in the Accounts Section, for instance. This was by all reports a very ornate piece of equipment, its doors embossed with masses of leaves, acorns, and flowers, and the key could only be inserted once the correct acorn had been selected and pushed aside. Having successfully negotiated the outer door, the, by now frustrated accountant, would be confronted by a locked inner steel chest. The curious thing about it was the fact that, being mounted on wheels, any potential thief could simply roll the whole thing away to be worked on at leisure.

One memento which eluded the efforts of the souvenir hunters was the painting said to have been the work of a Japanese officer during the occupation. On the wall of a room inside the flying boat hangar was a rather amateurish, though colourful, picture depicting the attack on the *Prince of Wales*.[54]

Gradually the station was settling down to its new peacetime role, and from all reports it certainly had much to offer. Christmas 1946 saw a grand dance being organised in the flying boat hangar, with the MT Section running a service to collect and return office girls and nurses from Singapore. Gallons of Tiger were said to have been consumed. And looking at Christmas lunch menus, the festive lunch at Seletar was better than most people in the UK could expect at that time, as seemed to be the case with most of the meals. An airman arriving on West Camp in

1947 stated, 'Five weeks after leaving the UK, where rationing was still in force, it was great to be able to order steak, eggs and double chips in the NAAFI. The mess would feature a huge bowl of fruit salad several times a week; a melange of chopped pineapple, oranges and bananas, all of which were seldom seen at home. Maybe the cinema wasn't so good, being subject to frequent breakdowns, and the screen image was often in "soft focus," but draught Tiger was only fifty cents (5p) a pint.'

The now extended married patch was again fully occupied by married airmen, and the sports field, swimming pool, and the two cinemas were being fully utilized (East Camp and West Camp each having their own, even if the one on West Camp only boasted a 16mm projector). Welfare facilities were opening up, and Singapore's nightlife was once again something to behold. The island had become a Crown Colony, the Raffles Hotel silver had been unearthed, cleaned and placed back in service. The hotel itself, after a period of acting as quarters for senior Japanese officers, then as a temporary transit centre for prisoners-of-war, was once again in full swing. The three "Worlds" were back, too: Happy, Great, and New. Another thing was that around this time, Seletar began to field a very good football team, and this continued for some time. It appears that with the onset of national service – football not being a reserved occupation – many professional players were being called up, a good few of them ending up at Seletar. The station put its name on a lot of trophies over the years. A contributing factor was possibly the fact that Seletar had magnificent sports facilities, especially when compared with Changi and Tengah.

But this period of tranquillity was the lull before the storm. In the background, fate was weaving a tapestry of intrigue, the long, grasping tentacles of Communism even now probing their way towards Malaya. As a military base, Seletar was about to become embroiled in one of the most prolonged struggles of modern times.

A shot of the 1950s swimming pool taken from the top of the nearby radio mast.   *Peter A Hughes*

Aerial shot of East Camp, RAF Seletar. The original hangar is in the centre foreground.   *Jim Brown*

CHAPTER ELEVEN

Troubled Days Of Peace:
The Malayan Emergency

As the Far East Air Force enters its eleventh year of the Anti-Terrorist Campaign in Malaya this month, it claims the distinction of fighting the longest war the world has known since Napoleon. (from the *Sunday Times of Malaya*, 22nd June, 1958.)

["Conflict" really, for war was never actually declared, this campaign being labelled "The Emergency." Or, in military terms, Operation "Firedog."]

• • • • • • • • • • •

Contrary to most people's expectations, the conclusion of the Second World War had not brought with it an era of peace and progress. People the world over had in some way been touched by events of the previous six years, many colonial powers beginning to experience latent unrest amongst their subjects.

Despite efforts to maintain the status quo, new forces had been set in motion. An "Iron Curtain" had been drawn across Europe, and direct confrontation between the two great power blocks – the Free World vs Communism – quickly developed into a potentially dangerous situation; to become known as "The Cold War." Asian and African countries were drawn in also, their steady push towards independence creating the kind of opportunities well suited to exploitation by the Communist block.

Conflicts began to flare up all over the place. In some cases, India and Burma to the fore, wise administration allowed for a comparatively peaceful transition to take place – as peaceful as

inexperience, political naivety and greed allowed, that is. Elsewhere, more ominous situations arose. Greek Communists were in control of a majority of their country, whilst West Berlin was fighting for the very right to survive. In Asia, Mao Tse-tung was ousting Nationalist armies from the Chinese mainland, and to the south, Ho Chi Minh's guerrilla army was battling a French expeditionary force for control of Indo-China, resulting in a humiliating defeat for the French three years later, at a place called Dien Bien Phu, in the north of the country. Indonesia had, of course, already gone its own way. With militant communism on the march, and the British Empire apparently falling apart, insurgent forces in Malaya decided the time had come to make their revolutionary bid.

The Malayan Communist Party (MCP) had existed well before WWII, supporting the Allied cause during the Japanese occupation. Its members, which had formed an effective part of the Malayan People's Anti-Japanese Army (MPAJA), had therefore been armed, equipped and trained by British experts in the art of guerrilla warfare. Throughout the war they had continually harassed the Japanese forces from within the shelter of the dense Malayan jungles, but it was not necessarily the Allies interests that the communist element had in mind. Their idea was that, with the cessation of hostilities, they would create a Communist State. Hence it was that Chin Peng, their eventual leader, had secreted away countless stores of weapons. He'd also had his followers indoctrinate the populace in the ways of Communism.

With the war over, the MPAJA had been disbanded, many of its members being feted as national heroes, one or two being invited to take part in victory parades in London. In Singapore, a number of them were acknowledged guests of honour at the main military establishments, including Seletar.

The British authorities had ordered that all arms held by the guerrillas should now be handed in, but the communist element, dominated by dissident Chinese, ensured that large numbers were retained for the inevitable confrontation with the government – especially those weapons which had been secreted away, thus never used.

By the spring of 1948, the party decided that, given the current international situation, now was the time to take the initiative. Malaya was about to experience the full force of a guerrilla war that was eventually to last for twelve years.

April and May saw violent clashes, the prelude to a communist operation in which the intent was to drive all Europeans, government officials, and police from isolated parts of the interior. The murder of three European plantation managers in the Sungai Siput area on the 16th of June was to result in a national state of emergency being declared.

Not actively affected during the initial stages, Seletar had been re-organized into a composite maintenance base, under the command of Air Commodore Carter CBE, only two days before the Emergency declaration. But Tengah-based 81 Squadron was in from the start, their Spitfires being used in the first strafing sorties of 'Firedog', a word that was to become familiar as the code–name covering all anti-terrorist operations. Activities were stepped up during August, aircraft starting to bomb the insurgent camps.

An indication of how serious the Air Force took the Emergency to be, was seen when a specially modified Lancaster was detached to the area to provide an early form of Airborne Electronic Reconnaissance. Possibly the first example of such a machine in RAF service.

One or two civilians working at Seletar were known communists, some even being reported as having gone off to join the terrorists. The remainder were quickly arrested, as were others throughout the island. From then on, the situation in Singapore was generally well under control for practically the whole of the Emergency. Communist-inspired strikes apart, the insurgent war was almost totally confined to the mainland. This meant that very few restrictions needed to be imposed on British personnel and their families. Apart from the rare periods of rioting which did occur, they were able to lead normal lives. In fact, Seletar's residents had little need to leave the confines of the station, for by 1949 it had been provided with every facility. An accurate account of the facilities available and the layout of Seletar appeared in the *Free Press* of October 18th:

> *Seletar's airmen have their own* Piccadilly. *Twenty-four bungalows have recently been built as additional married quarters for airmen and their families. More will be built as soon as the new roads are made. The base covers a large area and has many roads, all of which have been named after famous London streets. The road in which the bungalows have been built is known as* Edgware Road.

> *The sixteen SNCO's and 108 airmen's prewar married quarters are all pleasantly situated along the borders of* Oxford Street, Birdcage Walk *and* Lambeth Walk, *while in* Mornington Crescent *a pavilion and tennis courts for the occupants of these quarters have been built. In* Park Lane *are the residences of the Base Commander and other senior officers.* Piccadilly, *without a shop on either side except for a milk-bar, a tailor's, a hairdresser's and a curio shop, is almost as long as its London namesake, running right through the station and ending at the* Embankment, *washed by the waters of the Straits of Johore, where the clubhouse of the RAF Yacht Club is to be found.*

> *In* Piccadilly *also are the Astra cinema, Theatre Club and Seletar Social Club for*

married families. Leading up to Piccadilly Circus, *a roundabout into which* Edgware Road, Maida Vale *and* Piccadilly *also debouch is the main road from the entrance gates which is known as* Bow Street, *and in which, appropriately, are the Service Police Headquarters and the Main Guardroom.* [I seem to recall the guardroom being on Vine Street.] *Instead of Eros, in this* Piccadilly Circus *there is a high standard with four pendant lamps.*

In contrast to its counterpart, the Seletar Maida Vale *still retains some of its sylvan surroundings, being bordered by stretches of grass and woodland, interspersed with flowering shrubs and lined with an avenue of the vivid scarlet and yellow blooms of Flame of the Forest. Lying back from this road in London fashion, are the homes of the officers and warrant officers. The* Inner Temple *is the centre of learning where the Base School for the children of officers and airmen and the Information Room are to be found.*

Battersea Road *too is represented and leads from* Piccadilly *to the base swimming pool which is available to all ranks until bedtime, being floodlit at night. The swimming pool restaurant provides grills, steaks and ice-cream sundaes in a setting of lofty palm trees.*

Mincing Lane, *devoid of its tea associations, leads to the runway in front of the Officers' Mess, the entrance to which is immediately off the crescent-shaped* Halfmoon Street. *The Maintenance Base is now increasing the number of its buildings particularly in the airmen's married quarters which will require a larger road system.*

Some familiar names missing from that report (possibly built at a later date as part of that, "larger road system") include, *Regent Street, Baker Street, Sussex Gardens, Lancaster Gate, Brompton Road, Bayswater, Knightsbridge, Hyde Park Gate, Western Avenue,* and *Haymarket.* There was even an *Oval.* Further facilities were available in the form of a Malcolm Club; a social

club for airmen that was a recent concept at the time. The Malcolm Club differed from the NAAFI in that it had its own distinctive atmosphere, much like one of those friendly pubs back home. The idea had more or less originated with Marshal of the Royal Air Force, Lord Tedder, and his then boss, General Eisenhower, whilst both were in North Africa. The clubs were named after Wing Commander Hugh Malcolm, VC, the first RAF VC of the North African Campaign. The club at Seletar featured its own jazz group, the Steamboat Stumpers, and it was said that if an airman wanted a wedding party, the Malcolm Club staff could arrange everything but the bride. Very popular, the Malcolm Club.

Within a year, the renovated golf course – reputedly the best on the island – was re-opened. As if that wasn't enough, nearby Changi opened a luxurious Club for all officers and their families. It could hardly be wondered that the first WRAF personnel to be posted to Seletar – in February, 1949 – were elated to find they had come to such a "tropical paradise."

Not as Jean Hogg remembers it. 'Out of our entry I was the only one who didn't yearn to go overseas, yet I was the one that did! Facilities were poor to begin with, and the water in the taps was yellow. But I did get to enjoy it, often go back through there today.'

Seletar's ground staff worked hard in these seemingly idyllic conditions, the MU's gaining a reputation for efficiency. 209 was still the only flying squadron on the base, and, in the absence of an adequate civil airline system, or other military transport aircraft, their Sunderlands had been running a comprehensive round-the-clock courier service, carrying service and government passengers on important business, along with mail and freight. But later that month they were called upon to perform a somewhat more import-ant task.

With Burma having become an independent republic just the previous month, it now faced an uncertain future. Plans had therefore been formulated to evacuate any British nationals whose lives might become endangered in the event of violence breaking out during the transition. This appeared to be the case on February 22nd, for at 01:00 hours a message was received at Seletar requesting immediate assistance. By this time, of course, 209 Squadron's ground crews had long ago departed from the flight line, which delayed things somewhat. Nor did the weather help, monsoon-like conditions creating further difficulties. However, the first aircraft, piloted by Sqn/Ldr Hatfield, the Squadron Commander, was airborne within three hours; something of an achievement, considering the scratched-together groundcrew, minimal briefing, and just two flares marking the take-off run. With the most appalling weather conditions being encountered en route, upon entering Rangoon Flight Information Area, Sqn/Ldr Hatfield was then informed that all flying in Burmese airspace was forbidden, and that there were no night-flying facilities at all. But, after some delay, during which telephone calls had obviously been made, permission to land was eventually granted.

The intent had been to land on the river at Chauk – located between Mandalay and Rangoon, and site of the Burmese oilfields, but when the aircraft appeared overhead it was seen that a number of native craft were on the river, with fishing nets stretched out across the waterway. The authorities actually proposed holding a conference to decide on what action to take, however, after some brilliant manoeuvring, the aircraft landed and, managing to negotiate the obstacles, was eventually moored to an old buoy.

Only British families in the immediate vicinity could be organized and ready for take-off by late afternoon, and with Rangoon's ban on night-flying, the decision was made to await the dawn. This entailed an element of risk, for although the nearest rebel forces were thought to be twenty miles distant, one or two roving bands were known to be in the locality. So, as further security to the crew's anchor watch, a local guard was mounted.

Come dawn, the evacuees – 19 women, 15 children and six men – were taken aboard and the aircraft departed safely for Rangoon. The speed of the RAF's response was highly compli-

mented by officials of the Burma Oil Company, and the British Ambassador to Burma; a welcome shot in the arm for the Royal Air Force's reputation in the Far East. Other accolades were to follow. Upon their return to Seletar, the Commander in Chief complimented Sqn/Ldr Hatfield for an operation that "reflected great credit on you and your squadron, amply demonstrating to all, the efficiency of the Royal Air Force, and which earned the sincere thanks of the British community in Burma."

When 209 Squadron handed responsibility of its weekly Borneo courier service to Malayan Airlines, Sqn/Ldr Hatfield was in command on the last sortie. In Jessleton they were given the warmest of welcomes, being wined and dined royally. A football match was played against the police, and later His Excellency Mr Calder, on behalf of British North Borneo, presented the squadron with a cheque for one thousand dollars, and a ceremonial parang. The cheque was to cover the cost of a sailing dinghy for the use of the squadron, the parang was a beautifully mounted antique, its mother-of-pearl handle decorated with tufts of human hair and pheasant feathers! [A welcome addition to the squadron silver, perhaps?]

Always one to take up a challenge, Percy Hatfield had been one of a group of twenty pilots invited to fly the first jet to arrive in Singapore, a Meteor Mk IV. This event had taken place back in August 1947, and had been reported in *Flight* magazine. Percy had taken umbrage to the report which had branded him, *a pilot of the ponderous Sunderlands*, and he is said to have fired off an amusing reply.

The civil war in China was by now making headlines around the world, and while the attentions of the British were focussed upon day to day developments, Singapore's naval and air force personnel were about to become more intimately involved.

Although Seletar still had only one permanently based squadron in No.209, the Hong Kong based Sunderlands of 88 Squadron had been commuting between Kai Tak and Seletar on a regular basis for so long they were almost regarded as an integral unit. In fact the aircraft were originally Seletar based, being detached to Hong Kong as 1430 (Flying Boat Transport) Flight. 88 Squadron was reformed in 1946, using these aircraft as a basis.

● ● ● ● ● ● ● ● ● ●

The Yangtze Incident.

April 20th, 1949. This was the day Seletar received news that the Royal Naval Frigate, HMS *Amethyst* had come under intense fire whilst steaming past Chinese Communist gun batteries on the banks of the Yangtze River. A battle had been raging between Communist and Nationalist troops, the *Amethyst* sustaining heavy damage and the loss of forty-three crew, had eventually run aground, still within range of the enemy batteries.

At 22:45 hours 88 Squadron were detailed to dispatch an aircraft from Kai Tak to drop supplies or, conditions permitting, land alongside the vessel. Sunderland ML772, fully armed and loaded with medical supplies departed at first light, Flight Lieutenant Letford, DSO DFC, in command. Also on board was second pilot, Flight Lieutenant Marshal, Flight Lieutenant M Fearnley – an RAF doctor – Surgeon Lieutenant Morgan RN, along with the Station Commander, Group Captain Jefferson, and two Army dispatchers. Before arrival, they received a message from the cruiser HMS *London*, advising that, because of heavy shelling, the aircraft should divert to Shanghai. Here they learned that, although *Amethyst* had succeeded in refloating herself, conditions on board were becoming desperate. The frigate could proceed no further due to lack of an accurate chart, her Captain and his deputy were severely wounded, and her doctor was dead. There remained only four able-bodied officers aboard, plus one telegraphist to take care of all communications. Their morphine supply had run out, and attempts by HMS *London* and HMS *Black Swan* to reach her had failed. Shanghai then requested that the Sunderland should attempt to land alongside *Amethyst*, transferring a doctor and

medical supplies to the vessel, so at 17:30 the aircraft departed.

A low pass was made, attracting no gunfire. After a second fly-by, the Sunderland alighted, taxied close to *Amethyst*, and came to rest. A sampan, rowed by a Chinese, but with a naval officer aboard, arrived alongside the aircraft just as the Communist batteries opened up again. Flt/Lt Fearnley managed to scamble aboard the sampan, taking with him some medical supplies and the urgently needed morphine, and the naval officer boarded the Sunderland. But before it was possible to transfer Surgeon Lieutenant Morgan, the sampan pulled away.

The artillery fire was closing in, and as it seemed only a matter of time before they were hit, it was decided to take off immediately. The anchor was abandoned, a barrage of shells and bullets forcing a downwind, down-tide take-off, but the aircraft became safely airborne, returning to Shanghai without further incident. *Amethyst* was hit several more times, but once the aircraft was clear they managed to take shelter in a creek.

Under cover of darkness, *Amethyst* succeeded in evacuating a batch of her wounded to a nearby town. She then moved some miles downstream, to complete the offloading of her more seriously injured, including her gallant Captain, who later died of his wounds. There now remained on board three naval officers plus Flt/Lt Fearnley, fifty-two ratings and eight Chinese. But it was about this time that Lieutenant Commander OS Kerans, Assistant Naval Attache at Nanking, reached the vessel and assumed command.

The Navy requested that another landing be attempted alongside the stricken vessel next day, to facilitate the transfer on board of eight officers and ratings plus a Naval Chaplain, so at 13:00 hours the aircraft was airborne once again.

The aircraft did manage to land, but a strong current defeated all attempts to make a transfer. Then the heavy artillery and small-arms fire opened up again, and with its wireless aerial shot away, another take off under heavy fire was called for. Flt/Lt Letford circled the area for forty-five minutes, from where, as a helpless spectator he watched *Amethyst* being heavily shelled as she moved away. Unable to help, he then flew off to make a reconnaissance.

On the return to Shanghai, six Mustang fighters were observed, flying in line astern at a slightly higher altitude. Unable to see any markings, Flt/Lt Letford decided to treat them as hostile, taking his aircraft down to two hundred feet. A mistake, for they immediately encountered small-arms fire, the aircraft being hit. He climbed again, only to be pursued by a twin-engined aircraft. This he managed to loose at twelve hundred feet when he flew into thick cloud, using it as protective cover all the way back to Shanghai. Next day brought yet another request, this time for a reconnaissance of the Yangtze, to note any movements of Nationalist warships. It was proposed to move *Amethyst* downstream, preferably in the company of any Nationalist vessels which might also be trying to escape. The battered Sunderland took off once more, but a low cloud base forced the aircraft down to eight hundred feet, where it encountered heavy machine-gun fire. The port main fuel tank was hit, petrol gushing out to fill the aircraft with its fumes. The rear turret hydraulic lines were also hit, knocking the turret out of action, whilst that same burst partially severed a com-

pressor strut and an aileron cable. Evasive action was taken until they were out of range, but because of the fuel loss, and possible fire risk, Flt/Lt Letford elected for a return to Shanghai. Here the damage was assessed as being too serious for field repair, so, after some superficial patching up the aircraft was flown back to Hong Kong.

Four months after becoming trapped, HMS *Amethyst* was able to make a successful dash to safety and, as by this time Shanghai had fallen to the Communists, the RAF were not called upon to make any further patrols in the area.

Later that year it was announced that the Naval General Service Medal would be awarded to all those who had served on the Yangtze from April to July, including the crew of Sunderland ML772.

88 Squadron returned to their normal schedule, but at 22:00 hours on November 24th 1949, tragedy struck. A violent thunderstorm was raging at Seletar, but Flt/Lt DM Birrell judged conditions to be safe enough, so he positioned his aircraft, NJ176 (F "Freddie"), with its eight crew and four passengers, ready for take-off. Everything proceeded normally, but shortly after the Sunderland seemed to be clear, it crashed into an area of shallow water. With two thousand

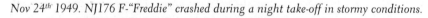

Nov 24th 1949. NJ176 F-"Freddie" crashed during a night take-off in stormy conditions.   ***Stan Ould***

SELETAR – CROWNING GLORY

gallons of aviation fuel quickly spreading into the surrounding area, there was a high possibility of a massive fire being triggered, either by a bolt of lightning, or the aircraft's shattered electrics.

A rescue party led by the Senior Medical Officer, Sqn/Ldr RE Wooley, was quickly on the scene, and, heedless of their personal safety, succeeded in rescuing the survivors, including two members of the crew who were badly injured. But the pilot was trapped, and Sqn/Ldr Wooley, unable to abandon a man who was still alive, nor wishing to prolong the obvious danger to his men, took the only decision possible: to amputate the trapped pilot's leg. With the assistance of Flt/Lt WB Kennedy, the operation began, heavy rain, the wind rocking their boat dangerously. A small torch, the only available safe source of light, showed the pilot – now pumped full of morphine – to be in an almost inaccessible position, his head having to be supported to keep it clear of the water. Tension was high throughout the twenty minute operation, for a single spark from the saw striking the surrounding metal would have meant a conflagration from which there would have been no hope of escape. The fumes were overpowering, but the foot was successfully amputated close to the ankle and the pilot freed. Unfortunately, the operation had been in vain, for Flt/Lt Birrell died in hospital the next morning, bringing the total number of fatalities in the crash to five.

In March, the following year, Sqn/Ldr Wooley was awarded the George Medal, Flt/Lt Kennedy and three airmen receiving the King's Commendation for brave conduct. The citation in the *London Gazette* included the following tribute:

Sqn/Ldr Wooley displayed great bravery, determination and skill. His devotion to duty was in keeping with the highest traditions of the Royal Air Force and set a high example to his subordinates.

Seletar's efforts in the Emergency had been stepped up considerably throughout 1949, 209 Squadron carrying out its first "Firedog" sortie in June of that year, in addition to its maritime reconnaissance/Search and Rescue (SAR) standby duties. The Sunderlands' initial role in Malaya was one of saturating a given area with twenty-pound bombs, followed by low-level strafing runs, fourteen operations of this type being flown during that first month. Initially there were problems, for although a Sunderland could carry three hundred and forty of these small bombs, it did not possess the means of delivering them quickly. The aircraft's retractable, underwing bomb racks were usually reserved for much heavier ordnance, or the SAR "Lindholme" packs). Sq/Ldr P. de L. Le Cheminant DFC, who was to assume command of 209 Squadron, (and in later years, as an Air Vice-Marshal, Senior Air Staff Officer, HQ FEAF), describes the method used:

'A chain of chaps used to line up inside the aircraft. When we were over the target area the twenty-pounders were passed from hand to hand until they were finally dropped over the side. This effective but unorthodox procedure continued until the Command Armament Officer accompanied us on one sortie. It then came to an abrupt halt, and we reverted to the slower but accepted method of using the bomb racks.'

How long this lasted is not known – possibly only until another armament officer took command – for during the author's time with the joint 205/209, in the late fifties, things seem to have reverted to that swifter, more personal method of hand delivery. After being unpacked on board, and the pins removed, the bombs were then passed down the chain (all volunteers) to be dispatched by hand through the aft hatches; hard graft, but no precision required. (A small propeller on the nose served to arm the bomb on its short flight earthwards.) The bomb racks seemed to be the sole reserve of the aforementioned Lindholme gear.

The operational strength of the station received a welcome boost in September 1949, when 205 Squadron's Sunderlands arrived from Koggala. After an absence lasting seven and a half years Seletar's very first squadron had returned to its spiritual home.

Terrorist activities were continually on the increase, with the Governor of Sarawak, Mr Duncan Stewart, being seriously wounded in a stabbing incident during December. One of 205's Sunderlands, under the command of Sqn/Ldr Le Cheminant, was rushed out to evacuate the injured Governor, who unfortunately succumbed a few days after being admitted to the hospital.

February 1950 saw the Far East Flying Boat Wing being formed at Seletar. This was made up from the two Sunderland squadrons – 205 and 209 – along with a Flying Boat Servicing Squadron. Amalgamating the Sunderland aircraft at Seletar – those of 205, 209, 230 and 240 Sqns – (230 personnel went to Pembroke Dock, 240 Sqn disbanded), rendered twenty-five aircraft surplus to requirements. As a result, personnel at Seletar were instructed to prepare eight aircraft for return to Shorts, where they were to be refurbished for sale to the Royal New Zealand Air Force.

As for the Far East Flying Boat Wing, tragedy was to strike just weeks after its formation.

● ● ● ● ● ● ● ● ● ●

LAC Ivor Gillett GC.

The George Cross is rarely awarded to personnel on military service, for it was instituted in 1940 by King George VI primarily in recognition of heroic acts by members of the civilian defence forces such as fire, police, etc. It was later seen to be an appropriate award for armed forces personnel to mark distinguished conduct not necessarily related to military action. The award is on a par with the Victoria Cross, and there are no higher awards for gallantry. Ivor Gillett was a recipient.

Arriving in Singapore in 1949, a national serviceman, and not yet twenty-one years of age, Ivor, a trained and skilled armament mechanic, found himself assigned to 209 Squadron at Seletar.

During Operation Firedog, Sunderlands were occasionally called upon to carry out heavy bombing missions over Malaya, each aircraft carrying twelve, two hundred and fifty pound bombs. The underwing bomb racks were able to accommodate four bombs per side, the rest being stored inside the hull, where there was ample capacity for up to twenty. The bombs were primed and made ready in the arming bay at 9X site: a huge, securely guarded compound within the confines of Seletar camp. It was the bomb dump, ammunition storage, and explosives site for the whole of FEAF (but never, as far as can be ascertained, for nuclear weapons).

From here the bombs would be transported to the jetty on trolleys, and thence by bomb scow (a small barge, towed by a dinghy) out to the aircraft. There was a winch on the jetty, and the aircraft's bomb racks also had built-in winches, these being utilized to facilitate loading at either end of the operation. Bombs were winched down from the jetty and onto the scow, then, on arrival out at the aircraft, the bombs were winched aboard. This called for the bomb racks to be tracked outboard, beneath the wing, lowered to the scow, bombs attached and winched up, then the racks to be tracked back inside the aircraft and their deadly cargoes to be lowered to the deck and secured.

A fairly complicated and labourious operation, and, considering the weapons were armed, with neither the scow nor the aircraft exactly stable, potentially dangerous. Although fairly immune to unintentional mishandling and vibration, a sharp tap in the vicinity of the firing pin, or anyone or thing twirling the propeller on the nose, would be enough to warrant at least a visit to the nearest loo, or worse! Fact is, there was ample scope for error were not procedures rigidly adhered to.

It was on March 26th, 1950, at around 10:00 that disaster was to strike the recently formed Far East Flying Boat Wing during just such a loading operation.

Ivor, along with Cpl Durk, was on a bomb scow, in position beneath the wing of SZ573. In the cockpit an officer was testing continuity of the bomb selector switch circuits – entirely different to the release switches, which were on a different panel, covered by safety guards – when a bomb fell from the rack. It dropped between the scow and the aircraft in fairly shallow water, the firing pistol priming itself on the way down.

The bomb exploded, and suddenly the sea was filled with bodies. Ivor, a strong swimmer, appeared to be in no difficulty, but "Taffy" Durk – "never one for swimming" – certainly was. He was struggling and spluttering, so when a lifebelt was thrown from a dinghy, Ivor passed it to his supervisor and helped him secure it. He is reported to have helped others as well.

The conjecture is that the blast had left Ivor conscious but numb, and he hadn't realized his legs were seriously damaged. The Sunderland's hull had been damaged, too, the aircraft quickly sinking to a point where it was supported only by the buoyancy of its wings, tail up. There had been eleven people in the vicinity at the time of the explosion, most now in a state of shock, and only at the hospital was it realized that Ivor Gillett was not among them. His body was washed up in a nearby cove the following day.

The lifebelt incident had been observed by the coxswain of the dinghy, and in October it was announced that Ivor Gillett, RAF, had been awarded a posthumous George Cross as a result of his actions.

Those are the basic facts as given by people closely involved at the time, but unconfirmed reports, or possibly rumours, allege that:

1) The officer was not really qualified for the job he was doing.

2) An RAF Regiment sergeant, seconded to the armoury, was in the nose playing at being a bomb aimer. It seems that due to a shortage of personnel, armourers from other units were attached to 9X site, a lot of them unfamiliar with the current operation, or with the aircraft. Not that these events, even if true, necessarily had anything to do with the incident.

Other snippets concerning the incident are as follows:

It was reported that a Medic/ambulance driver took off for the scene the minute he heard the explosion, then found himself on a charge for leaving sick quarters without a Medical Officer. This was later rescinded and he was in fact eventually commended for saving lives.

Bill Webb, who had just finished bombing up an adjacent aircraft and was being towed back to shore, suddenly found himself anchored to a buoy for a couple of hours; the scow he was on being cut lose by the coxswain when he took his dinghy back to the aircraft to help out.

Stan Pierce was playing darts in the nearby yacht club at the time of the explosion, and he reports the board jumping about six inches, just as he was lining up a double top finish.

● ● ● ● ● ● ● ● ● ● ●

Seletar's third operational squadron arrived in March 1950, No.81 transferring over from Tengah. It brought with it a number of aircraft: Mosquitos and Spitfires, plus one Anson. 81's speciality was in the field of photographic reconnaissance, a role that was of particular value during the Emergency, aircraft being dispatched to seek out and photograph terrorist concentrations. Flying at the usual height for photo-recce missions of around sixteen thousand feet, the terrorists would be oblivious of the fact their camps were being photographed; careful study of the results enabled Commonwealth land forces to spring a number of surprise attacks.

It was about this time that the RAF entered a completely new era, that of helicopter operations, Malaya being adjudged the ideal testing ground. Dragonfly C Mk II aircraft were assembled and test flown at Seletar, the aircraft which flew on April 22nd being a first for Singapore and FEAF. Although some aircraft continued to be "attached" to Seletar until May 22nd – when the unit relocated to Changi, becoming the Far East Casualty Evacuation Flight – few flying hours were actually achieved, mainly due to aircraft unserviceability, rotary flight proving to be a steep learning curve for all concerned. Despite this, the Casualty Air Evacuation Flight, Far East Transport Wing, was formed at Kuala Lumpur on May 1st, flying its first operational casevac mission on June 15th, 1950.

The planned communist expansion in Asia continued, when on June 25th, 1950, they mounted yet another challenge, North Korean soldiers crossing their southern border to invade South Korea – a member of the United Nations. The United States responded swiftly, moving forces from Japan to South Korea on behalf of the United Nations. Britain pledged support for the action.

At the time, Sunderland equipped 88 Squadron were taking part in summer exercises with the British and American fleets off the coast of Japan, and they quickly became involved. They were soon to be joined by the aircraft of 209 Squadron, and, by October, 205 Squadron had also joined the fray.

The Sunderlands, working alongside the USAF's Martin Mariner, were based at Iwakuni, Japan, located about one hundred miles from the southern tip of the Korean mainland. The flying boats' main task was to carry out round-the-clock reconnaissance flights along the coast, in support of the United Nations imposed blockade of North Korean ports, but they often found themselves diverted for the inevitable SAR missions. In December, for example, Flt/Lt Hunter made two open-sea landings in order to pick up twenty-three men from the mined, *MS Joseph S*. He flew his passengers to Hong Kong, landing safely at night.

Sqn/Ldr JE Proctor, Officer Commanding 205 Squadron, recorded how welcome these new activities were to his men. *'The morale of the squadron has reached new heights. The high standard of health is unaffected by the squadron's rapid change from tropical conditions to the winter weather prevailing in Japan'*.

Although generally in good spirits, many officers and airmen testified to the wretched weather conditions in which they were often required to work. Flights had a normal endurance of between twelve and fifteen hours, and could be quite hazardous, especially during the winter months. Fierce gales would blow down from the Arctic, as tempestuous as anything ever experienced by those wartime pilots over the Atlantic. In addition there were blinding snowstorms which lasted for hours, and sub-zero temperatures in which even the thickest clothing failed to provide adequate warmth. One airman recalled how bad conditions could get.

'We could be up there for hours on end until we really knew what it was to be a brass monkey.

The highlight of every trip was our tea break; boy did that go down well! The trouble was that sometimes it became so cold that if we left our piping hot tea to stand for a few minutes, it was frozen by the time we came back. On one east coast patrol I remember a temperature of minus 20°C was recorded at 41°N.'

Even summer presented its difficulties, low mist and haze would form, obscuring the low-flying pilot's vision; a potentially hazardous situation off a coastline which featured many high-peaked islands and islets.

There was also a strong possibility of encountering the hurricane-force winds which abound in the area in the form of typhoons. The breeding grounds for these storms is east of the Philippines, any time between May and September. Several pilots recalled experiencing wind speeds of one hundred plus miles per hour.

The difficulties imposed by these climatic conditions would appear to have accounted for the only losses inflicted on the Sunderland detachments in Korea. The first of these occurred on January 28th, 1951, when a 205 Squadron Sunderland, PP107, en route from Iwakuni to Hong Kong, crashed on Mount Morrison, in Formosa. Out of the fourteen occupants there were no survivors.

In December 1950, Singapore was subjected to what became known as the Maria Hertogh Riots. Probably an over simplification, but the basic story went thus: During the war, five year old Dutch girl, Maria Hertogh, had been left with a Muslim family for a day or two whilst her parents were away from home. But on their return journey, the parents were interned for the duration by the Japanese. The Muslim family looked after Maria, treating her as their own child and converting her to the Muslim faith. After the surrender, with the Muslim family refusing to give up custody, it took a court ruling for Maria to be returned to her natural parents. When Maria later married a Muslim, her mother, Bertha, became furious, the courts once more becoming involved. On account of Maria's young age (12), the marriage was annulled, the court ruling that she was to be placed in a

Catholic convent until things were sorted out. Now the Muslim community became incensed, and things were brought to a head when rioting erupted – seemingly communist inspired, the communists, as usual, taking advantage of the situation. Sadly, these riots were to result in the death of a Seletar airman. With the riot beginning whilst he was on duty, Cpl Bell was unaware of the situation until stopped by the service police as he was about to depart camp. Worried for his wife and new born child, recently arrived in the colony and living downtown, he sought and was granted permission to go to them. Unfortunately, the bus on which he was travelling was stopped at a roadblock, Cpl Bell being dragged off and beaten. Dead or not, his body was then thrown in a ditch, soaked in petrol and set alight.

June 1951 saw a major change taking place in the organization of Flying Boat operations. With the Korean commitment being scaled down, 88 Squadron was transferred to Seletar, the Far East Flying Boat Wing now encompassing all three of the Sunderland squadrons. It was planned that in future each squadron would take turns serving a six-week detachment in Iwakuni, the squadrons remaining at Seletar would devote themselves mainly to "Firedog" operations.

An upsurge of terrorist activities was largely responsible for these changes, for despite efforts to quell the Communists, Malaya was to log over six thousand incidents during 1951, with six hundred and thirty-three civilians being killed. One of these occurred on October 6th, and was a major tragedy. The High Commissioner to Malaya, Sir Henry Gurney was ambushed and killed on the road from Kuala Lumpur to Fraser's Hill. Civilian morale was now at a low ebb.

The Fraser's Hill retreat was one the places at which the RAF would occasionally be called upon to mount the guard, it being a jungle survival training area for courses run by the RAF Regiment. One airman recalls the time he was "volunteered" for this duty.

'We formed a military convoy to get there. Each airman was issued with a rifle and five rounds of ammunition, none allowed "up the spout," safety catch, "on". The "Gap" (where the ambush had taken place) was a winding road, steep, with many hairpin bends, and the terrorists would select the last vehicle in the convoy. If this happened, the vehicle would brake to a halt and all the occupants were supposed to dive into the jungle and return fire, with their five rounds! No doubt all the cartridge cases needed to be accounted for, too!'

Although the number of deaths was distressing, the authorities were seen to be gaining the upper hand, and it was largely a consequence of their efforts that the communists were being forced into making desperate attempts to reverse the trend. The brilliant "Briggs Plan" was already showing signs of success – this called for the grouping together of isolated sections of the community into defended, "new villages." The idea was to increase pressure on the terrorists by restricting their access to food supplies, hopefully starving them out.

The Royal Air Force was to play an integral part in the new operations by threatening and harassing them as much as possible. Paratroops and supplies were dropped, bombing and strafing attacks stepped up. 81 Squadron's aircraft were particularly successful, the top priority being given to photographic reconnaissance, for which a suitably equipped Avro Anson was found to be a very effective tool. Photographic mapping was also an essential requirement, the squadron's Mosquitos reaching new levels of attainment when, in May of that year, no less than nine thousand and sixty-four square miles of data was logged, the highest monthly figure ever recorded in the Far East, and six times the average for this class of photography.

A welcome change of routine, were the occasional flights during which the various squadrons transported distinguished visitors around. In July 1951, 205 Squadron was called upon to carry actor, Jack Warner and his party up to Iwakuni. The film and television personality was scheduled to entertain the troops in Japan and Korea. Later in the month author, Eric Linklater was flown to Japan. From there he travelled on to Korea, gathering data about the exploits of the British Forces in the war.

Not immune from danger, one of these flights was to end in tragedy, when, after their performance at Seletar – attended by Lord Mountbatten – Elsie and Doris Waters were scheduled to fly up to Hong Kong. Some of the ENSA (Entertainments National Services Association) party were to fly out that very night, but the Sunderland in which they were travelling had the misfortune to hit a native canoe on take-off. The aircraft crashed and there were no survivors, an indication of the ever-changing hazards that could lay in wait for flying boat crews operating at night.

It was in September of 1952 that an 88 Squadron aircraft was despatched on a unique assignment. Captained by Fl/Lt Houtheusen, and a specially screened crew, along with the Officer Commanding the Far East Flying Boat Wing, Wg/Cdr D Mackenzie DFC, they made two "top secret" transit flights to Australia. But, carrying as they did, Dr William Penny – a noted atomic scientist – and some heavily guarded equipment, revealed these flights to be in connection with the British Atomic tests off the Monte Bello Islands. Not so top secret after all.

The Duke of Kent visited the Royal Air Force in Singapore the following month, and at Seletar he was to visit the MU's, Marine Craft Section and the operational squadrons. Following that, a specially converted Sunderland of 205 Squadron carried the Duke and Duchess, along with the rest of their party, on a Royal Tour of Borneo and Sarawak. Captained by Flt/Lt Wells, the aircraft was accompanied by a second Sunderland. This, flown by Sqn/Ldr Ormston, the squadron's Commanding Officer, carried the baggage and acted as back-up. The detachment was again led by Wg/Cdr Mackenzie. The whole trip lasted ten days, and was deemed a great success.

On completion of the tour came the presentations. The Duchess expressed her appreciation by presenting Wg/Cdr Mackenzie with an autographed portrait, the captain and navigator of the Royal aircraft receiving monogrammed gold cuff-links. In turn, Sqn/Ldr Ormston presented the Duke of Kent with a mounted squadron crest.

It was on October 14th, 1952 that BOAC first flew the Comet into Singapore, but, in a repeat of the early days of flying in the colony, it had to rely upon the RAF, Changi this time, rather than Seletar, the runway at Kallang being too small to accept it. Time for a new civil airport to be built, at Paya Lebar, but this was not to open until 1957. (Changi was again called upon to temporarily accept commercial traffic in 1964, a BOAC Comet closing Paya Lebar for a while when it crash-landed on their single runway.)

Another change had been put into effect back in April that year: Seletar became a fully constituted RAF Group Headquarters. Known as 230 Group it also controlled Changi, as well as a number of non-operational units around the island. The new HQ came under Seletar's Base Commander, Air Commodore WA Opie, but early in 1953 the title was changed from 230 Group, to Air Headquarters Singapore, commanded by Air Commodore WML McDonald.

By 1953 the Royal Air Force in Malaya was entering a new era, being re-equipped with jets: Meteors, Vampires, Venoms, Canberras and Javelins putting in an appearance. A lot of the new arrivals came in by sea. It became a familiar sight to see aircraft being barged back and forth along the Straits, on their way to and from the naval base. Arriving from Britain and elsewhere aboard the Royal Navy's carriers, they would then be craned aboard a barge, secured, towed to Seletar and offloaded at the flying boat slipway, from where they could be towed across to 389 MU. This practice continued until well into the sixties, the first of the BAC Lightnings arriving in such fashion, although with the advent of in-flight refuelling, most were by then flying out. Some aircraft were subjected to the reverse journey, those that had been shipped out in crates, assembled and tested at Seletar before being forwarded by sea to other bases in the area, ie Hong Kong and the like. Few made it back to the UK. Most aircraft, after being withdrawn from service were reduced to scrap on-site at Seletar; very sad to see.

The jets would eventually replace the Spitfires, Mosquitos, Hornets and Tempests that were currently in use. But for all that, the Sunderland – Queen of the Skies – continued to give a good account of herself.

In March of that year, a serious fire broke out in Tawau, a small trading post in Santa Lucia Bay, North Borneo. With half the town the town being razed to the ground, Sunderlands of 205 Squadron came to the rescue, flying in with medical supplies, food, and other necessities, and generally maintaining contact with the outside world until such time as conditions were restored to normal.

The people of Tawau, in a show of appreciation for the services provided by the Air Force, presented the squadron with a ceremonial sword and flag.

But not all Sunderland stories would end on so happy a note, for away from base, aircraft were often required to operate in marginal conditions, and this could be fraught with danger. The same month during which the Tawau fire occurred, Flt/Lt Wilkinson of 88 Squadron, was the pilot of Sunderland PP148, returning to Iwakuni one wild, black night at the end of a patrol. Flying at five thousand feet so as to avoid turbulence below, he arrived overhead the fairly open waters at around 22:30 only for flying control to report a surface wind of thirty-five knots, gusting fifty. Descending to make a low run at fifty feet, after first switching on his landing lights, the pilot adjudged sea conditions to be unsafe for a landing, and, being advised that the wind was forecast to decrease, he decided to orbit. By midnight, with fuel getting low, the decision was made to attempt a landing. An emergency flare path was laid into wind and, once on the approach, the crew took up their crash positions.

Twice the Sunderland bounced off the water, so an overshoot was made. Things looked better next time, but, upon throttling back, it turned to disaster. The next thing Wilkinson knew he was under water. Struggling to the surface he saw the Sunderland was floating on its back, everything forward of the galley missing. Four of the crew died in the wreck.

On October 17th, 1953, another new aircraft was introduced to the area when a Prestwick (later, Scottish Aviation) Pioneer took off on a test flight from Seletar. A high wing monoplane with an excellent short field performance, this was the machine's first appearance outside Britain, and, capable of being flown at unbelievably slow speeds, it was to be found ideally suited to the Malayan campaign. This first aircraft was piloted by Flt/Lt MEF Hickmott, Commanding Officer of the unit especially set up to operate the Pioneer – 1311 Transport Flight. Capable of carrying four passengers or eight hundred pounds of freight, this STOL (short take-off and landing) aircraft possessed a speed range of from thirty to one hundred and thirty miles per hour; much faster than the helicopters it was to supplement in certain roles. It could land in, and climb steeply out of the isolated jungle forts from which it was to operate. In the peak year of their operation in Malaya, they flew four thousand seven hundred sorties, being mainly used for communications and casualty evacuation flights. A twin-engined version (ingeniously named, Twin Pioneer) was later introduced to the theatre. Once operational, 1311 Flight moved closer to the front line, being based at Kuala Lumpur, taking up the numberplate of 267 Squadron.

Throughout its years in Singapore, the Royal Air Force had been co-operating with the Police to prevent piracy and smuggling, which, as has previously been mentioned, had forever seemed endemic in the South China Sea. The official Royal Navy and Royal Air Force Anti-Piracy Patrol Order stated that acts of piracy were being committed on the high seas at the rate of one a month. Visibly armed flying boats did much to improve the situation.

In August 1953, they spotted and reported a transfer at sea between Thai and Singaporean fishing vessels, the resultant police swoop leading to the confiscation of a large quantity of opium. In October, the patrols received official backing, resulting in another opium-carrying vessel being stopped by the authorities in December.

Seletar airfield was again to find itself under attack in December 1953, but this time the bombs were nothing more lethal than the toilet rolls which showered down from one of 83 Squadron's Avro Lincolns, over from Tengah on a Christmas hell-raising mission.

A non-smuggling success occurred when, in June 1954, a 205 Squadron Sunderland, piloted by Flt/Lt Harrison, located a Malay fishing boat that had been missing for weeks, saving the entire crew. A month later, another 205 Squadron aircraft, piloted by Flt/Lt Robinson, was to intercept a suspected smuggling operation. Alighting on the open sea, the Customs Officer they were carrying was transferred to the vessel, and after some investigation, both boat and its contents were confiscated, the captain taken into custody.

81 Squadron's Mosquitos were also active on patrol work, playing a large part in co-operating with the Borneo Police to capture a group of Philippine pirates who had been marauding the coast of British North Borneo. The meticulous patrolling from the skies soon had an effect, and probably for the first time large expanses of sea became safe for local fishermen.

81 Squadron also featured prominently in the news in April 1954, when on the 1st of the month Spitfire PR19, PS888, flown by Sqn/Ldr Swaby, took off from Seletar to make what was to be the last operational flight of the type with the Royal Air Force. Strange, that, to all but 81 Squadron. Some months earlier they had been piqued to learn that, not only had 60 Squadron been credited with flying the last operational sortie back in 1951, but that Rolls Royce and Vickers Armstrong had actually presented them with silver model Spitfire to commemorate the event!

Sqn/Ldr W.P. Swaby, 81 Squadron Commander, decided to claim his, and the Squadron's, rightful place in history, taking the matter up officially. In a letter to Far East Air Force Headquarters he stated:

It is noted that the flying carried out by the Spitfires of No.81 Squadron should not have been classified operational with effect from

January 1st, 1951, and you are therefore requested to transfer the total of 1874.25 hours and 1029 operational sorties flown from that date to the training columns. Alternatively, the squadron will be pleased to accept an 18 inch high silver model of a Spitfire from the Commanding Officer of No.60 Squadron in commemoration of current operations.

A result of all this was that, on November 21st, 1954, Rolls Royce and Vickers Armstrong made amends for their error by presenting 81 Squadron with their own silver Spitfire. The presentation being made by no less a personality than Mr Jeffrey Quill, OBE AFC, who, as the former Supermarine Chief Test Pilot, had flown every mark of Spitfire, including the first prototype in 1936.

With operations against the terrorists still on the increase in 1954, all the aircraft were kept very busy. 81 Squadron, whose Mosquitos had completed their basic "Firedog" cover the previous September, were now required to carry out widespread reconnaissance. It was also the Mosquitos that bore the brunt of this task, covering Japan, in the north, Christmas Island – the Australian version in the Indian Ocean – along with the Cocos Islands in the south, Darwin to the east. Early in the new year, two Mosquitos flew west, the intent being to photograph the airfields in Ceylon, and to lend a hand during filming of the movie "Purple Plain." But on arrival the crews found their priorities had been reversed in favour of their aircraft becoming film stars, even requiring a visit to make-up; they needed repainting, and certain nose modifications had to be to be incorporated. A total of thirty-seven film sorties were flown, and the crews were said to have thoroughly enjoyed the experience, making many new friends amongst Gregory Peck and the Hollywood set.

March 9th, 1954, saw Countess Mountbatten of Burma visiting the Station, a special visit being paid to "Seletarville," by now a showpiece for the whole island. The inhabitants of were said to have been completely captivated by the

Countess' charm, photographs of the visit being proudly displayed on the walls of the Community Centre for years to come.

It was a month later that 88 Squadron were detached en masse to China Bay, Ceylon. Heavily laden with equipment and personnel, take-off from the Straits saw some unusually long runs, one Sunderland being logged at over three minutes before getting airborne. Their aircraft were to escort the *SS Gothic* as she carried the Queen and the Duke of Edinburgh on a State Visit to that country.

Five Sunderlands departed China Bay at 06:30 on April 8th, sighting the Royal convoy five hours later, still about five hundred miles from Ceylon. Led by Flying Officer Holmes, the formation flew past, signalling greetings, to which Her Majesty replied: *I sincerely thank all ranks in the Royal Air Force serving in Ceylon for their kind and loyal message.* Four of the Sunderlands then returned to China Bay, leaving F/O Holmes to escort the *Gothic* until dusk.

On the 21st of the month, three of the Sunderlands took part in the Queen's Birthday fly-past over Colombo, and the following day, in bad weather, four of them flew patrols around the ships upon departure. At midday, F/O Holmes closed in to take photographs of the *Gothic*, and half an hour later, being relieved by the little, twin-engined Short Sealand of the Indian Navy, the squadron formed up and flew past in a final salute. A final message was transmitted from the captain of the *Gothic*: *I wish to convey the message from Her Majesty the Queen – thank you for your escort.*

Although the fighting in Korea had ended in late 1953, it was to be well into 1954 before United Nations forces pulled out, the Royal Air Force withdrawing its units in accordance with the Commonwealth Plan. Before returning to Seletar, all three of the Sunderland squadrons were presented with some sort of memento by the Americans, but in 205's case this was to have somewhat dramatic repercussions.

● ● ● ● ● ● ● ● ● ● ●

The 205 Squadron Cannon – a tale of inter-squadron rivalry.

Two versions of this story make an appearance here, the first of which is as related in *Lion in the Sky*, therefore, at least second-hand, the other was told to me by someone who had actually been involved. Take your pick, but I think reference to the use of explosives probably rules version one somewhat out of contention as a clandestine operation, but version two also contains flaws. For instance, having never before set foot inside a Sunderland, this crew seemed to find out what was what rather swiftly. Still, a combination of both stories reveals more or less what happened.

Lieutenant Colonel CE Pannell, US Air Force, Iwakuni, made the official presentation at the end of May 1954, 205 Squadron's gift being a small cannon. A remnant of the 1904-5 Russian-Japanese War, this antique had until recently been gate-guardian at the entrance to Air Base Headquarters. (The USAF ran air operations over Korea, the RAF never fully committing an operational squadron to the conflict. The RAF contribution was in the form of detachments, the Sunderlands coming under US Naval Command, the three squadrons – 88, 205, 209 – rotating on a month by month basis.)

When 205 finally pulled out from Japan, the dismantled cannon was loaded aboard a Sunderland, for shipment back to Seletar. Unfortunately, due to engine problems, the flight was to suffer a delay at Kai Tak, the aircraft being taken ashore for repair. So the scene was set.

Version one – 205 Squadron's CO briefly explains things as he recalled them:

'It was stolen by another squadron, and cemented in front of their offices. I sent a crew back up to Hong Kong to recover it. With the aid of dynamite from the Royal Engineers, they blew it free one night but were caught carrying it to the slipway by the Duty Officer. Threats to throw him in the 'drink' were not appreciated, and they returned to Seletar empty handed. Meanwhile, the Commanding Officer at Kai Tak had the

Relic of the Russo-Japanese war, this cannon was presented to 205 Sqn by the USAF at the end of the Korean conflict, resulting in much inter-Sqn rivalry.
Stan Ould

cannon locked up until somebody established ownership.'

In the end, Colonel Pannell confirmed in writing that he had presented the trophy to 205, and the squadron was finally able to retrieve the cannon and set it up at Seletar.

Version two – Derek Jones, Cpl engine fitter with 80 Squadron, based at Kai Tak, fills in some details of the "James Bond" type operation when the cannon was "stolen by another squadron." He was one of those involved:

'Unfortunately for them, the aircraft went u/s in our domain, RAF Kai Tak, Hong Kong, and had to be beached for repairs. Whilst there it was visited by a number of senior NCO's who, upon noticing the unusual cargo, became more than interested in this example of Japanese artillery. But, being warned off by the Sunderland's crew, they withdrew, retiring to the bar of the yacht club, which was close at hand.

'There, also enjoying a Saturday afternoon pint of "San Mig" (San Miguel, the local brew) were three corporal engine fitters, "Jonah" Jones and Doug Murray of 80 Squadron, and "Doughy" Baker of ASF. They listened with interest as the SNCO's – Flt/Sgt Eustace, of ASF, in particular – talked about this cannon, and how

nice it would look mounted outside the Sergeants' Mess. He mentioned an upcoming dance, due to be held in the mess, finishing by saying " I'd like it to be there."

'Upon hearing this, and no doubt inspired by the promise of a plentiful supply of "San Mig," the collective corporals volunteered to see what could be done. The plan was simple: wait until all was quiet, board the aircraft, take possession of the gun and hide it in the sail loft of the yacht club until darkness fell, then wheel it to the Sergeants' Mess – about a mile distant.

'There was however, a small problem: none of them had been aboard a Sunderland, and it took some time to figure out how things operated inside that massive hull. "Jonah" and Doug gained entry through a hatch, with "Doughy" preparing a hiding place in the darkest recesses of the sail locker. With some of the yacht club's rope, the lighter parts were lowered through the hatch to the ground, but the barrel and shield required use of the internal bomb racks' winches. The beam hatches were opened ('Bloody things were spring loaded, made a hell of a noise. We nearly lost some fingers!), the gun swung out and was lowered to the ground successfully. The wheels were quickly fitted and it was trundled away, out of sight.

'After dark, we had to retrieve the cannon, drag it from the yacht club, across the grass and onto the perimeter track. All that remained now was to make our way to the Sergeants' Mess and claim our reward. But we did need to run the gauntlet of the dog handlers and the guards: RAF Regiment, Malaya. Trigger happy b...tards, and to be avoided at all costs! In this we were successful, skirting "Tin Town" – Nissen huts, home to 80 Squadron ground crew – we arrived unnoticed at the rear of the Mess, mission complete.

'Knocking on the kitchen door brought us face to face with a rather puzzled Chinese waiter, who was told to find Chiefy Eustace and tell him "IT" was outside, and "Jonah" and Doug awaited their reward. A more than surprised Chiefy arrived, took possession of the trophy, and we retired to a quiet corner to consume our prize: a case of "San Mig" and some chicken sandwiches.

'Ted Eustace, with some assistance, wheeled the gun into the mess, where a slight altercation took place. NCO members of the Sunderland crew attempted to regain possession, but failed. Then the Mess President decided that as AOC's inspection was imminent, the gun couldn't yet be mounted outside, so the decision was made to hide it. This was done in the long grass by the scrapyard; unadvisedly close to the 80 Squadron dispersal.

'The AOC came and went, as did the now-repaired Sunderland; gun-less, but not unarmed. Peace returned, and the jubilant sergeants' decided to recover their prize. But all the activity had not gone unnoticed by other 80 Squadron personnel, naturally, so a challenge for owner-ship now commenced, nay, a pitched battle, beneath the old Jap control tower, 80 Squadron winning through.

'It was taken to our armoury, stripped, cleaned, painted and polished, then, with due ceremony, mounted outside Squadron HQ, where Wg/Cdr Jim Kettlewell and the Squadron Commander, Sqn/Ldr Gerry Cullen reigned supreme.'

The mounting of this gun was said to be something of an engineering feat, concrete picketing blocks, chains, a five foot hole and lots of concrete being involved. With the wheels set in a concrete plinth, the cannon was at last secure. Well, for almost a year!

One morning in early 1955, squadron person-nel noticed a massive hole where there had once been a gun! Unknown to them, a heavily over-manned 205 Sqn Sunderland had flown in to Kai Tak – under the guise of a navigational exercise – determined to rescue their cannon. They'd apparently bribed an MT driver and his Coles crane, and with that, along with picks, shovels and brawn, managed to extricate the weapon and remove it. But a problem arose at Marine Craft Section when they tried to get coxswain, Cpl Harry Excel, to ferry the gun out to the waiting aircraft. Harry – who was in league with 80 Squadron – refused to do so, and the ensuing argument was cause for the RAF Police to put in an appearance.

Now things got nasty, with arrest being threatened. The station commander was next to arrive, and he decided the cannon had caused more than enough trouble at Kai Tak, and told the Sunderland crew to take it to Seletar. This they did, and it was mounted outside Flying Boat Wing Headquarters at the base, remaining there until long after 205 Squadron departed for Changi. Where is it now? The author for one would love to know.

● ● ● ● ● ● ● ● ● ●

It was around this period that the Astra cinema on East Camp was modernized, upgrading to the Cinemascope format. From now on, Fred Quimby's creations could be viewed in widescreen.

Early 1955, and the people of Tawau now found themselves able to repay their debt of gratitude for help received when their village suffered that disastrous fire of two years before.

The roles were reversed when a Sunderland landed at Tawau, suffering minor damage to a float and a propeller. A Police Superintendent promptly rowed out and took two of the crew off to find a suitable place in which to beach the aircraft. A number of people then assisted in the beaching, also building a sand-bag breakwater to reduce the effect of the swell. In addition, a local company provided a lighting system, so that a continuous watch could be maintained.

Repairs took eleven days, a new float and propeller being flown in by a Valetta, another Sunderland bringing in a servicing crew. Upon completion of taxying tests, the aircraft was ceremoniously named "Tawau Beach" by Mrs Chisholm, wife of the Resident Officer. The Sunderland then took off and returned to Seletar. Sqn/Ldr DJG Norton, who had flown in to supervise repairs, commented on the unselfish help and hospitality which had been shown by the local people and European residents.

On the morning of their departure, whilst awaiting high tide, a cricket match took place on the foreshore, an RAF eleven playing the resident team.

Immediately following the end of the Korean commitment on 2nd October, 88 Squadron was disbanded. In Korea it had contributed four hundred and sixty-seven out of the Flying Boat Wing's total of one thousand six hundred and fifty sorties. It also managed to squeeze in amongst those, one hundred and sixty five "Firedog" sorties back in Malaya. Now it was no more, its veteran aircraft were handed over to the two remaining Sunderland squadrons at Seletar.

Later that month, a signal was received at Seletar from the United States Consulate in Singapore. The request was passed on to Wg/Cdr Burgess, 205 Squadron's CO, in the middle of the night. It stated that a forty-nine year old American Missionary, Mr John Breman, had fallen seriously ill and required immediate hospital treatment. Mr Breman's location was given as the village of Singkawang, Indonesian Borneo, almost three hundred and fifty miles due east of Singapore. The pick-up point was to be Pamangkat, twenty-five miles north, on the mouth of the Sambas river. Arrangements were quickly made and a Sunderland was soon airborne, en route for a river that was said to be well known for a crocodile population that had

accounted for no fewer than eighty fishermen the previous year! Twice the aircraft circled over the muddy waters, the crew anxiously scanning the surface for anything afloat that may spell disaster. It looked OK, so the aircraft touched down, mooring with only six feet of water beneath the hull. Mr Breman was flown out safely the next day, and once in Singapore he received the necessary treatment at the General Hospital.

Seletar's Sunderland strength was further reduced when, on January 1st, 1955, the two remaining squadrons amalgamated to form 205/ 209 Squadron, under the command of Sqn/Ldr DJG Norton.

Although the Far East Flying Boat Wing now ceased to exist, the Sunderlands were not yet dead. With the squadron's full-time SAR commitment in Hong Kong coming to an end on August 1st – there being no Sunderlands on permanent duty at Kai Tak for first time in nine years – the emphasis was now on "Firedog" and anti-piracy operations,

The end of 1953 saw 81 Squadron begin converting to the Meteor PR Mk10, these working alongside the current aircraft. As previously mentioned, the first visit of a jet fighter to Singapore – a Meteor IV – had occurred as far back as August 1947, twenty selected pilots having been invited to fly the aircraft.

Although the Spitfire was now out of service, one of the type was still resident at Seletar, over on West Camp; at least that was its normal location. But on Christmas Day, 1955, it ended up on the parade ground at East Camp, pushed and shoved by persons unknown; quite a journey! Although a rather low key investigation was held, apparently no one had seen or heard a thing, but it can now be revealed that the group had been led by a somewhat "well oiled" F/O whose everyday job could be said to fit the description: driver, airframe, Twin Pioneer – not even Spitfire type-rated! And it was reported to have taken much longer to return the aircraft to West Camp than it had for it to find its way over to East Camp – despite the fact that the returnees had use of the proper towing equipment. It seems Tiger power won out over horsepower.

With the Meteors now operational, it wasn't to be long before Seletar, 81Squadron in particular, could log yet another "last operational sortie." No ifs or buts this time, and the sad demise was to be that of the Mosquito; RG314, a PR Mk34 completed a photographic sortie on December 15th, 1955, to mark the end of yet another distinguished career.

Never really suited to Far East operations, its wooden construction susceptible to the area's high humidity (fungus attacking the glue in the main spar), 81 Squadron's aircraft were the only ones not to be replaced by the Beaufighter and Brigand, mainly due to the fact that their specialized camera equipment could not be easily fitted to any other aircraft at present in the theatre.

This main spar problem had long been evident. Only two years after the war aircraft were being destroyed as soon as they became unserviceable, only the PR versions remaining. It must have been a sad sight to see coolies being supplied with saws and hatchets, then set lose to attack these aircraft.

A tragic example of this main spar problem was illustrated by an accident which occurred as far back as 1946. A Flt/Lt Stevens DFC, of Air Headquarters Malaya Communications Squadron, previously flying Dakotas, had been posted to Seletar to convert onto the Mosquito. Unfamiliar with the aircraft he was taken up on a familiarization sortie, only for the wings to become detached in flight, with fatal results.

• • • • • • • • • •

Although there was now a sharp decline in flying activities at Seletar, operations were on the increase elsewhere in Malaya, statistics for KL and Butterworth revealing just how large was the RAF's contribution. In addition to hundreds of supply drops and troop lifts, psychological warfare sorties were also flown; over fifteen million leaflets per month were scattered over the jungle, one hundred and seventy crop-spraying missions and hours of aerial broadcasts were made. ("Skyshout" Dakotas carried underwing loudspeakers, inducements for the terrorists to surrender being broadcast in their native tongue.) Seven hundred and fifty bombing missions and over nine hundred ground attack sorties were also flown during the year. But Seletar was still making a major contribution to the Emergency, not only through its two flying squadrons – 205/209 and 81 – but also through its Engineering and Supply Wings, these being largely responsible for maintenance and the supply of materials

The Astra in the mid 1950s, when Cinemascope was introduced. **John Smith**

for the whole of FEAF. Seletar also had a direct involvement in ground operations through the medium of No.92 RAF Regiment (Malaya) Squadron.

The RAF Regiment (Malaya) was commanded mainly by Europeans, with British and Malayan NCO's, but the rank and file were almost one hundred per cent Malay. Its primary concern was, naturally, airfield defence, but its squadrons also served – under Army control – to patrol the jungle on offensive operations. In time the Regiment was to become extremely proficient, being responsible for the death and capture of large numbers of terrorists.

Usually based at Seletar, from February to July 1955, No.92 took part in a successful anti-terrorist operation near Kuala Selangor, east of KL, and in 1957 they participated in one of the largest operations of the Emergency, in excess of ten thousand troops taking part. Some twelve hundred square miles of Perak State were targeted, the 8th and 9th Communist Districts being destroyed.

In late 1956, Singapore was suddenly subjected to communist-inspired strikes and demonstrations, some of which culminated in rioting. Service establishments were placed on immediate alert, ready to aid the civil authorities under the terms of the Defence Plan. Families were restricted to "safe" locations, and airmen were formed into Defence Squadrons, ready to assist in police actions. These squadrons, deployed to various parts of the island, were completely supplied and maintained from Seletar. From the 23rd to the 30th of October, the situation was so dire that vessels from the Marine Craft Unit had to be used to carry personnel and stores to and from Changi.

A firm and determined stand against the communists by the Singapore Government, headed by Mr Lim Kew Hock, soon brought the situation under control. The Royal Air Force's helicopters were especially helpful, observing trouble spots from the air, they enabled police and troop reinforcements to be quickly on the scene.

The whole episode was a frightening experience, particularly for the families of servicemen, some of who witnessed or were caught up in the violence. The wife of one airman recalled what happened one day when she was out shopping.

'I had been to town with another wife and had just got into my car when a crowd rushed towards us. Someone opened the car door and snatched my friend's handbag away from her. They then pulled her out and were trying to pull me out, but I clung on tight to the steering wheel. I don't think I've ever been so frightened in all my life. Thank God at that moment some soldiers appeared and the mob moved off. We were badly shaken but unhurt. The car was scratched a bit and one window broken, and my friend had lost her handbag containing about thirty dollars. We got back all right, and didn't leave our homes for weeks afterwards.'

Generally, the reaction of British families was reported to have been very sensible, the above incident being a rare exception. Civilians were given clear instructions on where to go and what to do, and many wives assisted with essential services. One example involved the telephone service. All locally employed telephone operators were advised to stay at home, the shortage of operators being partly offset by the voluntary efforts of three service wives who had past experience in the job.

Singapore was granted self-government status on April 11th, 1957, and their first crisis happened just a month later, the island caught up in an epidemic of influenza. This quickly spread to all sectors of the community, and Seletar's Sick Quarters were soon filled to overflowing, the medical staff hard pushed to keep the situation under control. The Asian community turned out to be more susceptible to the virus than the Europeans, 92 RAF Regiment Squadron suffering particularly badly.

A side effect of this epidemic was that as the Malay Auxiliary Police had their ranks decimated by the virus, extra guards and patrols had to be mounted by British service personnel.

1957 also marked the beginning of the end for Seletar's pride and joy, the Sunderland.

February saw the last two Sunderland squadrons in England, disbanding at Pembroke Dock, and some of their aircraft, after being reconditioned, were flown out to Singapore to swell the temporary strength of 205/209, which now became the RAF's last flying boat unit. The last aircraft, RN303, left Britain on September 11th, an event that was covered by BBC television and the press. With its arrival at Seletar on September 20th, the "Kipper Fleet" – as the Service affectionately called its flying boats – had little more than two years to live. Search and Rescue, maritime reconnaissance, mail-drops, these became the aircraft's main roles, with only the odd "Firedog" sortie to recall old times. Kenneth Poolman's book, *Flying Boat*, gives the following description of those last twenty-four months:

Inexorably, one by one, the Sunderlands became too unserviceable for further use. Then they were towed away from the water, up the road to the Sunderland Graveyard, a piece of melancholy wasteland deteriorating into a swamp, bordered on one side by "F" Block (*where the ground crews were billeted*), on the other by the compass base. There they would be dumped, to lie like huge, battered toys, and the scrap metal merchants would come in their cars to look them over. Slowly the serviceability of the ones that were still operating would decline until they followed the same path.

I saw that period quite differently, at least twelve months of it, for these were my days with 205/209. For me, this was the stuff of which dreams are made. I immediately fell in love with Singapore, the world, and my position in it. I especially fell in love with the Sunderland.

So excited was I that only brief fragments of my first waterborne take-off are lodged in memory. A launch had first made a sweep down the watery runway, checking for debris, our engines were running, we'd cast-off from the buoy, were lined up and ready. Then, with throttles pushed open and the roar of four engines at full power drumming in my ears, the spray flew back, obscuring the view in the lower-deck wardroom. There was a reluctant build-up

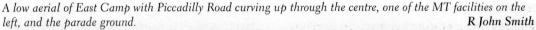

A low aerial of East Camp with Piccadilly Road curving up through the centre, one of the MT facilities on the left, and the parade ground.   **R John Smith**

of speed – degree of reluctance dependant upon hull cleanliness (barnacles, as usual, the problem here) – as hull and wing-tip floats cut creamy furrows in turquoise water. "On the step," and the foam subsided as we charged across the surface. A lunge, a couple of bounces, and we were airborne, water-streaked perspex clearing as we clawed our way into that vast blue waste of sky. A boat had become an aeroplane, time to put the kettle on. Fleeting but emotional recollections.

August 30th, 1957, was Merdeka Day; Malaya – Britain's last Asian Colony – becoming an independent country. This was a bit of a blow to the communists, for they had always stated that as being their eventual goal. OK, so maybe it had been, though not necessarily under a democratically elected government.

That October, the SAR commitment at China Bay was terminated after a three year spell, but a similar coverage was reinstated in Hong Kong. Next month brought with it a flare-up of "Firedog" operations for the Sunderlands. They flew in support of ground forces in Johore, the operation taking place some twenty miles northwest of Seletar. A new anti-piracy patrol was also started, a watch being kept on the north-east coast of British North Borneo in an effort to prevent further attacks on coastal villages and shipping. The aircraft no longer carried their impressive array of machine guns and cannon, it being hoped their presence alone would be enough of a deterrence. After all, pirates were unlikely to know whether or not munitions were carried.

• • • • • • • • • • •

The beginning of the end for the Sunderland.
1958 saw the introduction of the Avro Shackleton to the Far East. Early in the New Year a flight of 205/209 began to form at Changi, making preparations to receive the aircraft; 205/209 Squadron Headquarters also moving to Changi. This move became necessary because Seletar's runway was not long enough for the new aircraft, and it was not thought a practical proposition to develop it. And as far as the 209 element was concerned, this would be the first land-based

aircraft to be operated by that squadron since 1930.

Within three months the Shackleton flight had assumed 205/209's full identity, the flying boats becoming 205/209 Sunderland Detachment, even before the first of the new type had arrived. This event occurred in May, the aircraft piloted by the squadron's new Commanding Officer, Wg/Cdr R.A.N. McCready, OBE. He was met west of Singapore Island by two Sunderlands, and escorted to Changi in close formation.

More changes were to take effect in November, the two squadrons parting to assume their original, individual identities. No.209 reformed at Kuala Lumpur with the personnel and aircraft of 267 Squadron. Being variously equipped with Single Pioneers, Pembrokes, Dakotas, and Austers, through to the end of the Emergency in 1960, they eventually returned to Seletar during 1959. No.205 – the flying boat unit from which the Far East Air Force originated, back in 1928 – was still re-equipping with the Shackleton; but appropriately enough, it continued to encompassed 205 Squadron Sunderland Detachment, with the last of its water-borne aircraft still at their Seletar base.

Disaster stuck the squadron within months when one of their Shackleton's, VP254, with a crew of ten, along with Borneo's Deputy Commissioner of Police on board, disappeared in the South China Sea. The aircraft, on a routine anti-piracy patrol, had been diverted to investigate the reported sinking of a Chinese fishing boat, and to check for survivors. By 11:15 it had successfully completed this mission, resuming its normal patrol. There were no further messages from the crew.

An extensive search was carried out for the missing aircraft, but it was six days before anything was found. Flt/Lt John Elias and his crew, in another 205 Squadron Shackleton, spotted the missing aircraft's code, B – 205, marked out in white coral on the sandy beach of Sin Cowe Island. Next day, the frigate *Rotoiti* of the Royal New Zealand Navy sent a party of men to investigate. They discovered an RAF Officer's cap, a wristwatch, and a newly dug grave, marked with a large cross. From the grave they recovered a body – later to be identified as that of Flight Sergeant Dancey, VP254's flight engineer. Body, artifacts and cross were later flown back to Changi by an aircraft of 52 Squadron. The only other data available was the statement from a Chinese fisherman who said, after seeing the aircraft crash into the sea, he had recovered the body, buried it, erected the cross and, knowing there would be a search, had laid out the message. Despite a lengthy investigation, nothing else was learned about what happened to VP254. The flight engineer's body was subsequently interred in the military cemetery in Singapore, the cross being positioned outside St George's Church at RAF Changi, where it remained until closure of the RAF base in 1971. It now resides in the church at RAF St Eval, Cornwall.

April 17th 1959 saw Malaya signing a treaty of friendship with the Indonesian Government, little realizing it would become meaningless within six years.

It was during May that Seletar again dispatched an RAF aircraft on its last operational sortie, Sunderland DP198 "W" departing the waters of the Johore Straits on the 14th, to provide escort for the crippled naval vessel HMS *Caprice*. The pilot, Flt/Lt Ben Ford – a long time Sunderland man – was accompanied on this occasion by the Squadron CO, Wg/Cdr McCready. News reporters and photographers waited anxiously ashore, ready to record for posterity, the aircraft's return. But in the solemnity of the occasion they were at a loss to understand how the pilot and co-pilot had managed to disappear. The following story of how the press were duped was later revealed by the signaller, Flt/Sgt Jock Armitage. 'More newspaper men and photographers were on the pier to greet us as we came ashore, but the resulting news story never made the headlines to mourn the passing of an era. Dressed in naval-type monkey jackets, Naval officers' hats and resplendent in false whiskers, the captain and co-pilot solemnly came ashore. Nobody was particularly interested in the 'Naval officers' although they did look a little odd. They remained inter-

ested onlookers until the last cameraman had gone.'

One day after this last operational flight, two Sunderlands – DP198 "W" and ML797 "P" – the sole remaining airworthy examples – made a farewell flypast over the city and around the island, their crews being formed from men who had served longest on the type.

Five days later, on May 20th, 1959, "Papa" – ML797 was allotted the honour of making what would turn out to be the very last flight of an RAF Sunderland. Flt/Lt's Jack Poyser and Ben Ford were at the controls, and also on board was Air Marshal The Earl of Bandon, C-in-C Far East Air Force (Lord D'Lysle and Dudley; often referred to by service personnel as 'The Abandoned Earl'). The aircraft was hauled out of the water for the last time two days later. As she was winched up the slipway, stern first past an honour guard who presented arms, the aircraft was to be seen flying a paying-off pennant, in true nautical fashion. The 205 Squadron flag (crossed kris) was also on display.

All the aircraft with the exception of "Papa" were now in the graveyard. The original plan called for ML797 to be flown back to the UK, for preservation, and it was indeed fully refurbished ready for a re-launch. Unfortunately, during the time of refurbishment, a rethink brought about a reversal in policy. The politicians again? The cost of operating the aircraft, plus lack of suitable flying-boat bases en route to the UK, saw the idea consigned to the scrapheap, along with the aircraft.

By June 30th, after removal of engines and all useful equipment, plus the many and diverse souvenirs and mementoes claimed by squadron personnel, ML797 became the last aircraft to be officially Struck Off Charge. The remnants were sold locally, as scrap. The price? A reported six thousand Singapore dollars, which at the time equated to around fifteen hundred pounds. So, maybe that souvenir you bought, fashioned in downtown Singapore, had at one time been part of a Sunderland. (The going rate had obviously escalated over the years. For when David Stebbins – a national service airman – was stationed at Seletar during the period 1956-58, he tried to buy a Sunderland wing float for conversion into a boat, but was told he would have to buy the whole aircraft. Unfortunately, it was at a price he could not at the time afford – ten pounds!)

For the first time ever since the station's inception, there were no flying boats at Seletar – nor indeed were there any left anywhere in the Royal Air Force. Sunderlands did continue to serve in other parts of the world, with other air forces, and it was a very nostalgic moment in 1965 when a flight of these still magnificent aircraft paid a final visit to Seletar. They were remnants of the sixteen refurbished ex-RAF aircraft (eight ex-Seletar[55]), which had been bought by the Royal New Zealand Air Force in 1953, on the recommendation of their then Chief of Staff, AVM DV Carnegie, CB CBE AFC, his love of flying boats still evident. In 1928, "Andy" Carnegie had been with the Far East Flight, and had been Captain of "the first seaplane club in the British Empire," at Seletar, back in those pioneering days.

With 81 Squadron having packed their bags and taken their Meteors and Pembrokes across to Tengah back in March of 1958, this meant there were now no fully operational squadrons based at Seletar. But on April 6th 1959, the first hint of a new role was given when Air Headquarters Malaya left Kuala Lumpur, to reform at Seletar as Headquarters 224 Group. For the past six years it had been the operational Command for all the Commonwealth Air Forces taking part in the campaign against the communist terrorists.

Then, in October, Seletar was back in business, 209 Squadron returning, also from Kuala Lumpur, bringing with it five single-engined Pioneers and two Twins. The balance of its aircraft, four single Pioneers and a Pembroke, were scheduled to remain at KL for the time being, still engaged on "Firedog" operations. The squadron's two Penang-based Dakotas continued to broadcast their messages from the sky, advising retreating terrorists in northern Malaya to "Come out and surrender". In two months the squadron would begin activities in Borneo, this time in the transport support role.

On December 8th 1959, Seletar's new church hall was officially opened by Mrs P.A. Hughes, wife of the then Station Commander; it had been a long time coming. With the original church having been destroyed during the war, make-shift arrangements had served ever since; C of E and Catholic religions sharing a corrugated iron structure, converted from decontamination centre into dual-religion church in 1947. In the meantime, numerous attempts had been made to improve the situation, but only in 1957 did the Air Ministry approve funds for the construction of a new church. Assured that this would reach fruition during the early 60's, the

One of Seletar's three-storey barrack blocks. *Author*

One of the last Beaufighters prepares for a sortie over Malaya.

Chaplain and Parochial Church Council decided to proceed with the building of an associated church hall, and by way of donations, collections and sales, the necessary funds were raised.

February 1960 saw the last visit to Seletar by Countess Mountbatten of Burma. She was shown around Station Sick Quarters and made a tour of the Families Clinic at Serangoon. The whole visit was reported as being a happy and memorable affair, which made the shocking news of the Countess' death, just three days later, hardly believable.

• • • • • • • • • •

Last Flight of the Beaufighter?

Seletar was changing in many ways, although its function as a major MU was retained, as was, so it seemed, its penchant for staging honourable last-flights. The previous six years had seen the demise of the Spitfire, Mosquito, and Sunderland. Now it was the turn of Bristol's Beaufighter – known as "Whispering Death" to the Japanese – another event well worth recording. The Beaufighter had been the first night fighter powerful enough to take advantage of airborne interceptor radar, and the first versions had been issued to Fighter Command in the spring of 1940. Over five and a half thousand had eventually been built, the very last flying on target-towing duties from Seletar. The final sorties were flown by RD761 and RD809 on May 16th 1960, with an around the island flypast being made by F/O H. Marshall in RD761, a TT Mk10 belonging to the combined, Station and Target Towing Flight, a day or so later. And within a few hours of landing, that aircraft was said to have been

reduced to scrap, bringing to an end twenty years of Beaufighter service. Or was it?[56]

• • • • • • • • • •

1960 was also to witness the final Queen's Birthday parade to be held at Seletar – June 11th, on the main runway – and the seventeenth birthday of the Seletar Malcolm Club, a party being held on August 26th to celebrate the event. But the greatest cause for celebration must have been the culmination of the Malayan Emergency. After twelve long years, this was declared to have ended on July 31st, all "Firedog" designated operations ceasing from that date. The motto of the Far East Flying Boat Wing, "Defenders of Freedom" could well have been applied, not only to the men and women of Seletar, but to all those who fought against the Communists during the period of the Emergency. A defeat for communism, many experts agree, in which air power had been one of the decisive factors. A conflict that could well have ended differently, had it not been for the RAF's contribution.

The enemy within had been defeated, next to be faced, would be the enemy without.

ROYAL AIR FORCE
SELETAR

Open Day
Saturday 20th September
1958

COMMEMORATING
THE
BATTLE OF BRITAIN

PRICE 50 CTS.

OFFICIAL PROGRAMME

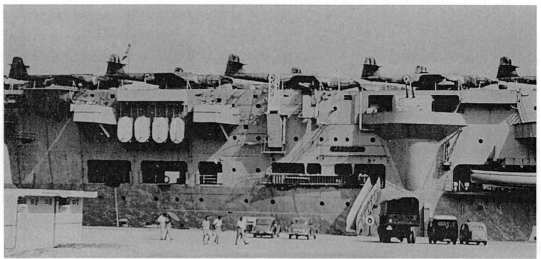

Meteors arrive in Singapore aboard a Royal Navy aircraft carrier. **Bill Richardson**

Before the days of in-flight refuelling, most of Seletar's arrivals and departures were by sea. Here a Meteor is picked up to be loaded aboard a barge for shipment from the naval base. On arrival at Seletar they would be offloaded on the slipway. A late mark Spitfire gets the same treatment. **Bill Richardson**

CHAPTER TWELVE

The Sixties & Beyond:
Confrontation

.... the government of the Federation of Malaya will afford the Government of the United Kingdom right to maintain bases at Singapore for the purpose of assisting in the defence of Malaysia and for Commonwealth defence and for the preservation of peace in South-East Asia.

(Extract from joint statement issued in London by Prime Minister MacMillan and Tunku Abdul Rahman, on November 22nd, 1961.)

● ● ● ● ● ● ● ● ● ●

The early sixties saw increased military expansion taking place on Singapore Island, Royal Air Force bases to the fore. Changi, for instance, apart from accommodating Far East Air Force headquarters and the RAF hospital, also became the main transport base in South-East Asia, and a major stopover on the UK – Australia run. Tengah's development as a jet fighter and bomber station was equally rapid, with new types to the area entering service.

As for Seletar, it just grew and grew until it was reputed to be numerically the largest single establishment in the Royal Air Force, although it was once again being commanded by a Group Captain. (The practice of an Air Commodore commanding the station – which became the norm after re-occupation by the RAF in 1946 – appears to have survived only until mid 1951.) Seletar's growth began in 1960, it's maintenance units once again becoming independent entities. 389 MU formed the main Royal Air Force equipment base in the Far East, stocking well over two hundred thousand separate items;

everything from clothing to furniture, vehicles, munitions, aircraft. Its storage areas were eventually to occupy almost one third of the station site. 389 MU Headquarters were located in the ex flying boat hangars, opposite the slipway and yacht club – close to the site of the original Station HQ's. 390 MU also covered many acres, its motto, "Repair to Prepare" adequately describing its aims. It had a need for those large tracts of land and numerous hangars, being required to provide deep servicing back-up – ie: repair, refurbishment, modification and salvage – of all aircraft and associated equipment in use in FEAF, as well as for aircraft of the Army and naval aviation units in the Far East. In other words, Seletar was required to carry spares for all the aircraft of all services, an array which at that time included: Javelins (60 Sqn), Hunters (20 Sqn) and Canberra's (84 Sqn), from Tengah; the Changi operated Hastings, and later, Hercules (48 Sqn), Shackleton (205 Sqn), Argosy (215 Sqn),along with the Britannias and Comets passing through on their way to and from Australia and elsewhere. Then there were the Austers and Beavers of the Army Air Corps, not forgetting Seletar's own squadrons: Beverley (34 Sqn), Single and Twin Pioneer (209 Sqn), Belvedere (66Sqn), and the Whirlwinds and Sycamores (110/230 Sqns), quite an array all told. The vast numbers of servicemen and civilians required to be based there accounted for it being largest unit on the island. According to Air Chief Marshal Sir Robert Freer, who as a

Grp Cpt was Station Commander from August 1963 to July 1966, the total population of Seletar grew and grew, until at one time it was in the order of fifteen thousand people, including dependants. But Seletar was not solely a gigantic maintenance unit, for there were now no fewer than six flying squadrons based there, along with one Surface-to-Air missile squadron; No.65, with its Bloodhounds. On top of this were to be found, 15 Army Air Dispatch Regiment – along with 130 Flight and their Beaver aircraft; FEAF Mobile Air Movements Squadron; 51 Field Squadron (Airfields) Royal Engineers – ex 5001 Airfield Construction Unit, RAF; 1124 Marine Craft Unit; 15 (Field) Squadron RAF Regiment; Headquarters of 224 Group – a formidable line up.

Naturally, this growth brought with it numerous administrative problems, particularly as far as the accommodation of families was concerned. With a dire lack of facilities on the station, a big drive was made to find suitable homes in the surrounding area, a lot being housed on the nearby estates at Jalan Kayu, Seletar Heights, and Serangoon Gardens. Even so, some people were still forced to live up to sixteen miles away. This entailed two long tiring journeys per day through Singapore's bustling traffic.

This influx of families created a host of ancillary problems, such as the requirement for a number of auxiliary services. Clinics needed to be set up, creating a requirement for extra medical staff; these being brought out from the UK. Additionally, existing hospital facilities at Changi were extended, thus creating the RAF Hospital, Far East, a large, modern establishment which served all bases in Singapore. Extra schools were another priority, the number of children seeking places was stretching existing capacity to bursting point. The situation required urgent action, and in May, 1963, a new grammar school opened its doors at Changi, Seletar chipping in with a secondary modern school the following year. It all took time. Moreover, with the grammar school being at Changi, and a lot of children living away from Seletar, there was a need for the MT section to provide an efficient bus service that covered almost half the island. (As long ago as 1957, I recall being on "school bus duty," and in those days we were armed. Never did figure out if that ancient Lee Enfield was meant as protection for the kids, or to protect us from them.)

Not only did Changi provide for the grammar school education of the RAF in Singapore, but the village outside the camp gates was *the* place on the island to shop for a bargain: Charlie Photo Store; Curly's Ever Green Store (Charlie and Curly had their bases covered, so to speak, for both also had branches in Jalan Kayu, though for some reason the prices always seemed to be lower at Changi); Sew On Tong shoe store – for the ever-popular "Desert boots"; Hup Hing Watch Maker – clocks, watches & gramophone (or "music box") repairers; and for all your uniform requirements, Bombay Silk Store. But I reckon Seletar had the edge when it came to the matter of *makan*. Unless it was egg and chips you were after – Changi Milk Bar, egg and chips, seventy-five cents (about 30p) – nothing in Changi could match "Pop's," the Indian curry shop on Jalan Kayu. It was in this rickety, open-fronted affair that my room mate had first introduced me to the delights of the curry platter. Here the air was spiced with a combination of coriander, turmeric, cumin, chilies, garlic. Not an English smell. A different form of cooking from a different land.

So here we were, 1960, the Emergency now declared to be at an end, yet the station was expanding dramatically. Who would have believed such a thing? Indeed, many suspected there would have been a reduction if anything; just as well there wasn't, as things turned out.

By the end of 1960, Seletar was once more well on the way to becoming fully operational as a short and medium range transport base. 34 Squadron had transferred across from Changi, bringing with it the massive Blackburn Beverley freighter, and the Pioneers of 209 Squadron were already resident.

By now, Seletarville had a much needed community centre, and in December, at long last, the foundation stone for that promised, long-awaited C of E church was laid. The station even had a new gymnasium; the camp appeared to be settling in for a period of peace. There was the Sea Angling Club, where catches during competitions were usually weighed in ounces by the thousand, and the Kingfishers swimming club had quite a reputation. There were clubs for rowing, yachting, and power boating, and the golf club had been thriving for years. There were also clubs for bowling, judo, table tennis, football, rugby, cricket, darts, badminton, photography, motoring; you name it, Seletar had it.

Even the international scene in Asia seemed to be settling down to a period of peaceful coexistence, apart from the odd incident, one of which occurred on December 17th, 1960. That was the day 34 Squadron were ordered to despatch an aircraft to Laos. It was to carry medical teams and supplies, eventually flying a total of almost forty hours, taking in medical aid and food, etc, bringing out refugees – including the Dutch, Russian, and French Ambassadors.

This apart, the outlook looked fairly promising. "Up country," the remaining communists were still quietly and efficiently being "mopped up," while on the political front, first reference to the possibility of combining Malaya, Singapore, and the Borneo territories into a wider federation was voiced in May1961.

Helicopters had been associated with Seletar throughout the Emergency, 389 MU being responsible for the assembly and issue to squadron service of the majority, if not all, of FEAF's rotary winged aircraft: Dragonfly – RAF Casualty Evacuation Flight (Changi, 1950); Sycamore – 194 Sqn (KL, 1953-58); Whirlwind – 155/110 Sqn (Mk4 – KL, 1954-58/Butterworth, 1958-60, Mk10 – 1963-71. But in April, 1962, Seletar was to acquire its first operational helicopter unit when the Belvederes of 66 Squadron arrived; long, twin-rotor affairs, to which the locals in Borneo attached the name, "Flying Longhouse". These aircraft went into action almost immediately, supporting operations against the surviving terrorists, who were now operating from across the Thai border. 34 Squadron was also active that year, one operation revealing what the Beverley was really capable of by transporting an entire unit, 20 Squadron (Hunters), to the Thai – Laos border during the civil war that was threatening to spill over into Thailand; a fair demonstration of the aircraft's load carrying capacity.

But it wasn't to last, and the relative calm was once more disturbed when, on December 8th, 1962, a rebellion broke out in the independent State of Brunei – a British Protectorate. The implications of this uprising completely threatened the fulfilment of a dream – the creation of

The waterfront in 1959 from the top of the radio mast. Marine craft section & yacht club but no longer any flying boats.   ***Peter A Hughes***

Malaysia. The contentious issues were Brunei's basically autonomous government – the Sultan himself – and the suggestion that the State may join the proposed Malaysia. The oil town of Seria was now effectively under the control of armed dissidents, as were police stations in the villages just inside the border with Sarawak.

Seeking refuge in Brunei's main police station, the Sultan immediately asked Britain for assistance in restoring law and order. In accordance with the terms of its defence agreement with the tiny State, the response from Westminster was immediate. Within hours, 34 Squadron had three troop-and-vehicle-laden Beverleys airborne, with orders to proceed to Brunei airport, and within twenty-four hours 209 Squadron had five of their Twin Pioneers on detachment at the offshore island of Labuan, twenty miles off the coast of North Borneo. This small staging post, its runway capable of taking the largest jets, was destined to assume operational importance over the next few years, becoming a station in its own right.

The first of the Beverley aircraft, piloted by Sqn/Ldr Bennett, had departed Seletar at 14:45 hours. By 19:15 it had landed, its complement of Gurkhas disembarked, ready for battle.

The whole operation had been a triumph of efficient organization as far as Seletar was concerned, requiring, as it did, the co-operation of almost every aspect of the station's facilities. The equipment section in particular were worked hard, some of their personnel putting in well over twenty-four hours continuous duty during the initial stages. A special Transit Centre had been set up, chiefly for the kitting-out and arming of personnel on the Brunei detachment, and to take care of all air movements.

The results achieved were nothing less than spectacular. A particular highlight was undoubtedly the operation which took place on December 10th. After reconnoitring the area, air assault landings were made at Seria by five Twin Pioneers and a Beverley. The "Twin Pins" were able to land on open ground by the police station, their troops quickly disembarking to recapture the town. The Beverley had no option but to use the rebel-held strip of Anduki. Making a low approach along the coast, to avoid detection – quite a feat in a Beverley – the pilot pulled up over the trees at the last moment, touched down and braked to a halt using less than a quarter of the runway. In doing so it did receive a couple of hits from an automatic weapon located in the control tower – the rebel's reply to a "permission to land" request, maybe? – but the troops safely disembarked, rushing off to recapture the strip. The Beverley then executed an immediate short-field take-off becoming airborne after a stay of well under two minutes.

Prompt action by the British, with the immediate dispatch by air of troops from Singapore, had proved to be very effective, the revolt being crushed within days. But it became almost immediately apparent that, Indonesia – having probably instigated the unrest in Brunei – was certainly intent on pursuing the policy. With her national press backing the rebels, her Government officially announced support for these, "new emerging forces." Less than a month later, President Sukarno was expressing strong opposition to the "Malaysia" project, and had very soon inserted the Indonesian word "Konfrontasi" in the dictionary of political jargon.

Indonesian guerrillas now moved over the border into Sarawak, and with help from the local communist element, attacked villages and police stations. With British and Malayan forces committed to safeguarding the Sarawak border so as to counter such attacks, Seletar's helicopter force was to find itself deployed away from base. It was to remain away for some years.

34 and 209 Squadrons, were, during this initial phase of Confrontation, concerned with the build-up of troops, vehicles, servicing personnel and equipment on Labuan island, along with the aerial resupply of the border patrols in Sarawak. 66 Squadron's Belvederes soon joined the fray, departing Seletar on December 17th to carry out trooping, freighting, casualty evacuation and reconnaissance operations. Other helicopters were dispatched to the area, either under their own power, or being carried across. On Christmas Eve, two Beverleys departed Butterworth

carrying three Sycamores of 110 Squadron. Twenty-four hours later, after being off-loaded and reassembled, they were flying on operations.

Indonesian guerrillas began to increase their infiltration of the North Borneo territories of Sabah and Sarawak in April 1963, penetrating the border and stepping up their raids, but the worst violence did not occur until after the establishment of Malaysia, on September 16th. (Malaya, Singapore, Sabah and Sarawak; Brunei opting out at the last minute.) On the 17th, thousands of Indonesian demonstrators stormed the British and Malaysian Embassies in Djakarta, and in Medan, North Sumatra, the Consulates of both countries were sacked; Indonesia was clearly not happy about something!

Two days later, the British Embassy in Djakarta again faced the wrath of the locals, a huge mob sacking and burning the building. They then went on to wreck and loot the homes of British subjects. Because of the depth of anti-British feeling, the Ambassador in Djakarta, Mr A. Gilchrist, recommended that all British subjects should leave the country, and, with the consent of the Indonesian Government, an airlift began. It was operated by 34 Squadron's Beverleys, assisted by other RAF transport aircraft and a Qantas 707. Within twenty-four hours, over four hundred women and children had been evacuated to Singapore. Some later told of Indonesians running amok, screaming, "Kill the British" and, "Crush Malaysia." Rioting mobs had ransacked, looted and burned their homes. One evacuee described how children of an Indonesian neighbour had hidden her under their bed, saving her from the howling mob that was burning down her home.

Britain informed Malaysian Prime Minister Tunku Abdul Rahman she was prepared to assist in defending Malaysia's independence, under the terms of the Mutual Assistance Treaty. The build-up at Labuan continued, and by year's end British and Commonwealth forces were ready to face any threat.

No.5001 Airfield Construction Unit (Light) RAF had moved to Seletar during 1963, and on August 1st, 103 Squadron's number plate was transferred to the station when the Whirlwind flight of 110 Squadron – already resident – was enlarged and given squadron status. Amid all the support being given by Seletar's squadrons and MU's to the troops in Borneo, one heroic act occurred on the station in June; totally unrelated to the Confrontation. An explosion occurred in the cockpit of a Gloster Javelin, causing a fire. Chief Technician C.T. Yates immediately climbed into the burning fighter, disconnecting the batteries and directing a ground party to bring the fire under control. His "courage and presence of mind" resulted in him being awarded the Queen's Commendation for brave conduct. Recalling the episode, Ch/Tech Yates paid tribute to his Royal Air Force training. 'My action was instinctive and part of my training. Anyone could have done it.'

Another fire of the period was to have more disastrous results for one specific section of the community.

Ever since its inception, in 1949, the Theatre Club had always been an important feature at Seletar. Born in a Nissen hut, later productions were staged at the Astra Cinema, a modest, purpose-built theatre appearing in only 1957. Disaster struck, when, on August 6th, 1963, fire broke out in a backstage store-room, and by the time the resultant conflagration had been brought under control, little remained. Stage, auditorium, workshop, foyer and lighting box, were totally destroyed. With only the clubroom and dressing rooms remaining intact, club members resigned themselves to the task of starting again. Insurance money, supplemented by generous donations from the Nuffield Foundation and various station funds, plus a degree of resolve, were enough to build a newer, more modern theatre, which was later to become one of the most active drama groups in South-East Asia. In the mid-1960s an airwoman photographic interpreter with a pronounced Berkshire accent was said to be a member, Pam Ayres actually served at Seletar.

The build-up at Seletar continued into 1964, a time when Singapore was once again living under the threat of attack from the air. Now they were better equipped to deal with such a threat, for 65 Squadron had been established at Seletar back on January 1st, the RAF's first overseas Surface-to-Air Missile (SAM) squadron. Equipped with the Bristol Bloodhound, the squadron became responsible for the installation of the missile complex, and for carrying out the tropical and environment trials such a sophisticated weapon system required.

Six days after the arrival of 65 Sqn, the Whirlwind contingent of 110 Sqn moved from Butterworth to Seletar – to be followed in October by the Sycamore Flight. In April, the De Havilland Beavers of No.15 Air Dispatch Regiment were based at Seletar, although for the next three years, they too would operate out of Borneo. Also arriving at Seletar in 1964 were the seasoned jungle fighters of No.15 (Field) Sqn RAF Regiment, moving across from Changi, where they had been based for the past four years.

These additional reinforcements had arrived just in time to counter punitive attempts by Indonesia to carry the war onto the Malaysian mainland. Several incidents occurred on Singapore Island, and during April 1963, guerrillas landed on the Malay peninsular, but lacking popular support they were quickly eliminated. A second attempt was made early on the morning of August 17th, but the one hundred men who came in from the sea to land at Pontian, southwest Johore, suffered a similar fate to the first group. On September 2nd, a more serious incursion took place when an Indonesian Hercules managed not only to penetrate Malaysian airspace, but dropped a large group of parachutists – again believed to have numbered around one hundred – in Labis, central Johore. If a transport plane could approach and complete such a mission, presumably strike aircraft would find it much easier. With the realization that Singapore was once again living under the threat of an attack from the air, airfield defence was stepped up, and at Seletar, 65 (SAM) Squadron was ordered to place one section of Bloodhound missiles on immediate readiness. (Exactly two years after their arrival at Seletar, 65 would also

deploy an operational missile section to Kuching, and in the months following, up to the end of the Confrontation, most of the missile crews would have served in the operational area.)

Seletar's aircraft had been active in opposing these incursions. 209 Sqn's Pioneers had maintained effective communications and reconnaissance at Labin, with helicopters from 66, 103, and 110 Squadrons providing tactical support. RAF aircraft, in conjunction with those of the Army and Navy, came under the centralized control of the Army. The rapid deployment of helicopters and Pioneers enabled our troops to isolate, and, in time, account for all the Indonesians. Similarly, the terrorists at Pontian were demoralized and rounded up, this operation being assisted by air strikes from Hunters, and voice broadcasts by the Pioneers.

The pace of activity at Seletar was increasing, with 1964 proving to be a busy year for the RAF. By now it was clear that the Indonesians had little hope of making headway in Malaysia, and that its leaders were determined to stand firm. Mr Lee Kuan Yew, the dynamic Prime Minister of Singapore, was certainly showing the kind of attitude appreciated by the British forces. This became apparent in the way his government quickly dealt with rioters and restored the situation after civil disorder broke out on the island in July – a situation that was bad enough to require all service personnel living in Jalan Kayu to be moved into the camp perimeter. It was therefore quite an occasion when, on August 4th, Mr Lee Kuan Yew, accompanied by one of his Ministers, Mr Rajaratnam, visited Seletar to address civilian employees on the Seletarville Padang.

On the offshore islands to the south, Indonesian artillery began to fire indiscriminately on any aircraft approaching or departing Singapore, forcing airlines to deviate their flights from the regular airway which passed close by these islands.

Given the strength of the air defence mechanism, no attacks were attempted, but the threat was ever present, so defensive measures could not be relaxed.

On the step. With the front turret now locked in the in-flight position, RN303 Romeo, charges down the Straits. A safety launch would sweep the area to ensure it was clear of debris. The danger at night was local fishermen straying across the take-off run!
Author

The Sunderland graveyard, within sight of F block.
Ron Wilkinson

The Sunderland cockpit. A basic blind flying panel with the addition of a radio altimeter and the remote reading compass of the DRC.

Conditions were not always so good, and with a bit of sea the transfer from launch to aircraft could be exciting.
Author

Tail trolley failure, and at this stage of the game, 1958, those wrinkles told the story; the aircraft was a write-off.
Author

Seletar's squadrons were still in the thick of things over in Borneo, and transport aircraft were kept busy on the route between Singapore and Labuan. The work wasn't always repetitious and dangerous, and jobs would occasionally drift away from the routine, a different kind of challenge being presented. In an article for the *Voice*, Seletar's last station magazine, Flt/Lt D. May, of 34 Squadron stated that, *'among the more unusual loads were a consignment of cats to rid a village of a plague of mice, and live chickens to Ghurkha troops for religious ceremonies.'*

The carrying of Ghurkha families could also present problems, the passengers themselves sometimes creating the hazard, as recalled by one Beverley pilot. 'We had a number of wives aboard, and during the trip one of them decided to "brew up," extracting a primus from beneath the folds of her robe and stoking up in the gangway! I nearly had a coronary at the time,' he said, 'but as so many other crews experienced the same thing, the story doesn't even raise a laugh these days.'

Perhaps even more devastating an experience is that of the 209 Squadron pilot who, in May 1963, took off with three passengers aboard his Single Pioneer, and arrived at his destination with four; a baby girl being born en route. Too good an opportunity to miss, a unknown "friend" sent a telegram advising that "Mother, pilot and baby are all doing well." But even this episode would not cause the average helicopter pilot to blink, for babies seemed frequently to be born on their flights, one pilot keeping score on the cockpit side, in storks.

From January to October 1966, helicopters in Borneo flew more than two hundred and forty casualty evacuation sorties. Such invaluable flights have always been standard with the type, "Casevac" being the original role of the aircraft. Even so, it took some time before "choppers" came to be accepted by the aborigines. That they eventually did was proved the day one elderly native, after agreeing to be flown out of the jungle, refused to be transferred from the airfield by ambulance because "it didn't have a propeller on top." It was the first time in his life he had left his village, and he had never before seen any vehicle but a helicopter.

Early in 1964, 110 Sqn were to find themselves detailed for a rather unusual task, to be known as "Operation Eagle." In order to improve their poor coverage, Sabah Radio planned to build a relay station and associated power-house, nine and a half thousand feet up Mount Kinabulu, the highest mountain in South-East Asia. Sqn/Ldr Eley flew up with a reconnaissance party, and, after waiting some time for the cloud to clear, managed to set down – the landing zone (LZ) being at the six thousand five hundred feet level. They then found themselves stranded for six and a half hours when a wind shift swiftly brought the clouds back down. It was some months before deployment of the installation was ready to begin, Flt/Lt Lord and Master Pilot Leyden flying dozens of sorties to lift sixty-one thousand pounds of equipment – including some very expensive radio parts and switchgear – to a height of eight thousand feet, under treacherous conditions. But the station became successfully operational in August, and the Royal Air Force had enhanced its reputation in the area.

Flying over tropical jungle always had the potential of being hazardous, and there were several unfortunate and extremely unpleasant accidents. One problem faced by aircrew forced to bail out over such territory was that they were liable to end over two hundred feet up, parachute snagged in the jungle canopy. With rescue from such a position impossible by helicopter, and unlikely by land, the unfortunate airman would be faced with a no-go choice: die of dehydration, or chance falling 200ft to the jungle floor. Thus it was that then AOC FEAF, Air Commodore Greenham, directed the General Engineering Flight at 390 MU, Seletar, to design a device with which an airman could safely lower himself from such a height. It had to be both small enough and light enough for aircrew to wear at all times. With Sqn/Ldr Pricket of GEF producing the initial design, to be further developed by Ch/Tech George Reeve, they eventually produced the "Treescape", a device that – now much modified – is still in use in jungle areas.

Never for one moment did the men of the Royal Air Force flinch from their responsibilities. Throughout the whole period of Confrontation they continued in the traditions of an Air Force which had won respect over the whole of South-East Asia. (It is a little known fact that the RAF School of Jungle Warfare, based over the Straits, in Johore, actually trained units of the American Forces in the art of jungle fighting, readying them for service in Vietnam.)

As 1966 entered its twilight months so confrontation faded to a conclusion, the increasingly powerless President Sukarno apparently the only person unhappy with the outcome. Seletar's aircraft had operated in Borneo throughout the entire three years, and even a superficial examination of the contribution made by this base alone shows how invaluable the Royal Air Force was to the whole campaign.

Statistics for 110 Squadron alone reveal something of the extent of the effort. Between December 1962, to the end of September 1965, the squadron's aircraft logged almost seven thousand flying hours during the course of nineteen thousand plus sorties. Over forty-one thousand troops were carried, along with well over three million pounds of freight and five hundred plus casualties. 110's achievements were honoured by the award of a Squadron Standard at Seletar on December 3rd, 1965. The squadron badge, the heraldic Hyderabad Tiger, and the motto "Nec Timeo Nec Sperno" (I do not fear, neither do I spurn) are surrounded by selected Battle Honours: Independent Force and Germany 1918; Channel and North Sea 1939 – 1940; Norway 1940; France and Low Countries 1940; Malta 1941; Fortress Europe 1940 – 1942; Arakan 1943 – 1944; Burma 1945.

Once again peace had returned to this corner of South-East Asia; although not too far distant, war was raging away in Vietnam.

The surprise secession of Singapore from Malaysia the previous year did not alter the position of the bases on the island, since Mr Lee Kuan Yew had promised to retain close economic and defence co-operation with Malaysia, and asked that the British bases should remain intact; but history is continually being written, changes always taking place.

In December 1966, three Hawker Siddeley Andovers of 52 Squadron arrived at Seletar from RAF Abingdon, Oxfordshire. These short-range tactical transport aircraft were to replace 34 Squadron and their Beverleys by the end of 1967, until which time both squadrons would fly from Seletar alongside the Pioneers, helicopters and Beavers belonging to the other units based there.

209 Squadron celebrated its 50th Anniversary on February 1st, 1967. With twenty-one of those years having been spent at Seletar, it was therefore appropriate that the Reviewing Officer for the occasion was AVM P. de L. Le Cheminant, DFC, who, as a Squadron Leader, had commanded the squadron here during its 1949-51 Sunderland era.

The squadron also took the opportunity of paying tribute to German fighter ace Rittmeister Manfred Freiherr von Richthofen, the "Red Baron" of the First World War. One of 209 Squadron's pilots had been credited with shooting down von Richthofen in 1918. To commemorate the episode, craftsmen at Seletar built an almost life-size replica of the German's Fokker Triplane, especially for the Anniversary. The squadron was also able to invite His Excellency Oswald Baron von Richthofen to the ceremony, as "Guest of Honour." By remarkable coincidence, this second cousin of the Red Baron just happened to be the German Ambassador to Singapore at the time.

It appeared in some respects as though the station was now returning to those heady, between-wars days of the Thirties, when everyone who was anyone seemed to visit Seletar. In August 1967 it was the World Champion Table Tennis team from Japan. They visited the station to give an exhilarating exhibition to a packed gymnasium. A few months earlier an English First Division Football Team had dropped in. Over the years all manner of people had visited Seletar: the upper ranks of the services, Princes, Rajahs, Prime Ministers and even Kings, all had paid their respects, but perhaps no visit was so poignant as that made in the January of 1967.

The occasion of 205 Squadron's 50th Anniversary was to be an historical moment all round. Although no longer based at Seletar, for most of its long and distinguished service in the Far East it had been so; the very first of Seletar's many squadrons. So what could be more appropriate than they invite Group Captain GE Livock, DFC AFC, to be Reviewing Officer for the occasion. He had after all been the first man to fly over Seletar, as well as being the first RAF officer to set foot on the base. He had been lead pilot of the Far East Flight, and the first RAF officer to command the station. Thirty-five years after departing Seletar, Gerry Livock was about to make a memorable journey "home."

The invitation had been eagerly accepted by Grp/Cpt Livock, who, along with his wife, had retired to Blandford, Dorset. A programme was quickly drawn up, a uniform purchased and a flight booked through the RAF at Lyneham; a Britannia on the Changi Slip would carry him back to Singapore.

With the anniversary celebrations due to take place at Changi – 205 Sqn's present base – Grp/Cpt TWA Hutton, OBE DFC, Officer Commanding RAF Seletar, arranged for a special dining-in night to commemorate the occasion. Unfortunately, Gerry Livock's arrival was delayed, the aircraft carrying him experiencing problems en route. Now, not due to arrive at RAF Changi before 18:20 hours on the evening of his commemorative dinner – thirty-six hours behind schedule – a message had duly been signalled from Seletar whilst the travel-weary guest was still airborne. The basis of this message was that, in view of his lengthy journey it would be quite understandable if he couldn't make it. But Gerry Livock was not one to let such an opportunity pass by, and, barely hours after his arrival on the island, he was occupying a place of honour at the top table. After the meal, Grp/Cpt Hutton said how delighted everyone was to see their guest, particularly after such an exhausting trip. Then, to an ovation which lasted for several minutes, Grp/Cpt Livock, obviously moved by his reception, went on to say, 'The last time I made the journey out here we didn't have any trouble. The flight just took a little longer, that's all!'

The party that night was described as being one of the most delightful ever to be held at Seletar, and the next day Grp/Cpt Livock reviewed "his squadron" at Changi. During the memorable week which followed, he was taken on conducted tours of both Seletar and the island, revisiting many of his old haunts, before finally returning to England.

Forty-three years separated Grp/Cpt Livock's first and last visits to Singapore. They had been forty-three colourful and historic years for Seletar, the Royal Air Force, and South-East Asia. Whatever the future had in store, the Royal Air Force could already look back on this base with pride, as could the men who had worked and flown from there. Its place in aviation history was already assured

Although Confrontation had ended in August 1966, it was 1968 before the Royal Malaysian Air Force was ready to take over control of Labuan, so Seletar's squadrons remained actively detached.

The ill-fated VP254. 205 Sqn Shackleton that mysteriously disappeared on December 8th 1958.   **Author**

Photo from an RAF Seletar Xmas card, undated, but judging by the formation, pre 1959.   **Peter Cox**

The ex flying boat area in 1970 during the disbandment ceremony for 1124 Marine Craft Unit on October 1st.
Seletar "Voice"

Seletar Yacht Club as viewed from the top of the flying boat hangar. Note radio station over in the trees, the swimming pool was also located in this area. ***Seletar Yacht Club***

CHAPTER THIRTEEN

An Uncertain Future:
The RAF Departs

Rumours were rife during the early months of 1967, seemingly every man and his dog speculating over, not only Seletar's future, but that of the whole of the Far East Air Force. Economies proposed for the British Government's defence expenditure made reference to the possible closing down of Seletar, as did several articles in the British press. There was, however, as yet, no official confirmation...

...Until, in July of that year, the government published what they called a Supplementary Statement on Defence Policy, in which it was announced that:

> We plan to withdraw altogether from our bases in Singapore and Malaysia in the middle 1970's; the precise timing of our eventual withdrawal will depend on progress made in achieving a new basis for stability in the South-East Asia, and in resolving other problems in the Far East.

As if in confirmation, Tengah's Javelins were being phased out, as were 215 Squadron, flying the Argosy from Changi, all part of the reductions. 1967 saw 64 Squadron disbanding, their remaining aircraft being transferred to 60 Squadron, also at Tengah. Less than a year later, it was the turn of 60 Squadron itself, the remains of the Javelin fleet ending up at Seletar as training airframes for the fledgeling Singapore Air Force, for which Seletar was now a technical training base. Then, even though it had been announced back in 1966, the axe again fell on December

31st, 1967. 34 Sqn's seven year spell at Seletar came to an end, its Beverley aircraft – after claiming yet another final operational flight for the station – dispersing or being scrapped, the squadron disbanding.

Adverse weather was to feature strongly in the 34 Sqn's disbandment, for not only was the parade – scheduled for Jan 5th – cancelled due to intermittent showers, the ceremonies were also clouded by the fact that the squadron had suffered their first loss only sixteen days previously, a Beverley crashing in mountainous North Central Malaya. The sad details are recorded in the squadron's operational diary, F540:

Friday 15th (Dec, 1967)

The crew (of XL150) took off around 10:00 for a practice run for the Bennett Trophy. It ought to have landed around 11:45 but with the weather as it was, a slight delay would not have been unusual. At 12:38, the Ops Officer instigated overdue action. The aircraft was then "Missing." The first reaction was bitterness – at flying in the existing conditions of low cloud and bad visibility, bitterness at the events' proximity to Christmas and the unit's disbandment. Then a slow feeling of fear mingled with horror as we recognised the closeness of the crew and their families. As the day wore on, the anxiety reluctantly rolled on to an acceptance of death. Beyond the melodrama, the worry, the hysteria and the calm, lay the cold fact that Sqn Ldr Bacon, F/Os Brodie and Hudson, and Sgts

Curtis, Trigwell and George, are missing. Even if they crash-landed, the odds against them surviving are colossal.

Sunday 17th.

Wreckage of 150 found by a "Twin Pin" of 209 at 02.32N 103.27E at a height of 1400' agl on the side of Bukit Kendok. (No survivors.)

Monday 1st January (1968)

Although officially we are no longer in existence, much activity is taking place around the squadron. Files to be destroyed, diaries to be completed, aircraft inventory to be handed over. Secondary duties to be re-allocated, offices to be emptied, telephones to be withdrawn... ad infinitum.....

Friday 5th

Our disbandment parade was cancelled owing to sporadic rain showers. The reception went off well.

• • • • • • • • • •

Although 34 Squadron could justifiably claim the last *operational* flight, Beverleys did continue to fly at Boscombe Down for some years to come, XB259 making last flight in RAF service in 1974.[57]

Then came another bitter blow, for in February 1968 the Government announced that the plans for the future of our bases in the Far East had been amended. The new policy was outlined in a White Paper on Defence, in which it was stated:

We shall accelerate the withdrawal of our forces from Malaysia and Singapore and complete it by the end of 1971.

It seemed as if the end of the Royal Air Force presence in Singapore was in sight, but with the establishment of a training centre for the air element of the Singapore Armed Forces over at West Camp, RAF Seletar, on June 17th, 1968, there was some hope that the base would continue to play a vital role in preserving the peace in South-East Asia.

Meantime, things went into a steady decline, with the cuts beginning to take effect amongst Seletar's flying squadrons, 209 Squadron disbanding in December 1968.

At 20:20hrs on March 28th 1969, upon completion of the exercise, Crowning Glory, the death knell finally sounded for Seletar's flying squadrons. At that hour, on that day, a 103 Squadron Whirlwind – crewed by Flt/Lt T. Lloyd, Flt/Lt B. Hall and Flt/Sgt J. Neal – departed Seletar from the lawn fronting the officers' mess, after which the airfield lights went out one by one. This symbolic event that was to mark Seletar's end as an RAF operational flying station, a role it had performed for the past forty-two years. The rest of 103 and 110 Squadrons' aircraft had already departed for Changi, 52 Squadron's Andovers having also previously redeployed there. March also saw the closure of JARIC (FE), after twenty eight years continuous service in the Far East.

As for 66 Squadron, it was disbanded, its Belvederes reduced to scrap, or ceded to the Republic of Singapore Air Force, to join those Javelins as training airframes, (all, that is, apart from "Oscar," XG474, an aircraft that has operated in all theatres in which the Belvedere has seen service. This airframe was transported back to the UK courtesy of the MOD, Royal Corps of Transport, and the Royal Navy, via the Commando Carrier, HMS *Albion*, and is now on display at the RAF Museum, Hendon). And so, to 66 Sqn fell the honour of being the last of the last; it flew the last operational Belvedere sortie, thus completing RAF Seletar's formidable list of last flights.

Although the run down continued, the station itself was far from finished. It still had a couple of years to function as an MU for the Far East Air Force, even if its personnel were forever being reminded that the end was nigh. With the Singapore Air Force taking control of ATC and Flying Wing HQ in April 1969, this did ensure that flying would continue at the base, embryo pilots of the Singapore defence forces puttering around on their initial training in civilian registered Cessnas, with only the occasional burst of obtrusive sound from an SAF Strikemaster, over from Paya Lebar for a few noisy circuits.

In May of that year, a further sixty buildings in West Camp were handed over to the Singapore Government for use by the SAF, and, sadly, August saw the last of Seletar's airwomen being posted out, the WRAF block being closed. In the year 2000, Mrs Jan Moore told me: "As SACW Jan Wake I was one of the last WRAF to serve at Seletar. There were about a dozen of us, led by F/Sgt Gerry Lynch. We had a massive 'de-WRAFing' party before we moved over to finish our tour's at Changi; not in the same league as the elegant lifestyle we led at Seletar, I'm afraid.

• • • • • • • • • •

No.15 Sqn RAF Regiment held their farewell parade in November 1969, although it was to be a further six months before their compound was handed over to the Singapore Government.

Next squadron in line for disbandment, in January, 1970, was 81 – long since transferred to Tengah, and one of the few squadrons to be based at one time or another at each of Singapore's three military airfields.

In May 1970 the final death knell was sounded by the announcement that RAF Seletar would close on March 31st 1971. To the shop-keepers in Jalan Kayu, a fixed date was absolute confirmation that the end was definitely nigh, and there was now real anxiety about the future. With eighty per cent of the village's business being generated by servicemen and their families, there were seen to be lean times ahead.

April, and it was the end for 65 Sqn. With their disbandment on March 31st, all their buildings and equipment were now handed over to the Singapore Government. And so the steady decline continued. July – closure of the infants school; August – the last AOC's inspection, this being carried out by AVM O.S. Hennock CBE DEF RAAF; September – Hygiene Section transferred to Singapore Ministry of Health; October – disbandment ceremony of 1124 Marine Craft Unit.

November 1st saw the closure of the Corporals' Club, Eros (airmen's club), and the ever-popular Malcolm Club. All were to be replaced the following day by a combined all ranks club known as, would you believe, the Fare-Well Club. This was expected to remain open until July/August 1971.

But the writing really was on the wall, and not just for Seletar, for with the advent of such aircraft in the transport fleet as the Comet, Britannia, Belfast and VC10, it meant a brigade of troops could be deployed almost anywhere within seven days, thus the need for expensive overseas bases was reduced considerably. And with the Cobham Group's advances in air-to-air refuelling, fighters could be on the scene even sooner.

An institution came to an end in January 1971, the RAF Seletar Yacht Club being taken over by the Singapore Armed Forces, and with the closure of the Officers' Mess in February, this must have really seemed like the end, or perhaps, for some, the beginning, for it re-opened at No.1 Park Lane, home of the original Mess back in 1929. Full circle.

An editorial in the February 1971 edition of the Seletar *Voice* stated:

One rumour that I would like to quash is that Voice *will finish next month. This is not true, although next month's issue will be a special one as March is the last month of RAF Seletar.*

It seems the March issue was very special indeed – it was the last, even if the editorial in that issue did state that the publisher had agreed to continue producing it – free of charge to the station – from April onwards to August.

October 31st, 1971 saw the end of Changi-based 205 Squadron – Seletar's, and the Far East Air Force's first ever squadron; appropriately, it had also been FEAF's last.

Seletar was transferred to the Singapore Government on March 30th, 1971, Changi on November 28th, and although this marked the end of the Far East Air Force, it wasn't quite the end of the Royal Air Force's presence in the Far East. An agreement had been drawn up between Australia, New Zealand and the United Kingdom

(ANZUK), along with Singapore and Malaysia, to ensure the defence of South East Asia. The RAF element, to be based at Tengah – now a base of the Singapore Air Force – was to consist of a detachment of helicopters (Whirlwinds of 103 Squadron), and one of maritime reconnaissance aircraft (ex 205 Sqn Shackletons, now carrying the 209 Sqn numberplate), these being replaced in January 1972, by Nimrods of 206 Squadron. This situation was however destined to be short-lived, for the 1975 Defence White Paper announced the government's intention to withdraw the British contribution to this force almost immediately. 103 Squadron was duly disbanded in August 1975, and the Nimrod detachment withdrawn back to the UK. As a result, the only remaining RAF presence in the Far East was 28 Squadron at Kai Tak, flying the Wessex HC Mk2 helicopter.

In a letter to the Air Crew Association magazine, *Intercom*, in 1989, Air Vice-Marshal Alec Maisner, CB CBE AFC, remarking on a series of articles which had previously appeared in their newsletters, wrote:

> '*Dear editor,*
>
> *As last Station Commander at RAF Seletar, I read with interest Raymond Flack's articles on the history of that station which appeared in recent numbers of the Intercom. I hope he will carry on with this history to cover also the postwar period until Seletar's closure in 1971.*'

The AVM then appended the following, as he thought it might provide a useful epilogue to this series of articles. I now use it as an epilogue to this book.

ROYAL AIR FORCE SELETAR FAREWELL CEREMONY – 30ᵀᴴ MARCH 1971
Address given by the Reviewing Officer, Air Vice-Marshal NM Maynard,
CB CBE DFC AFC RAF Commander Far East Air Force.

The ceremony we are participating in this evening marks the closing down of this, the oldest, and at one time the largest Royal Air Force Station in the Far East. Its history spans almost the entire period of existence of our service, since it was in 1921, only three years after the formation of the Royal Air Force, that the British Government decided to establish an air base in Singapore. The site they chose for it, then a rubber plantation bordered to the north by extensive mangrove swamps, is where we are this evening.

The long and illustrious history of Seletar is outlined in the programme ...

It was at Seletar then that the history of the Far East Air Force began, and it was here that the pattern and standards of Royal Air Force life in the Far East, which we follow by and large to this day, were first set.

Very few stations have known such a chequered career as this place, and not many housed such an amazing variety of units within their perimeter: in addition to the force of five to eight flying squadrons, Seletar contained at various times, the Royal Air Force Far East Command Headquarters, a Group Headquarters, a missile squadron, two large Engineering and Maintenance Units, a Marine Craft Unit, the Far East Joint Air Reconnaissance and Intelligence Centre, RAF Regiment squadrons, and several small, Army, Joint Service and RAF units. Over and above this, Seletar has also had parental responsibility for a number of units outside its boundary.

The picture which emerges from all this, is one which I, an erstwhile Commanding Officer of its sister station at Changi, always had and will retain, is that of a large, diversified and intensely active station, which has given valiant service in peace and war, during the Malayan Emergency and during Confrontation. Always a tough opponent on the sports field, Seletar has never been found wanting in the discharge of its wide support responsibilities to stations in the Command.

But now Seletar has been called upon in her own demise to lead the way in withdrawal. This – probably the most difficult and painful of all the operations and responsibilities which Seletar has had to discharge in the past – has also been accomplished with quiet skill and efficiency.

This is a sad moment for me, as I am sure it is for all of you, and the countless many who have served at Seletar over the years. But there are some thoughts which should help brighten our mood tonight. There is no doubt that Seletar's long, loyal and efficient service has firmly established her a place of honour in the history of the Royal Air Force, alongside such famous names as Shaibah, Habbaniya, Khormaksar and El Adem.

But in Seletar's case there is also the pride and satisfaction in which we all share, of knowing that most of the facilities and amenities which have been built-up here by the Royal Air Force, will continue to be used by units of the Singapore Armed Forces and by the various civilian firms which have established themselves here, and that the name of Seletar will continue for many years to come, to be associated with military and civil aviation activities in this part of the world.

It falls upon me now as the last Commander of the Far East Air Force to say, on behalf of myself and all my predecessors, to you remaining personnel and all your predecessors: "Thank you for a job well done." You and your predecessors have made a part of Royal Air Force history, and in doing so you have enhanced the name of the Royal Air Force, and of the Far East Air Force. The move of the Royal Air Force from Seletar is the end of an era, and a very great era. But it is encouraging to know that this great organisation will continue to function under a new management, albeit in a somewhat different role.

So I would like to wish every success for the future units of the Singapore Armed Forces and for all the aviation firms which will be taking our place.

And on behalf of the Royal Air Force, I say: **'Farewell Seletar!'**

High altitude aerial shot of Seletar Camp & surrounding area.   **Public Records Office**

CHAPTER FOURTEEN

Today: Singapore & Seletar in the New Millennium

And what of Singapore itself? How has that changed over the years? An extract from my own book, A *Suitcase Full of Dreams* (ISBN 0 9534082 0 5) answers that question.

● ● ● ● ● ● ● ● ● ●

It wasn't quite as I remembered, this place. None of the familiar smells greeted me as the aircraft opened its doors once again on Singapore. It was now the aroma of jet fuel which pervaded the senses, rather than those of mimosa and frangipani. It was also different in that I had arrived in the harsh light of day, rather than the softness of a tropical night. But these, I was soon to discover, weren't the only changes.

Was this really the place where it all began, forty years back – my overseas tour, that is? It certainly wasn't the same any more, but where is? Few places are untouched by the passing of time, but this country seemed to have changed more than most. For a start, it was now a Republic.

As an International Airport, Paya Lebar was a thing of the past. Opened shortly before my arrival in 1957, it had replaced the old Kallang airport, out on the waterfront, just as Changi has now replaced Paya Lebar, switching from military status to become one of the most modern airports in the world. Paya Lebar too has seen a role reversal; now a transport base for the Singapore Air Force.

Changi was now a huge complex, much larger than when it had been an RAF base, as was the island itself, and the city. Land reclamation has imposed vast changes to the south coast, completely redefining the waterfront area. The coast road we had so often followed out to Bedok Corner was now well inland. The city has changed, too. As well as growing out, it has grown up. Cloud-piercing up. Raffles Hotel now lay in the shadow of the world's tallest hotel: the seventy-three storey Westin Stamford and Plaza. Orchard Road, once on the outer fringes of almost everything, was now the hub; a shopping Mecca for tourists. The Cathay Cinema was still in place, at the eastern end, although this too – previously the most prominent building in the city – now finds itself dwarfed almost into insignificance.

There is an underground system, known as the MRT – (Mass Rapid Transit). This links many of the of the island's most popular destinations, though, strangely, not yet the airport. The trip to and from Changi is via either the Pan Island Expressway (PIE), or the East Coast Parkway (ECP), magnificent, tree-shaded, flower and bush-lined multi-lane super-highways, which become choked with traffic as you approach the city. Tampines still exists, for the moment. But it too is scheduled to become an expressway in the very near future.

Water is still imported across the Causeway from Malaya, only now, after being purified, the majority is re-exported, back from whence it came, at a considerable mark up in price. Good business practice.

Bedok Corner – well remembered for late night/early morning eating and drinking – is alive and well, though now as picnic area, well inland, with ten-pin bowling, the inevitable Macdonalds, other restaurants and family play areas. One thing remains constant, so it seems: as it was back in Gerry Livock's days, cricket is still played on the Padang, against the backdrop of City Hall and St Andrew's Cathedral – they too almost lost amongst the multi-storeyed architecture.

Occasionally, amid all the modern buildings, one will stumble across one of the old, trad-itional, merchant's homes. Concrete and wood structures, raised above the ground on cement piles so as to allow cooling air to pass beneath, and with an encircling veranda. Due to high humidity, the burnt-orange tiled roof will likely be darkened with moss and fungus, walls black-ened with mould, but the structure will be set amid a cool greenness of coarse grass and traveller's palms, with flame-of-the-forest, hibis-cus, bougainvillea and magnolia adding colour to the oasis. But the most famous oasis of all is still to be found within the grounds of Raffles Hotel. But even the Raffles hasn't escaped the changes. Expensively refurbished, I was saddened to find their oasis, the Palm Court – where I had once sat and sipped on a "Singapore Sling" – was now out of bounds to all but registered guests; though none sat out there, for even the tables and chairs had been removed. The laid-back era of Coward and Maughan, it seemed, was no more.

The Singapore River has probably seen the biggest changes of all. One-time hive of activity – lighters carrying cargo to and from the ships lying at anchor offshore, in what were known as the inner and outer roads – its waters were now deserted. Even the inner roads have disappeared beneath reclaimed land. Back then those lighters would discharge their freight into the heaving clutter of godowns (warehouses) which lined the banks. Interspersed amongst the godowns were dozens of rickety, open-fronted shops, packed with everything from spices to incense, clothing, raw cotton, and silks. There were fruits galore, dried fish and sharks' fins.

An aromatic clutter of herbs and pungent spices would be piled all around, open sacks and tins, in bowls, and on trays. A dazzling kaleido-scope of colour. Greens and browns, saffron, white and orange. The red of the hot chili peppers, the green of the capsicums.

It was all gone now, replaced by touristy restaurants and bars. One compensation, the river was cleaner; much cleaner, sweeter smel-ling, by far. Of the lighters – still with an eye painted on the bow, so they could see where they were going – the few that remained had been modified to run tourists up and down the river.

Change Alley? Would you believe Paris chic? High class art, Havana cigars, designer clothing, the real thing these days. There *is* a touch of the old place, if only in name: Change Alley Aerial Arcade. It spans the highway, but bears only a passing resemblance to the original. Still, there is one thing – you are much less likely to have your wallet nicked these days.

The only thing to remind me of earlier times were the barrows which served fresh drinks, a hand-turned mill squeezing the juice from sugar-cane, or tropical fruits.

Not bad then, the changes, though not all good. For although it is probably one of the safest, cleanest, and greenest, cities to be found anywhere, it seemed to me that a lot of the character had been swept away. As in Tanjong Pagar Conservation Area. The original buildings remain, repainted, neat and tidy, yet the spirit seems to have departed.

Gone too, is Bugis Street. At least the Bugis Street that Seletar-man knew. Officially "Out of Bounds", it was a raucous playground where, come the witching hour, certain young men turned into something rather more exotic than pumpkins! Nor is one now able to witness the ritual that was occasionally performed there, seemingly by the lower ranks of the Royal Navy. This involved a lighted, rolled up newspaper, inserted in an unmentionable part of the anat-omy. The area is now renamed New Bugis Street; correctly so, for it too retains little of the original character. The boy-girls who used to entertain us with their antics have moved to another area.

Out of sight, out of mind. Also missing – and no bad thing this – was that familiar Black, Standard Vanguard Estate, which used to patrol these "Out of Bounds" areas during the late fifties. Registered SS660, this vehicle was an unmarked car belonging to the RAF's vice squad.

Albert Street has suffered likewise; its roadside kitchens, its rickety stairs, its balconied parlours, all gone, to be replaced by something called the Albert Street Mall. And there are very few trishaws remaining; as well, really, given today's traffic.

The open storm drains, too, have disappeared, as has the stench of rotting vegetation, and most of those huge cockroaches. Not really gone, more like, rarely seen. The majority of mosquitoes also seem to have packed their bags, headed for pastures new.

● ● ● ● ● ● ● ● ● ●

It was a shock. A familiar place in a once familiar area – Stamford Road. I peered through the window. Yes, of course. The basic layout appeared to have changed hardly at all, though forty years ago it hadn't been known as Harry Keely's Pub and Lounge, just a plain old bar. One other change: the place was now air conditioned. It reminded me of how the MU had been, at Seletar; freezing if you were dressed in anything less than a suit. In this bar we would sit in the heat to drink cold beer, an electric ceiling-fan stirring up the air enough to keep us comfortable, and to deter the mossies. And what of the Worlds; Happy, Great, and New? Yes, they also failed survive the cleansing. Or have they? I did see what was called, The Great World Centre, yet another shopping and apartment complex. It couldn't have been... could it? It was.

So, better, or not? I wasn't really sure. Cleaner, yes, but perhaps a little too clinical, and at a price, for it certainly isn't cheap these days. But mine are the memories of an ex-Seletarite, and therefore pure nostalgia. For me, Lee Kuan Yew and his government have done a magnificent job, and Singapore remains one of my favourite cities. I'll go back, anytime.

So much for the city, then, but what of the camp itself?

● ● ● ● ● ● ● ● ● ●

Our arrival at Singapore's International Airport, Changi, had coincided with that of a tropical downpour; torrential rain, thunder, lightning, the whole shebang. And once clear of immigration and customs, we were greeted by that human tornado, Yeo Kuan Joo, our guide.[58] Even though our arrival was at the end of a long day, he guided, advised and organised, and generally whipped us into shape. And once we were installed in the River View Hotel, he held our attention until well into the second or third jug of Tiger – slightly more expensive than the Tiger Tops we used to consume by the gallon in the Malcolm Club.

Day one was spent becoming acclimatised, with various groups exploring the town, and taking lunch in the Britannia Club. Although now known as the Warrant Officers' & Specialists Club, it seemed little changed from days of yore, though not for much longer. A brand new facility is at present being built out at Jurong, and when complete the old Brit Club building will be no more, the whole site being scheduled for redevelopment.

Day two, and thirteen "moonies" - along with Ron Seddon, who had come across from Papua New Guinea to join us - presented themselves in the hotel lobby, ready for a return to Seletar. We had a coach, the inimitable Kuan Joo - along with his aptly named "side-kick," Billy Ho - and the aforementioned fourteen eager bodies, so away we went. Kuan Joo gave an entertaining, non-stop commentary en-route, pointing out once familiar landmarks, including Woodbridge Hospital. Most ex-Seletarites may recall that name – described by Kuan Joo as "a place people go when they have computer short in the head." And then we were there, at the main guardroom, seventy-two years after the base first opened.

The aeroplanes were back, though none flew this particular day; what there were sat still and silent on West camp, now the home of various aviation related service companies. Nor were they military types; mainly Cessna, various adaptations of Piper's Indian tribes, and the usual flying club type aerosystems, along with a few commercial models: Hercules and charter jets. But the aircraft didn't matter, we hadn't come to see those, this trip was to be steeped in nostalgia.

Aircraft apart, not a lot else seemed to have changed. The layout was as remembered, especially those once familiar street names: Piccadilly Circus, Mornington Crescent, Maida Vale, Park Lane, et al. But, being largely unused, the place was generally quite run down; one could say, well camouflaged – the bush reclaiming various sites, especially over on West Camp, which is sparsely occupied by civilian users. We were allowed to wander around at will, and to take photographs, no problems whatsoever. We even had a group photo taken at the main gate, "No Photo Taking" sign to the fore. Only the old 9X site was to be denied our presence, well hidden behind a high fence and the aforementioned undergrowth. The swimming pool and cinema were no more; pool abandoned, cinema put to another use.

As we wandered around East Camp, there were the obvious discussions as to which building had, or had not been, the Malcolm Club, A, B or C block, etc, although the parade ground, WRAF block and cookhouse seemed to pose few problems. The blocks have change only insofar as most were now deserted; no more the hive of activity of old, no more the bearers, no more sew-sew, no more the mattress' out to air – to rid them of the bed bugs. Even the blocks which were occupied showed little evidence of being so.

All the while we looked for signs of the aircraft which had once graced this place: Southampton, Vildebeest, Sunderland, Beaufighter, Beverley, Belvedere ... and, believe it or not, we saw them all – apart from Southampton, Vildebeest, Sunderland, Beaufighter, Beverley, Belvedere, that is.

As stated previously, no 9X visit was allowed, so no confirmation as to whether or not the ghost stories referred to by various Seletarites actually carried a grain of truth.

After a quick visit to Jalan Kayu, itself not as I remembered, it was time to visit the area most affected by major change: the waterfront, down by the slipway. A huge island has been created where once flying boats reposed, and the old concrete jetty has been replaced by a smaller, steel and wooden affair – a lesser control tower, no crane. It was sad to see these changes, for this was the area in which it all began: the Far East Flight; this station; FEAF itself. It was especially sad in my case, for I too had been one of those web-footed airmen. Even the commemorative plaque marking the site of the original Station Headquarters building has disappeared; history down the drain. The yacht club, where I once spent so many happy hours, was still in place, more or less, only it is now the Officers' Mess for 35 Combat Engineers, Singapore Armed Forces – the original mess, at one time the biggest in the RAF, now housed the Army School of Logistics. We were to be royally entertained in that ex-yacht club mess later that evening, where, out on the veranda, one could almost have been back in the fifties, had it not been for that tree-laden island less than 100 metres out in the Straits! But at least it shielded from sight the major changes taking place across on the Johore coastline; industrialization on a large scale.

First, there were to be yet more group photographs, this time on the slipway, a quick stroll back in time to the bridge over the creek – mud, water and mangrove, just as the whole area had been back in 1925 – and then on to the Officers Mess. This too, was also a step back in time, for the Tiger flowed freely, with the emphasis on "free," and there was "Makan" aplenty.

Out on that verandah, glass in hand, storm clouds clearing to allow the stars to peek through, night air washed fresh, scented with frangipani, I once more gazed out across the water, eyes closed. In the background, nature's symphony was tuning-up, just like those days of old: frogs and cicadas providing the percussion, mosquitoes, the strings. Only now, the island was gone. Out at anchorage, Sunderlands bobbed on the water, mooring lights aglow. I opened my eyes, shook my head, went and got a refill at the bar. Ah well.

From then on we covered pretty much all of what Singapore has to offer, which is quite a lot. There were visits to the Botanical and Orchid Gardens, Kranji War Memorial, Sentosa Island – originally known as Blakan Mati [59] army and naval base – and Changi Prison, where, although we arrived too late to visit the museum, we were able to pay our respects at the little chapel. What a revelation this trip must have been for those among our party who had not visited Singapore since their Seletar days. Still, we had all once more tasted life in the orient.

Now known as Seletar Airport, the facility lives on today, a joint military/commercial base, the runway forming the demarcation line between the two: West camp being the commercial side. The ex married quarters are now leased out by the government, and the golf course is run under the auspices of the Seletar Golf Club. The Singapore Flying Club operates from West Camp, having been evicted from Paya Lebar when that facility became the Republic of Singapore Air Force's (RSAF) transport base. East Camp is restricted to military use.

So, life still ticks over at the base, and this may continue for another year or so, though one thing is for sure, Seletar's heydays are over; the future will never be so colourful and action packed as had been the past. With land at a premium in Singapore the base has been ear-marked for housing and industrial development within the next ten years. When these plans reach fruition, Seletar camp will disappear into the sands of time. And of the events which were enacted on these lands? Nothing will remain but memories, and pages of words in the history books.

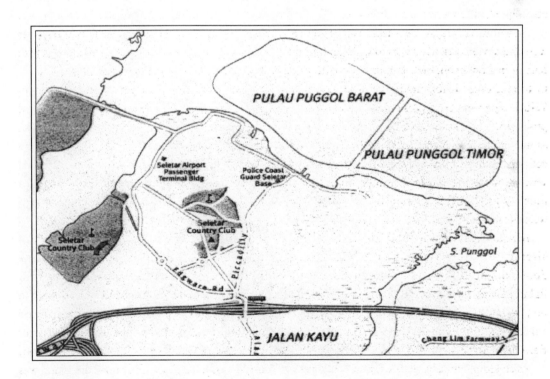

Seletar Area 2001 – Barat & Timor are reclaimed land, the old flying boat moorings.

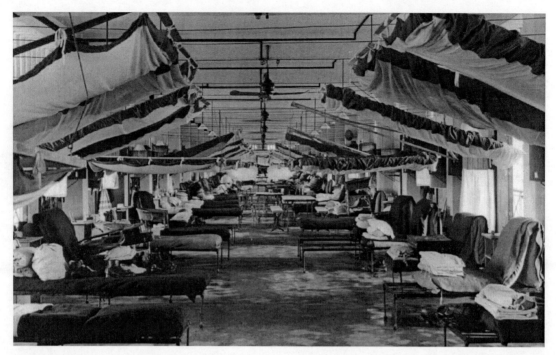

1935 kit layout beneath the mosquito nets in one of Seletar's barrack blocks. I doubt if it would have passed muster at Cosford in 1953! **RA "Scotty" Powell**

Yacht Club verandah from the beach at low tide. Ah, the memories. It is almost the same today. **Seletar "Voice"**

APPENDIX 1:

NOTES

¹/ Lion – after Lion City. A direct translation from the Sanskrit: Singa, meaning lion, Pura, city; the city, and island, of Singapore. The name apparently came about after a Sumatran Prince, visiting the island, encountered what he thought was a lion. It was a time when tigers roamed the jungles which still covered acres of land. No lions though; never had been.

²/ Nostalgie de la boue – literally, nostalgia for mud: craving for a debased physical life lacking civilized refinements.

³/ To third century Chinese it was known as Pu-luo-chung; island at the end of the peninsula – on Long Yanen; Dragon's Tooth Strait.

⁴/ Later renamed the Town Club, an institution that did not even consider accepting women members prior to 1988.

⁵/ The Singapore CC was located on the Padang (Malay for plain ground) where it still remains to this day, an oasis in the midst of high-rise architecture.

⁶/ Kiaochow Bay: The German navy, using the murder of two missionaries as a pretext, annexed this area of Shandong Province, north-east China, with a view to developing a naval base there.

⁷/ Although an official enquiry was later held into the cause of this mutiny, its findings were never disclosed.

⁸/ This may have seemed a trifle ambitious at the time, but Sir Alan Cobham was to become the pioneer of air-to-air refuelling, the company he formed – In-flight Refuelling – a leader in the field to this day.

⁹/ Get in some serious cricket Gerry Livock certainly did, playing three games for Middlesex in 1925, and later representing his country in an English Gentlemen's XI vs Australia match.

¹⁰/ An amusing aside on the Raffles Hotel, fairly typical of the area, as those who served in Singapore may well recall: Apparently a Swiss lady reprimanded her room boy when he woke her one morning at 05:00, walking in without knocking. She found his reply, though possibly amusing, to be not very encouraging. "Don't worry, madam, me always lookie-lookie first keyhole before come-in!"

¹¹/ Although open to traffic in September 1923, the Causeway was not officially declared open until the following March.

¹²/ Despite the existence of an early 1920's document from the Governor of the Straits Settlements to the effect that: "The sites selected were acquired by the Straits Settlement Government, to be handed over as a free gift," there later seems to have been some dispute about this. In August of 1929, telegrams were flashing back and forth between the Secretary of State for the Colonies and the Governor of the Straits Colonies, a final one missive stating: "The

Air Ministry now confirm they will meet a cost not exceeding £3000. Please take steps to purchase land on behalf of the Air ministry as soon as possible." Or could this have been an extesion to land already being developed?

13/ The original Headquarters building was actually constructed out over the water on stilts. This hut was eventually destined to become the RAF Seletar Yacht Club and, in a later life, after much reconstruction, Officers' Mess to the Singapore Armed Forces, 35 Combat Engineers. A plinth which had been erected to commemorate the site of the original building was no longer to be found during a May 2000 visit to the area.

14/ A fine testament to the construction of these hangars is the fact that both have withstood the ravages of war and time, and are today still in use.

15/ As well as being an excellent pilot, Gerry Livock was also very competent behind a camera, as photographs in his book *To the Ends of the Air*, show. The complete "Livock Collection" is available for viewing at the IWM Photographic Archive, All Saints Annexe, Austral Street, London SE11, or in the reading room at the RAF Museum, Hendon (both by prior appointment).

16/ Tanglin area was a fairly isolated outpost at the time. By the mid sixties the city had spread out far enough to incorporate the area, and today it is well inside the city limits.

17/ Only one aircraft had previously circumnavigated Australia – a Fairey seaplane piloted by Groble and MacIntyre, who were said to have 'scrambled' round after many trials and tribulations.

18/ The forced landing off Sumatra was due to a problem with the aircraft's accumulators, they caught fire whilst being charged, filling the cockpit with smoke and fumes. Within quarter of an hour of landing the crew had cured the problem, the aircraft rejoining the flight.

19/ JJ Moll, who along with K D Parmentier flew the then new Douglas DC2 into second place behind Scott and Black's DH88 Comet on the London-Australia race of 1934. An airliner against a pure-bred racer.

20/ In actual fact this aircraft only carried the mail on from Karachi; a regular Croydon to Karachi run, using a variety of aircraft, had been established the previous year.

21/ Considering the route can be flown today, sixty-seven years later, for only about fifty pounds more, this was an enormous sum.

22/ These Holt flares hung from brackets on the wing-tips, rather like a suspended tin can. They were triggered electrically, a wire running from the cockpit into an "illuminating composition."

23/ With fabric and plywood skinned wings, surprised it wasn't on fire; there were reports of it happening to an HP42, on the approach to Le Bourget in 1932.

24/ Reference to "hauling her up the slipway" adds confusion to this report. Was this aircraft land-based, or a seaplane? If the latter, it would seem the reporter was probably commenting on the arrival of an Imperial Airways, "C" or "G" class, Empire flying boat, neither of which entered service on the Singapore run before 1938. If so, the landing would have taken place at Kallang rather than Seletar. This airport – with a grass strip, and a slipway for flying boats – sited on Singapore's south coast, opened in June 1937, and civilian traffic ceased to use Seletar. We must therefore assume it wasn't the arrival of a flying boat being reported; reference to a slipway being erroneous.

25/ The Burmese rebellion had been ten years ahead of its time, in that it used a system of guerrilla warfare that did not come into its own until WWII.

26/ Some residents of later years had been born in Seletarville, were christened in those churches, married there, and brought up their own families there. This self-containment was to prove beneficial over the years. It meant the labour force was partially insulated from what was happening throughout the rest of the island. This is why the strikes and unrest of 1964 barely affected the base and its operations. The combined British Services were after all the biggest employers on the island.

27/ The "Worlds" remained popular long after the war, too, right up the their closure in the sixties. Although, at least during the fifties and sixties, those unwritten conventions regarding officers and other ranks, appeared to have been consigned to the scrapheap.

During a May 2000 visit, it was noted that the Great World had reopened, only now, merely as yet another shopping complex.

28/ In a letter to Sqn/Ldr N. Shorrick in 1970, Mr HR Shawyer says: "I like to think that an LAC Bristowe and myself were responsible for the initial encouragement of Wg Cdr Burling... we spent much of our spare time paddling and sailing native canoes around, usually with a square rigged towel! On one of these trips we were spotted by the Wing Commander and questioned as to the possible popularity of a sailing club..... From little acorns...

29/ The club served none members, too, being especially convenient to the crews of 205/209 Squadron, whose headquarters and hangar were located just yards away. The first-line crew room was closer still, the small wooden hut often being forsaken in favour of the yacht club's verandah, from where they could sit and savour the atmosphere, as it were, whilst still keeping an eye on their aircraft.

30/ When afloat, flying boats are required to comply with the laws of the sea, even so far as being required to carry an anchor. In later years it was a piddling little thing that would have found difficulty holding a rowing boat in position, but it did adhere to the letter of the regulations if not the spirit. There was also a hand-bell, for use in foggy conditions, and mooring lights needed to be displayed during hours of darkness.

31/ Changi: the name is said to have been derived from the Chengel or Dhengai trees (balanscarppusheimii), or possibly the Changi Ular (apama cerymbosa), a climbing shrub, both of which at one time were known to have grown in that area. The so called "Changi tree" of 1942 was a different species entirely. The Japanese artillery were seen to be using this 200ft tall specimen as a rangefinder, so British Army engineers blew it up (or maybe down?). Stories about it being a navigational aid to incoming pilots have to be totally disregarded, Changi did not become an RAF airfield until 1945/6, by which time that tree was long gone.

Between 1942 and 1944 Changi military base became the infamous Prison Camp – as opposed to Changi Jail, which was initially used to house civilian prisoners of war. In 1944, due to airfield construction work at Changi, military prisoners were also squeezed into the jail; twelve thousand people in an area originally intended for no more than six hundred!

Work on converting Changi into an airbase was begun by the Japanese, in late 1943 – using POW labour. The site was finally handed over to the Royal Air Force in 1946.

Sembawang, likewise, is also said to be named after a tree – (kayoe ferruginea)? *Got me beat. Maybe it's something to do with the Malay pronunciation.*

32/ A safety feature of this drop-down panel was a micro-switch operated engine cut-out, ie the engine could not be started unless the panel was up and secured.

33/ Following the RAF's departure in 1971, a civilian operation was set up to maintain aircraft of the Singapore Air Force and those of foreign air forces, the USAF's Viet Nam effort in particular.

34/ Shortly after the RAF took the Tung Song on contract they changed the name to Anne, only it seems they failed to notify the appropriate authorities. During the early days of the war the vessel was intercepted and boarded by the Royal Navy, suspected of being a possible enemy ship in disguise, for the navy had no record of an RAF Auxiliary vessel named Anne. But on inspecting the ship's papers, all was revealed. The vessel smartly reverted to being the *Tung Song*.

[35]/ Apart from his escape aboard the *Tung Song*, Robert Hampson was also dealt a favourable hand at the start of the air war in Malaya. He was the WoP/G normally assigned to W/O Webb's Catalina, *W8417, FV-W*, the aircraft lost on that fateful day, December 6th 1941. I suppose one could say it was fortunate that Bob was at the time confined to hospital, having contracted malaria. Such is the fickle finger of fate.

[36]/ War in all but name. As war was never officially declared, it became the Malayan Emergency, just as a later affair was to become the Indonesian Confrontation.

[37]/ Strange coincidence here: Dick Fowden was also the medic who was sent out on pinnace 105 to pick up an airman (Peter Masters) infected by malaria, as detailed on page 74. Both gave their impressions of the Vildebeest collision, although neither one knew the other. Dick later said he was unsure of the fate of his malaria victim, but he had heard tell he'd survived the war. He knows now, for both are members of the Seletar Association.

[38]/ Different people, different recollections. As Terence Kelly tells it in his book *Hurricane over the Jungle*, relating to his, admittedly short stay on the island, Jan 29th – Feb 4th 1942. "In fact I don't recall any night bombing of Singapore, nor for that matter any bombing in the afternoon."

[39]/ The Remorseless Road, *ISBN 1-85310-886-3 Published by Airlife, 1997.*

[40]/ There is a story of one "old sweat" W.O. of not very high educational qualities, who made out a demand for so many feet of "crinkly tin." Stores thought it so hilarious they had the demand framed.

[41]/ By all reports, not the first mistake by Tengah's CO. When five new Hudsons were delivered, their squadron commander suggested that, as a precaution, they should be flown out over Java when the morning bombing raid was due, to return when the raid was over, the station commander had refused permission for this. Next day, two of the aircraft were destroyed on the ground, two more damaged, none of them having yet flown a sortie.

[42]/ Close by Batavia; now Jakarta Airport.

[43]/ The propeller of one of these valiant aircraft, one of the last British aeroplanes to depart Singapore in those dark days, was said to have survived. Upon being informed that it actually adorned the crewroom wall of the Northumbrian University Air Squadron, at RAF Leeming, Yorkshire, I made plans to visit. Disappointment. Despite a plaque proclaiming – "This propeller is from a Vickers Vildebeest and is reputed to be from the last aircraft to leave Singapore in the final hours before the surrender of 15/2/42.

"It is known that two such aircraft, both of 36 Sqn RAF, escaped before the Fall, and continued the unequal struggle in Java and Sumatra during March of that year and it is to one of these Vildebeests that the propeller belonged." – this propeller was nowhere near large enough (8 ft diameter rather than 14ft plus). Checking with the person who presented the propeller to Leeming, Flt/Lt Richard Allen, an ex-instructor at the base, he says the prop came from a local pub, and the person who placed it in the pub was an ex-Royal Navy rating who said he had removed it from a bar on Gan. *If anyone has further information on this story, both myself and Richard Allen would be interested to hear from you.*

[44]/ It says much for British resourcefulness that one petrol store which had been sited underground was so well camouflaged that the Japanese failed to discover it at all. In fact it was said not to have been rediscovered by the RAF until 1947, two years after the end of the war!

[45]/ It is amusing to note that by an unbelievable oversight, these regulations remained incorporated in civilian orders for over twenty years. Once it had been brought to someone's

notice, the offending clause was hastily removed, though the reasons for its retention by the British remained a mystery.

46/ Could this story possibly tie in with the one which had a ghost apparently wandering around 9X (explosives) site in the fifties and sixties? See, *Seletar's Ghosts*, Appendix 2.

47/ MAD: a sensor which detects localized distortion of the earth's magnetic field; a possible indication as to the presence of a submerged submarine. A very much more sophisticated version is today used by the Nimrod fleet.

48/ A few of the very lucky ones, for, of the estimated fourteen thousand seven hundred airmen of the RAF, RAAF, and RNZAF captured in Malaya, Sumatra, Java and Burma, between December 1941 and April 1942, less than three thousand five hundred were found alive in 1945.

49/ As a memento of the occasion, Cpl Jenkins was not only presented with the Japanese flag which had flown over Seletar for so many years, but also Vice Admiral Kogure's ceremonial daggers, known as a Naval Tanto's. Flag, Tantos plus other items from Cpl Jenkins' collection are today on display in the RAF Regiment room at the Yorkshire Air Museum; donated by his relatives.

50/ Rumour has it these tins of sardines had been buried out on the airfield before the Japanese arrived, and had remained there throughout the war!

51/ Given the prevailing conditions, ie, those involved were still on active service, the strike could have been classed as a mutiny from the outset. That it was not, was seen as an effort by the authorities to dilute the situation.

52/ The Imperial War Museum photographic archives contain a good selection of shots recorded as these flights took place.

53/ Data from this survey became invaluable in later years, with the Indonesian desire to expand their territory.

54/ Although now long gone, this painting survived until at least July 1960, for an entry in the station F540 for that month referred to it as "A mural on the wall of hangar 500." The entry went on to state that "although of no great artistic merit, it has, nevertheless, over the years, attracted considerable attention and speculation as to the meaning of the inscription above the painting. The services of the Japanese Consul General in Singapore were requested, and as a result, the Japanese characters were transcribed as reading, Display of Fighting Spirit. Whether this was in reference to the British or Japanese is not known. An appendix to the F540 contained a colour photograph of the painting – reproduced in this book in monochrome.

55/ Ex Seletar Sunderlands sold to New Zealand, RNZAF crews picking them up from Pembroke Dock after refurbishment by Short Bros: PP124 – ex 205 Sqn; PP129 – ex 205 Sqn; RN280 – ex 205 Sqn; RN306 – ex 205 Sqn; RN291 – ex 88 Sqn; VB880 – ex 88 Sqn; VB883 – ex 88 Sqn; SZ561 – ex 209 Sqn.

56/ The following report would suggest that the actual "last" Beaufighter flight may have taken place at a later date.

A direct casualty of the 1960-61 defence cuts was the Queen's Birthday Parade, and the associated day off. Before this took effect, it was decided that Singapore should have a final fling, one large parade to be held on the pan at Changi, all Armed Forces on the Island being represented. It was also decided that the oldest aircraft left on the island would be readied for a flypast during the event. The aircraft selected was to be one of two Beaufighters which were by now rotting away at 390 MU, Seletar. A team of selected tradesmen were detailed to prepare one of these aircraft to a standard of "airworthiness for one flight only." All non-essential items and systems were removed, and by dint of robbing Peter to pay Paul, one aircraft was made ready, until it was discovered that all the tyres were rotted beyond help. An urgent signal was sent to the Avon Tyre Co., Melksham, requesting their assistance. Ivan Rowe, Avon's technical manager at the time, recalls receiving the message, "but with Avon having never manufactured aircraft tyres, I had our service manager pass the request on to Dunlop, where someone actually managed to unearth the moulds." Dunlop were thus able to present RAF Seletar with two sets of tyres.

A "single flight" certificate was now issued, and a volunteer crew scratched together, including a "type experienced" pilot. The plan was for the aircraft to make a low pass, timed to coincide with the Royal cheers.

The parade was performed amidst the pomp and splendour, with much banging of drums, skirling of pipes, the shouting of orders, the stamping of many booted feet, until it came time for the salute. The order, "Caps Off," was issued, and the moment four thousand SD's were tossed into the air, "Whistling Death" did its thing. Pulling out of its famous, near vertical dive manoeuvre, it passed overhead at zero zero feet. Spectacular indeed, especially when the draught

from those two large propellers deposited a goodly percentage of four thousand SD caps against the perimeter fence. The parade was wrapped up with as much decorum as was possible without headgear, and it is reported that once the aircraft landed back at Seletar, the wings promptly fell off! Well, the certificate had been for one flight only. And whatever the date, Seletar definitely had staged the last flight of a Beaufighter in RAF service.

[57]/ As well as being the last Beverley to fly, XB259 was also the first. It is now the only surviving aircraft of the type, residing in the Army Museum of Transport, which, appropriately enough, is located in Beverley, East Yorkshire.

[58]/ Commanding Officer at Seletar from 1980-84: see Appendix 2, Seletar Boy.

[59]/ The name Blakan Mati translates as, behind/ beyond death.

"Roll on the Nelson, the Rodney, Renown, you can't sink the Hood 'cos the ...."

Goodbye Seletar: Misdeeds, Musings & Nostalgic Memories

First, a note for those purists who are concerned with my spelling of Vildebeest; you are correct, the original spelling was Vildebeeste, but the last "e" was for some unexplained reason dropped sometime in 1934. Just thought you should know.

● ● ● ● ● ● ● ● ●

FLYING BOAT DAYS

Flight engineer Dicky Knott was on 230 Squadron the day the first Sunderland arrived at Seletar, he was also serving there, still on Sunderlands, on May 31st 1959, the last official day of an RAF flying boat squadron.

● ● ● ● ● ● ● ● ●

The story goes that flight sergeant RAF policeman had developed the habit of cycling to the swimming pool for his mid morning break, his chosen route taking him along the waterfront (The Embankment), past the top of the slipway. If a beached aircraft's engines were being run, barriers would be lowered to halt the traffic, these, however, did not deter our policeman. Arrogantly chastising anyone attempting to stop him, he'd carry on his merry way. Well, for any airman worth his salt this was a too perfect an opportunity to miss.

One fine day, with a fully chocked aircraft carefully positioned between the hangars, restraining lorry attached (no brakes on a Sunderland, you see), all four engines on tick-

over, and... sure enough, here he came. Mounted on his trusty steed, KD immaculate, white webbing, shiny boots, stockings and white gaiters – even though wearing shorts – he once more ignored the verbal warnings, negotiated the lowered barriers. Unfortunate really, for, with perfect timing... er, I mean, purely by coincidence, this was the point at which all four throttles were advanced; whoops! For here on it was totally down to the science of physics, something relating to Newton's third law, I believe; there was only one way he and his bicycle could go – down the slipway and into the sea. Hope you enjoyed your swim, Chiefy.

● ● ● ● ● ● ● ● ●

An entry in 205 Sqn records for December 3rd 1941 (all times GMT), reads: 2330 – Catalina FV-W took off for Labuan en route to Manilla, carrying Admiral Sir Tom Phillips, newly arrived C-in-C Far East Fleet, for a strategic conference with leaders of the Defence Forces of the USA.

December 5th: 06:00 – Catalina FV-W departed Labuan for Manilla.

December 6th: 23:50 – Catalina FV-W left on a hurried recall to Seletar. Her crew was devoid of Sgt Hamlin, who had leave from the aircraft and could not be found in the short time available.

A scribbled note in the margin states:

Some say Sgt Hamlin was still in a brothel! I hope he enjoyed it.

Another 205 Sqn story, this one told me by Bob Hampson, concerns a certain LAC rigger serving with the Sqn during 1938/39.

"Bugger" Bayhan, who was a bit of a loner, often wandered along to what he called "The Ulu," a bit of bush out by the radio station – where, at the end of 1939 the swimming pool was to be opened. Here was located a workmen's basha, where he could be alone with his thoughts and brew up a cuppa. In there one day, he was suddenly confronted by a stranger who had wandered by. "Fancy a cup of char, mate?" Bugger asked.

"Yes, thanks," replied the stranger. So the tea was produced and they sat and talked, sorting out Seletar's problems, as airmen are prone to do. Then, preparing to depart, the stranger posed the question, "What's your name then?"

"I'm Bugger Bayhan," replied our resident char wallah. "What's yours?"

"I'm Batcherly Cox," replied Wg/Cdr Cox, the station CO, as he took his leave.

During WWII, Iwakuni had been an airfield of final departure for *Kamikaze* flights – and, presumably, their pilots, too! One such pilot had been scheduled for such a flight on the day of the surrender, so, in effect, had been saved. The Korean conflict found him in employment as a dinghy driver at what had since become a flying boat base. Nicknamed, "Suicide," this now referred to the way in which he drove his vessel rather than his previously planned, somewhat short-term occupation. He would circle the flying boats at great speed, causing the aircraft to rock in his wake, making things rather difficult for all on board.

David Kane was an engine fitter with the Far East Flying Boat Wing during the 1950s, but he was also a cartoonist, his work often featuring in the station magazine. Whilst at Seletar he produced a book of cartoons which mainly related to the Sunderlands. This one is said to portray the above mentioned character, "Suicide".

A safety feature to be incorporated in the Sunderland's drop-down leading edge panel was a micro-switch operated engine cut-out, ie the engine could not be started unless the panel was up and properly secured. One prankster engineer was said to have deliberately left the port inner panel unsecured, and when the engine failed to start, he suggested to the pilot that he climb out and check things over. Upon dropping the panel and opening the engine cowling, he reached into his overalls and extracted the piston and con-rod he had secreted away – ex scrap dump. Calling the pilot's attention, he waved the useless lump of metal in the air, dispatched it into the sea, secured the engine cowling and wing panel, then requested the pilot to try again. Of course, the engine started, and away they went.

390 MU – You Want It, We Got It – You Try & Get It

As is stated in the main body of text, Seletar, as a Maintenance Unit, was responsible for all RAF aircraft operating in the Far East Air Force, along with those of many other units in the theatre; an important position. But with regard to procedure for the issuing of aircraft spares, I heard tell of an incident which would cause one to question the commitment of certain personnel stationed at the base. It concerned a 155 Sqn Whirlwind, at the end of a visit to Seletar in the mid fifties. The aircraft was urgently needed back at KL, but the pre-flight inspection revealed a blade to have been damaged, requiring replacement. Well, that shouldn't pose a problem, the MU was at Seletar, West camp, so they were contacted.

'Yes,' the NCO in charge of aircraft stores confirmed, they did have a blade in stock. And, 'Yes,' he would dispatch it to Seletar, East camp – where the aircraft was located. 'Just a moment, though. Isn't 155 squadron based at Kuala Lumpur?' he questioned.

'Well, they are, but this aircraft is on detachment, here at Seletar.'

'Ah, but any replacement parts must go via the squadron, otherwise it will take forever to sort out the paperwork. I'll have it dispatched immediately, shouldn't take more than three days.'

'Three days! But this is an AOG situation' (aircraft on ground – the second highest priority, being eclipsed during the Cold War by VOG – V-bomber on ground).

'Which is why I'm dispatching it forthwith.'

The next call stores received, apparently less than ten minutes later, was from 155 Squadron's Commanding Officer, in KL, via the station CO at Seletar. He was said to have issued a curt reminder that Seletar was actually an active service posting, and that as, presumably, we were all working for the same Queen, they had better get that aircraft back up to the front line, immediately.

Within thirty minutes the blade had been transported from one side of the camp to the other, direct. A ten minute drive. The aircraft was back on operations the following day.

● ● ● ● ● ● ● ● ● ●

SELETAR'S GHOSTS?

There are many stories of mysterious sightings around Seletar, most seeming to favour 9(X) site, which could indeed be very spooky after dark, most guards being posted in pairs. So first, a brief rundown re 9(X) site. This explosives and dangerous chemicals storage area covered around one third of Seletar's area, and was totally fenced in; only those with business there were allowed inside. It contained concrete bunkers, underground storage, and around nine miles of roads. People working there seemed to enter and

just disappear, only to reappear at lunch time, or at the end of their shift. An article in the last edition of the Seletar Voice states, "Whilst the main camp roads were named after London streets, on 9(X) they were named after the London Underground: Circle Line, etc, although no one I have spoken to who worked there can confirm this. Anyway, back to the ghosts.

One airman's experience: "One of our guard duties was that at 9(X) site. We were locked in with a rifle, five rounds and a whistle, and the NCO i/c would advise us to keep our eyes open for the ghost of a Japanese General who was said to have committed Hari-Kari here. I never heard any reports of him being seen, but I always had this creepy feeling that someone else was around."

Well, maybe there was, for another report concerned two airmen patrolling the bomb compound in the early hours when one of them suddenly issued the challenge, "Halt! Who goes there?" His colleague, seeing nothing, was said to have questioned the reason for the order, but his mate, shouting, "Halt, or I fire," did just that. After calling out the guard sergeant, the lad was taken to hospital. He was said to have stated that he'd seen a Japanese officer walking towards him. All five rounds were discovered in a tree trunk, very tight grouping – this from an airman who had been rated, "a very poor marksman."

The above story was repeated to me by LW Simpson, although no mention of a Japanese General. He did say that Singaporeans would shun the 9X area on a certain day in August,

wouldn't go anywhere near it, this is due to the fact that the Japanese were said to have executed a group of people in there on that date.

• • • • • • • • • •

There is also mention of various sightings of a Japanese General on a white horse riding around the station. Then there was the Japanese lady, dressed in black, who was said to haunt one particular barrack block; she was thought to be searching for a son who had been killed at Seletar. This apparition was said to have been seen only by people who slept in the old style beds, as used by the Japanese before all metal beds had been shipped off to Japan. The barracks had been refurnished with the same style of bed shortly after the war, although they were soon to be replaced. Nothing to do with ghost stories, one would hope.

• • • • • • • • • •

PERSONAL RECOLLECTIONS: **The Author**
During my service at Seletar in the late 1950's, our after-dark escapades would also feature the "Worlds" – transport via the ubiquitous trishaw. Other favourite haunts were the bars and cafes along Stamford and Bras Basah roads with their "egg and chips" type menus. This must have been early on in my tour, for later, when my taste buds had been acclimatized, and especially at night, it was a good curry, or Chinese from the kitchens located along Albert Street. The Albert Street kitchens were sited on Tilly-lamp lighted barrows, positioned at the roadside. One could eat out there, or venture inside. Marble-topped tables were sited in the mysterious-looking depths of the buildings behind, up rickety wooden stairs. Up there the floors were polished wood. Solid, yet uneven. The lighting was dim, but the inescapable cockroaches didn't seem to mind. But forget the decor, the food was great, the aromas, out of this world. Real flip-flop food. Fatty's seems to strike a chord. His place was popular, therefore possibly better, and perhaps a little more expensive; but we are talking pennies here.

Occasionally we'd call in at the Raffles, just for a look-see, couldn't afford even to have drink there, especially with the Britannia Club right across the road; on the seafront then, it is now well inland. Also popular was the Union Jack Club, on North Bridge Road – or maybe Victoria Street – close by the Capitol cinema, a favourite for the midnight show on a Saturday. After the film we would often congregate in Bugis Street to be entertained, or maybe we'd take a run out to the beach at Bedok Corner: good seafood, and cold Tiger from the hotel across the road.

• • • • • • • • • •

PERSONAL RECOLLECTIONS: **Sqn/Ldr Case**
From the final edition of the Voice, in an article entitled *Goodbye Seletar*, Sqn/Ldr Bill Case recalls some memories and amusing incidents recorded during his tour on the station. He too remembered Fatty's, in Albert Street, and sailing at the weekends. He tells how his five year old son, who, like all youngsters, had great faith in his father. He would often voice encouragement, such as the time they took a friend out sailing, "Go on Dad, capsize it now. My dad's a good capsizer, Mr Hiscock, go on, Dad.....

Then there was that Standard Vanguard the SWO and I lost. On a visit to the Secondary School, I noticed a ramshackle Vanguard rotting away in the school playground and, being a tidy chap I asked the SWO to get rid of it, which he did. Then came a check of the school inventory. Well, whoever heard of a car being on a school inventory?...."

And what of the story told by Sqn/Ldr Ron Baker about his greengrocer? He asks.

One day the greengrocer was looking unhappy, so Ron asked him what the trouble was. The man told him that during the weekend he had been driving his car along, then suddenly – CRASH, BANG – he collided with another car. The driver, a British Serviceman, climbed out and "he tell me I naughty driver. He say nasty words to me. He say I to blame. But master, I not know if I to blame. I talking to friend, so not looking. How do I know if I to blame if I not looking?"

Sqn/Ldr Case also reminisces about visits to such places as Mersing, Cameron Highlands, Port Dickson, Penang and Hong Kong, and of barbecue parties on Seletar Island, of white sands and crystal clear waters (not the Straits of Johore then!). He finishes the piece by posing a question about his next posting: "I wonder what Old Sarum's like?"

• • • • • • • • • •

There is an amusing story from the sixties that involves a Valiant tanker aircraft accompanying a flight of Javelins on their way out to Singapore. With the Valiant itself due to refuel in Karachi, the AEO – a man who prided himself on his mastery of accents – called up the tower in his best Peter Sellars Pakistani.

"Karachi, this is RAF JET Bravo Oscar Papa, requesting your latest vether and wisibility."

To which the controller answered in his best Etonian English: "RAF JET Bravo Oscar Papa, this is Karachi. Our weather is fine, visibility 25 nautical miles... and when you land you'd better be a Pakistani!"

• • • • • • • • • •

PERSONAL RECOLLECTIONS: **Jan Moore**
'I can honestly say that if you are going to have flu, then the best place to be was Seletar Sick Quarters. After the initial 'I'm dying' phase, I was well enough to sit out in the garden. Friends brought me my music, soft drinks, books, magazines and titbits, so I could sit out on the sun lounger, in the shade of the frangipani tree, sipping ice cold cokes and nibbling. Seletar may have been small, WRAFwise, but hospitality like this was unsurpassed; Changi definitely lacked the personal touch.

'As a sports enthusiast, I swam, table-tennised, hockey'd (badly), even walked for Seletar. I found the rivalry that existed between Seletar and Changi exhilarating – "Never on the field ..... was so much effort made against so many by so few," to paraphrase Winston Churchill. It was such a good posting.'

On the de-WRAFing party mentioned in chapter 13, Jan Moore goes on to comment: 'It was a cracker! We spent the whole day getting ready. A boxing ring floor (I think) was set up at the front of the WRAF block, with lights in the big tree which was there, and one of the girls' record player was set up on the front balcony to provide music. The B-B-Q was courtesy of the Caterers. We had just got everything organised for a 7pm start, when the heavens opened – and continued to open.

'With no time at all before our guests arrived (Station nebbies, and two guests per WRAF, as far as I can remember) something had to be done. The music machine was hastily moved to the WRAF NAAFI, as was the red-hot BBQ – relocated on the covered pathway between the block and the NAAFI. As for seating, we stripped the block of all the mattresses, cushions etc, we could find, threw them on the floor, scatter-style. As guests arrived they were offered a mattress – Make your self comfortable, relax, etc – very laid back.

'Ah Heng, the barman who worked in the WRAF NAAFI, was in his element – having our own bar was a great boon (and not just for that final party).

'Needless to say, the party was a blast. But there is one mystery which has had me pondering ever since – who shredded the plantain tree?

'There was this little plantain tree which stood between the NAAFI and the WRAF Block. It was cosseted by F/Sgt Lynch ("Keep your hands off my plantains!"). The morning after the party, when I staggered into the NAAFI for brunch, the tree was laid out on the ground, in perfect symmetry, still attached to its roots, but completely flat – and I mean flat. If you tried to pick it up by the trunk, it would just drape over your arm. No-one ever admitted to it.'

• • • • • • • • • •

HOW LOW CAN YOU GO?
Bob Symons – a wireless operator with the Marine Craft Unit, Seletar 62/63 – tells the story of a trip he made on RTTL 2755, a late afternoon detail involving a 205 Squadron Shackleton.

'We arrived at the range area early, and were cruising around waiting for the aircraft.

'I saw the "Shack" come out of the cover of the sun, preparing to beat us up from the stern. The aircraft was very, very low, and appeared to be approaching at full chat. I could see one of the crew laying in the bomb aimers position, grinning as the aircraft roared overhead. Then I looked at our mast and noticed the ground planes of our UHF aerial had been broken off and were hanging limply. This antenna was only about ten metres above the water-line! Miraculously, the stub of the antenna was still intact, and we managed to make contact with the aircraft. When informed of the "hit", the reply was along the lines of, "Oops! Sorry about that," like he'd bumped into someone in the cafeteria queue.

'The wireless fitters back at Seletar weren't too chuffed when they saw the mess; there was a lot of work involved in changing the aerial. There were no comebacks though, the true cause was kept quiet. We chalked it up to maritime boyish pranks.'

● ● ● ● ● ● ● ● ● ●

WEST SIDE STORIES

The smaller, West Camp, seems to feature a tad strongly when stories of mischief and wrong-doing at Seletar are recalled: the Christmas 1955 Spitfire episode for instance, as related in chapter 11. A similar, though more serious, incident apparently occurred during Christmas 1958. Said to have been a drunken protest as to the quality of food on offer in the mess, especially the Christmas lunch, a group of airmen manhandled a scrap Harvard on the West Camp parade ground, overturned it then doused it in fuel. Fortunately, the police arrived before the aircraft could be set alight.

To discourage breakage of beer glasses in West Camp NAAFI – thus creating a shortage – it was decided that a twenty cent charge would be levied on each one. This scheme backfired somewhat when it was discovered that airmen were collecting any abandoned glasses found at the end of the evening and hoarding them. They would be cashed in when funds ran low, usually during the second week of the two week pay schedule. Once the shortfall in glasses was noted, the deposit idea was abandoned, thus foiling the beer-fund backup ruse. No problem, someone decided, no levy, no glass; the empties were tossed over the balcony. This more than upset the taxi and car drivers; due to shards of glass on the road, they were unable to pick up their passengers when the cinema -located below the NAAFI – turned out. The levy was soon restored, and West Camp life assumed normality.

Another failure was the jukebox that was installed in the West Camp NAAFI, for a time! The lads quickly learned how to by-pass the mechanism, resulting in the machine playing all its records for free – no profit for the club. Changes to the system corrected this, until it was discovered that judicious juggling with a dinner knife was effective in avoiding the necessity of depositing coins. The machine was further modified, successfully combatting all efforts to fiddle the system short of breaking in and selecting a record manually, which is what happened. Again the machine was modified, steel bars and a protective grill rendering the system foolproof – well, almost. Apparently, a group playing a darts match took umbrage to the intrusive music. They unplugged the machine and heaved it over the balcony. End of the jukebox.

● ● ● ● ● ● ● ● ● ●

SELETAR BOY

Stan Pierce was based at Seletar in 1948, and when he and two colleagues discovered a young Chinese boy, still struggling to survive in the aftermath of the Japanese occupation, they decided the time had come to do their bit. Suffering from malnutrition and very thin, this lad had seemed none the less very intelligent. Placed in a hospital for a nutrition course, several airmen then arranged for him to attend a local school. Towards the end of his tour, Stan and his wife, Molly, were allotted a married quarter, and they invited the boy – known to them as Kuangi

(Yeo Kuan Joo, Yeo being the surname; it is customary with the Chinese to place the family name first), to stay with them at weekends. Content with his lot at Seletar, Stan extended his tour for another eighteen months, during which time, Kuan Joo continued to visit at weekends, and for holidays.

Finally, the time came for Stan and Molly to return to the UK, which led to a very emotional goodbye, though they agreed to keep in touch by mail. Sadly, after four years the letters suddenly went unanswered, being returned "unknown." After trying to trace the boy through the Singapore High Commission, to no avail, Stan and Molly feared the worst.

Thirty-five years later, out of the blue, Molly received a phone call; it was Kuan Joo – he was on holiday in England with his wife and daughter, and would be arriving at the local station in one hour, could Stan collect him?

Seletar Boy. Major Yeo Kuan Joo, Singapore Armed Forces, CO at Seletar 1980-1984, President of the RAF Seletar Association **Author**

Stan could, and did, and after a tearful reunion he asked Kuangi what he'd been doing over the years. The answer? He was now Major Yeo Kuan Joo of the Singapore Army, and had been the Commanding Officer at Seletar from 1980-84!

Despite his seemingly, face to face, extrovert nature, Kuan Joo is really a very shy, retiring character. When he was guiding a group of Seletar Association members around the camp in the year 2000, I pointed out his name, embossed in gold, on the board at station headquarters that listed past commanders, and he was genuinely embarrassed. He had never seen it before.

Kuan Joo has since retired, after pursuing a second career in civil aviation at Changi International airport.

Which leads nicely into that airport. Although not strictly part of the Seletar story, it is part of the overall story of the RAF's involvement with Singapore, for it could be said that Changi took over from Seletar in many ways.

The decision to convert the RAF's premier transport base in the Far East, into an international airport – one of the world's finest – was taken in 1975. Although open for operations on July 1st 1981, the official opening did not take place until December 29th. But the first landing at the now redeveloped Changi International Airport was credited to a Singapore Airlines Boeing 747, this touching down at 07:25 on May 12th 1981, upon completion of flight SQ692.

● ● ● ● ● ● ● ● ● ●

W.H.O.R.E. AT 205/209

R John Smith – Seletar-based from 1957 to 1960 – recalls a management course he attended whilst working with Cathay Pacific Airways, long after his RAF career had come to an end. A visiting lecturer from Hong Kong University was discussing the importance of production targets, and of the importance of acknowledgement, if and when targets were reached. He enthused particularly about the significance of recognition by one's peers, and referred to an illuminated scroll he had once seen in an RAF crew room. John asked if it might have been that of The Wise and Honourable Order of Revered Elders, in Singapore, on the flying boat squadron at Seletar. When told that it was, John pointed out that it had been the acronym that had given him the clue. One's name was added only after contracting an unfortunate affliction. Apparently unaware of that 205/209 crew-room scroll's true significance, it had been a linchpin of this speaker's management lecture for years.

• • • • • • • • •

PERSONAL RECOLLECTIONS: Ron Seddon

Whilst on that very nostalgic 2000 tour of Seletar, we had to pass by the guardroom, a very familiar place to Ron Seddon, so he told us, and after hearing the following, we could well believe how that might have been so...

Although I personally don't ever recall running across the Station Warrant Officer during my time at Seletar, Ron stated his and the SWO's paths had crossed quite often during his time on the base, something I can well visualise. Imagine the scenario:

Ron, walking to the mess, passes a pilot officer and, being sans berry, does not salute.

Eagle-eyed SWO, spotting this from afar, called Ron over:

"Airman. Why didn't you salute that officer?"

Ron: "I'm not wearing a hat."

SWO: "Not wearing a hat, what?"

Ron: "On my head."

SWO, apparently becoming agitated, as one could well imagine, points to brass warrant on his wrist: "What do you think that is, lad?"

Ron, after peering closely at it: "Looks like a couple of dogs fighting." This of course led to a request for Ron to report to the SWO's office later that day, which, naturally, resulted in more visits to said guardroom.

Ah, well. Ron is now, er.... let's just say, very well off. I wonder how the SWO finished up!

• • • • • • • • •

PERSONAL RECOLLECTIONS: Pam Jones

I was there during the 'Uprising in '65' (Confrontation). We had something like 6 months of incursions from Indonesia and we were on 'Alert' It came out on Station Orders that in the event of a air-attack at night the lights would be doused blacking out the Station. One night I awoke to

1939. Seletar Girl Guide troop collecting salvage.

Joan Booth

complete darkness and the fans slowing down. I lay there ears straining for the sound of aircraft, adrenaline running high. The phone in the duty WRAF's bunk rang, and about five minutes later she came out yelling, 'OK everyone, 'it's only a power cut' with that to a girl we all got from beneath our pits rather sheepishly, we'd thought we were in for noisy night.

During the same period, I was at work in Flight Planning when a Sqn/Ldr came in and asked if I would go out and give a bottle of 'coke' to a couple of people. OK, off I go only to find that the couple of people were two very small 'locals', they could only have been about 12 or 13, if that, dressed only in shorts, their flip-flops fashioned from old tyres and string. They were being guarded by two Military Police, and both had their hands tied behind their backs. The poor kids were prisoners, having being picked up in the Ulu up country. I had to feed them their coke as the guards would not untie their hands. That was the communists for you.

● ● ● ● ● ● ● ● ● ●

RAINBOW CREEK – Maurice Whincup

Does anyone from the early '57 era recall crossing the bridge over the creek on their way to the swimming pool, and noticing that, for a period, the tide marks on the mud flats had taken on a rainbow hue? Read on.

In 1956, the sergeant in charge of the transmitters had a very orderly mind, and for the AOC's inspection he repainted all the buildings. The accommodation block was one colour, stores another, the tech site yet another. Workbenches, furniture, fire points, everything a different colour, very smart. However, he was only able to get the paint in large containers – five gallons or more – which left him a problem of what to do with the surplus. No problem. In the freshly painted store he identified every item, section and ref; description; quantity; including part used tins of paint. The AOC was impressed, complimenting the sergeant, then upon seeing the paint, he said, "With everything so well looked after, I don't suppose I have to ask if the paint is tumbled regularly?" "Oh, yes, sir," the sergeant replied.

After the AOC had left he rang a friend in stores and asked, "What does tumbling mean?" He was told that paint in storage had to be shaken up, or tumbled , to prevent the oil and pigment separating, thus rendering the paint unuseable. Records of tumbling had to be kept for each batch.

With the next CO's inspection coming up he was sure he would be asked about the AOC's comment, and would need to produce records he didn't have.

Over the next few night's, deciding to get rid of the evidence, he tipped the paint over the side of the bridge, into the creek. What he didn't realize was that the paint had spread and marked the different tide levels in different colours. Fortunately, everyone but the signals W/O had forgotten about the AOC's comment, and as the W/O and the sergeant were mates the mystery of the rainbow creek was never revealed.

● ● ● ● ● ● ● ● ● ●

Out on the airfield stood a wooden hut that housed the VHF/DF equipment, and for some long forgotten reason the hut had been entered on my inventory. In time it became riddled with termites, and the D/F operator refused to climb the aerial mast as he felt it was unsafe. The W/O, deciding to prove him wrong, climbed up, only for the ladder to collapse and some of the roof timbers to give way. A replacement, brick D/F hut was built, and most of the equipment transferred over. The remaining equipment had to be returned to stores. The new building had a water supply whereas the old one didn't. We had used a tea urn, which now became surplus. I raised the vouchers to strike it off inventory, but as it had only been used to carry water, the strainer had been lost years ago. Stores would not accept the urn without a strainer as serviceable, nor, because it didn't leak, would they accept it as unserviceable. I found an old strainer in the scrap yard but it was too long to fit; no good , said stores. I cut the bottom off; not fair wear and tear, said stores, 664B, you will have to pay for a new urn. After about three months I finally got the urn struck off, then the old hut disappeared. Not another battle, I thought, but this time stores accepted a certificate from DoE, "Destroyed by fire to prevent spread of infestation."

• • • • • • • • • •

Personal Recollections: Joan Booth

Joan, who can claim to have been one of the first into the new swimming pool upon its opening, was a school girl at Seletar during the years 1939 – 41, her father was Station Warrant Officer up to the fall in 1942.

Christmas at Seletar was a very happy time, parties were arranged and Father Christmas arrived with presents for all the children. Dad would ride around on a "Stop me and buy one" tricycle, dispensing free ice cream to all the kids.

The parents had their celebrations in the Families Club whilst the amahs looked after the children. I remember dad won a piglet – little did I realize it was for eating, not a pet. There were chickens and turkeys, too, bottles of whisky, boxes of chocolates and biscuits, and tins of fifty cigarettes; DuMaurier, Players, Senior Service.

Christmas 1941 was spent in a house in Singapore, being bombed every day and never knowing if we or our father would survive. My father used to go to HQ carrying a hand gun.

I remember standing on the quayside saying "Goodbye" to dad; myself, my sisters and brother. His last words as we climbed the gangway, "Look after your mother." Taken captive by the Japanese we were not to see him again until October 1945.

• • • • • • • • • •

FAR EAST AIR FORCE

The Far East Air Force was formed from Air Command South East Asia at the end of the Second World War. The headquarters were at Royal Air Force Changi and it consisted of the RAF stations at Seletar, Tengah, Kai Tak, Kuala Lumpur, Gan, and Negombo, plus smaller units in Burma, Ceylon, Java, Malaya and Thailand

When the Command closed in 1971, the Principal Chaplain, the Reverend W.E. Mantle MA travelled to Singapore and arranged for the collection of various items of church furnishings, and their subsequent return to the United Kingdom. These items were reassembled at RAF Finningley, and on the 29th January 1972 the Far East memorial Chapel was formed and dedicated to the glory of God in remembrance of all those who served and died in the Far East Air Force.

At the closure of RAF Finningley in 1995 the Chapel was moved to St Andrew's Church, Royal Air Force Cranwell.

The Seletar filling station, but not for aircraft.   *Ron Wilkinson*

Squadrons Based At Seletar

Aircraft type and dates refer only to a squadron's time at Seletar.

No. 205 (Formed from the Far East Flight of 1928)

Seletar's first permanent Squadron. Last RAF unit to fly the Sunderland, 1959.
Squadron disbanded 31ˢᵗ October 1971 (Changi – Shackleton MR2).

Southampton Flying Boats:	January 1929 – February 1935
Singapore Flying Boats:	November 1935 – December 1941
Catalina Flying Boats:	February 1941 – January 1942
Sunderland Flying Boats:	September 1949 – May 1959*

*Includes a duo-squadron period with 209, and one as 205 Sunderland Detachment.

No. 36

Horsley Torpedo Bombers:	September 1930 – April 1935
Vildebeest Torpedo Bombers:	April 1935 – January 1942, to Sumatra.
Albacores:	December 1941 – January 1942

No. 100

Vildebeest Torpedo Bombers:	January 1934 – January 1942, to Sumatra.

No. 230

Singapore Flying Boats:	November 1936 – June 1938
Sunderland Flying Boats:	June 1938 – February 1940, to Egypt
Sunderland Flying Boats:	December 1945 – March 1946, Pembroke Dock
Whirlwind HAR 10:	1964 – 1966, returned to UK (Odiham)

No. 232

Hurricanes:	January 1942 – February 1942, to Sumatra.

No. 89

Mosquito/Beaufighter:	September 1945 – April 1946, disbanded.

No. 84

| Mosquito/Beaufighter: | September 1945 – January 1946 |
| Mosquito/Beaufighter: | September 1946 – September 1947, to Tengah. |

No. 110 (Hyderabad)

First formed November 1917. Squadron aircraft took part in both first and last sorties of WW2. Named in commemoration of the Nizam of Hyderabad's gift of DH9A aircraft to the British Government in 1918; aircraft which were used to equip 110 Squadron. Another unit which gave sterling service during the Emergency, when on June 3rd 1959 it was re-formed from elements 155 and 194 Squadrons. The Squadron moved to Seletar from RAAF Butterworth on January 7th, 1964, flying the Whirlwind Mk10 and the remnants of its Sycamore 14's. Disbanded 15th February 1971.

| Mosquitos: | October 1945 – February 1946 |
| Whirlwind/Sycamore: | January 1964 – March 28th 1969, to Changi. |

No. 11

| Spitfires: | September 1945 – January 1946, to Japan. |

No. 17

| Spitfires: | September 1945 – January 1946, to Japan. |

No. 681

| Spitfires: | January 1946 – April 1946, to India. |

No. 81

Reformed from No.684 Sqn September 1946. Flew RAF's last Spitfire and Mosquito sorties. Moved to Tengah March 1958. Served at all three of Singapore's RAF bases.

Mosquitos/Spitfires:	September 1946 – October 1947
Meteors/Pembrokes	
Anson:	March 1950 – March 1958

No. 209 (Hong Kong)

Sqn selected to perpetuate "Hong Kong" title after 114 Sqn (the original holder) disbanded.

| Sunderland Flying Boats: | April 1946 – November 1958* |
| Single/Twin Pioneers: | October 1959 – December 1968 – disbanded. |

*Includes a duo-squadron period with 205

No. 88

| Sunderland Flying Boats: | June 1951 – October 1954, |
| | disbanded, remaining aircraft to 205 and 209 Sqns. |

No. 34

Re-formed at Seletar 31st October 1960, by redesignating the Beverley flight of 48 Sqn, Changi.

| Beverleys: | October 1960 – disbanded, December 1967. |

No. 66

Re-formed at Odiham in 1961 with the Bristol Belvedere twin-rotor helicopter – the first Squadron to be so equipped – the unit began to deploy to Seletar in April 1962, in support of the Far East Land Forces.

Belvederes: April 1962 – March 1969 – disbanded.

                                         Aircraft ceded to SAF as training airframes.

No. 103

Its SAR Whirlwind Mk10's were originally a flight belonging to 110 Squadron, detached to Seletar, but in 1963 the flight was enlarged and given Squadron status.

Whirlwinds: August 1st 1963 – March 28th 1969

                                         moved to Changi.

                                         Squadron finally disbanded at Tengah, August 1st 1975.

No. 65 (East India)

"East India" title is a result of the squadron being presented with eight Spitfires by the East India Fund in July 1940. Disbanded as a flying unit in 1961, it reformed at Seletar in 1964 as the first overseas surface-to-air missile unit, with the Bristol Ferranti Bloodhound Mk2.

Bloodhound SAM's: January 1964 – March 30th 1970

No. 52

After years of sterling service during the Malayan Emergency – operating variously from KL, Penang, and Changi in the Supply Drop and Psychological roles; leaflet dropping and voice flights – the Squadron reformed at Seletar on December 1st 1966, receiving the first of its Hawker Siddley Andover short-range tactical transport aircraft on the 22nd of that month.

Andovers: December 1966 –

                                         Disbanded, December 31st 1969, at Changi.

They really did dress like this. A group of smart looking airmen in West Camp Cpls Club.   **Ed Noonan**

1124 Marine Craft Unit

Given a numbered unit status in 1961, well after the demise of the flying boats it had served so well. Its tasks included SAR, high speed target towing, sea survival training, and general logistical support for the China Rock bombing range. Disbanded October 1st 1970.

5001 Airfield Construction Squadron RAF

Disbanded in 1966, its function being taken over by 51 Field Squadron, Royal Engineers, based at Seletar.

Far East Air Force Mobile Air Movements Squadron (FEAF MAMS)

Based at Seletar from its formation in 1960.

No 15 (Field) Squadron Royal Air Force Regiment

Moved to Seletar on September 28th 1964, being accommodated by the Malcolm Club.

No 2896 (Field) Squadron Royal Air Force Regiment

Arrived Singapore September 5th 1945, disbanded June 1946.

15 Air Despatch Regiment, Royal Corps of Transport

An Army unit whose role, in conjunction with transport squadrons of the Royal Air Force, is the maintenance of ground forces by the aerial delivery of supplies and equipment. Part of this unit was **130 Flight**, their Beaver aircraft based at Seletar from January 1967.

Seletar's Commanding Officers

Far East Flight

Grp/Cpt HM Cave-Browne-Cave, DSO DFC	Feb 1928 – Jan 1929

205 Far East Squadron and Seletar Air Base (from Jan 1929)

Sqn/Ldr GE Livock, DFC AFC	Jan 1929 – Dec 1929

RAF Base Singapore (from Jan 1st 1930)

Grp/Cpt HM Cave-Browne-Cave, DSO DFC	Jan 1930 – Oct 1930
Grp/Cpt AH Jackson	Oct 1930 – Nov 1933
Grp/Cpt S.W. Smith, OBE	Nov 1933 – Dec 1933
Wg/Cdr EJP Burling, DSC DFC AFC	Dec 1933 .....

RAF Station Singapore (from Apr 1st 1935)

Wg/Cdr EJP Burling, DSC DFC AFC	.....Mar 1936
Wg/Cdr C.L. Scott, DSC	Mar 1936 – Nov 1936

RAF Station Seletar (from Nov 13th 1936)

Wg/Cdr CR. Cox, OBE AFC	Nov 1936 – Oct 1939
Grp/Cpt V. Buxton, OBE	Oct 1939 – Mar 1940
Grp/Cpt HMK Brown	Apr 1940 – Feb 1942

Seretar Hikojo – Japanese Occupation
Commanded directly from the Naval Base, but at station level it was really a joint command as follows
Logistics (No.101 Maintenance and Supply Unit)

Capt Hideo Sawai	Feb 1942 – Apr 1943
Capt Natsuo Muda	May 1943 – Dec 1944
Capt Chinae Kawasaki	Jan 1945 – Jun 1945
Capt Yutaka Hara	Jun 1945 – Aug 1945

Operations (No.40/936 Air Unit)

Capt Yoshio Furuta	Feb 1942 – Jul 1943
Capt Seizo Konishi	Jul 1943 – Sep 1944
Capt Yoshio Furuta	Sep 1944 – Aug 1945

RAF Station Seletar (from 21st Nov 1945)
Grp/Cpt G. Francis, DSO DFC   Sep 1945 – Jan 1946
Grp/Cpt CE St J Beamish, DFC   Jan 1946 – Mar 1946

RAF Base Seletar (from Apr 1st 1946)
Air/Cdr G.H.Q. Vasse, CBE   Apr 1946 – Nov 1946
Air/Cdr GPH Carter, CBE   Nov 1946 .....

RAF Maintenance Base (Far East) Seletar (from Jul 1948)
Air/Cdr GPH Carter, CBE   ..... Mar 1949
Air/Cdr HJGE Proud, CBE   Mar 1949 – May 1951
Air/Cdr WA Opie, CBE   May 1951.....

Royal Air Force Base Seletar (from Jun 1951)
Air/Cdr WA Opie, CBE   ..... Mar 1952

R AF Station Seletar (from Jun 1951)
Grp/Cpt RF Shenton   Jun 1951 – Mar 1952
Grp/Cpt HW Marlow, OBE AFC   Apr 1952 – Nov 1952
Grp/Cpt RG Seymour, OBE   Nov 1952 .....

RAF Maintenance Base Seletar (from May 1st 1953)
Grp/Cpt RG Seymour, OBE   ..... Nov 1954
Grp/Cpt T. King   Nov 1954 – Jan 1956
Grp/Cpt DD. Rogers, OBE   Feb 1956 – Oct 1958
Grp/Cpt FC Hopcroft, DSO DFC   Oct 1958 .....

RAF Station Seletar (from Jul 1959)
Grp/Cpt FC Hopcroft, DSO DFC   ..... Oct 1959
Wg/Cdr G. McKenzie, DFC   Oct 1959 – Nov 1959
Grp/Cpt P.A. Hughes, DFC   Nov 1959 – Jan 1961
Grp/Cpt RD Williams, CBE   Jan 1961 – Aug 1963
Grp/Cpt RWG Freer, CBE   Aug 1963 – Apr 1966
Grp/Cpt TWA Hutton, OBE DFC   Apr 1966 – Mar 1969
Grp/Cpt A. Maisner, CB CBE AFC   Mar 1969 – Apr 1971

GREAT WORLD CABARET
DANCE COUPON
GOOD FOR ONE DANCE ONLY
NIGHT DANCE

Further Reading

Smithy. Ward Mcnally. *(Robert Hale Ltd)*

British Rule in Burma, 1824-1942. GE Harvey. *(Faber & Faber)*

To the Ends of the Air. G E Livock. *(HMSO 1973) SBN 11-290151-4*

Singapore – The Japanese Version. Col Masanobu Tsuji. *(Ure Smith Pty, Sydney)*

The Remorseless Road. James McEwan, *ISBN 1-85310-886-3 (Airlife Publishing)*

The Sea Gypsies of Malaya. WG White *(Seeley, Service & Co Ltd)*

Last Flight from Singapore. AG Donahue *(MacMillan & Co. 1944)*

You'll Die in Singapore. Charles McCormac, DCM *(Pan Paperback)*

A History of Early Photography in Singapore & Malaya. J Falconer *(Singapore Times 1987)*

Action Stations – Overseas. Sqn/Ldr Tony Fairbairn *(Patrick Stevens) ISBN 1-85260-319-4*

Spotlight on Singapore. Denis Russell-Roberts. *(Times Press & A Gibbs & Phillips)*

Civil Aviation in Singapore. Dunleep S Kaulsay. *(Univ. Of Malaya, Singapore)*

Hurricane Over the Jungle. Terence Kelly, *(William Kimber 1977) ISBN 071830405-5*

The RAF and the Far East War 1941-1945. (RAF Historical Society & RAF Staff College, Bracknell) ISBN 0-9519824-4-3

Flying Boat. Kenneth Poolman, *(William Kimber 1962).*

Tomorrow You Die. Eric S Cooper, *(E S Cooper & Sons) ISBN 0 9525 3610-2*

So Long, Singapore – RAFAux Tung Song. H. Campbell & R. Lovell, *(Hugh Campbell 2000) ISBN 0-646-39525-8*

Coastal Command & Special Squadrons. JDR Rawlings. *ISBN 0 71060 187 5*

Squadrons of the RAF. ISBN 0 85130 083 9

Flying Units of the RAF. Alan Lake. *(Airlife) ISBN 1 84037 086 6*

History of the Second World War / Campaigns / War Against Japan-Vol 1. (HMSO)

The RAF at the PRO. (Public Record Office) ISBN 1 873162 14 6

SOME SELETAR PERSONALITIES

SERVICE:

Lord & Lady Mountbatten	Supreme Commander, Far East, 1945
ACM Sir Keith Park	Allied Air Commander-in-Chief, 1946
AVM The Earl of Bandon	C-in-C Far East Air Force, 1959
Air Commodore Tedder	Officer Commanding Far East, 1937
Wg/Cdr Stamford Tuck	B o B pilot. Senior Admin Officer 1947
Sqn/Ldr "Ginger" Lacey	B o B pilot. Officer Commanding 17 Sqn, 1945
Australian PM, John Gorton	232 Sqn pilot, 1942
Pilot Officer Peter Townsend	36 Sqn pilot, 1930's
Pam Ayres	WRAF, Photo Interpretation, 1960's

CIVILIAN:

Amy Johnson	Record breaking aviatrix, married Jim Mollison
Bert Hinkler	Pilot
Captain Ross Smith	First England – Australia race winner
Charles Ulm	Pilot, often accompanied Kingsford-Smith
Charlie Chaplin	Actor, stage and screen
Douglas Fairbanks Snr	Actor, stage and screen. Husband of Mary Pickford
Duke of Kent	
HE Oswald Baron von Richthofen	Grandson of the "Red Baron"
J. J. Moll	Early KLM pilot
Jean Batten	New Zealand's record breaking aviatrix
Jim Mollison	Record breaking flyer, married Amy Johnson
Jimmy Melrose	Pilot
Jimmy Youell	Test pilot and adventurer
Lord Baden-Powell	Father of the Boy Scout movement
Mary Pickford	Actress, stage and screen. Wife of Douglas Fairbanks
Mr Lee Kuan Yew	Singapore's first Prime Minister
Noel Coward	Actor, performer, writer; a regular visitor
Parmentier	Early KLM pilot and racer
Paulette Goddard	Actress, stage and screen
Reg Harris	Racing cyclist
Sir Francis Chichester	Trail blazing pilot and yachtsman
Sir Phillip Sassoon	
Sir Charles Kingsford-Smith	Australia's most famous record-breaking pilot
Sir Alan Cobham	Early flyer, innovator of in-flight refuelling
The Aga Khan	Super-rich playboy, racehorse owner

Index

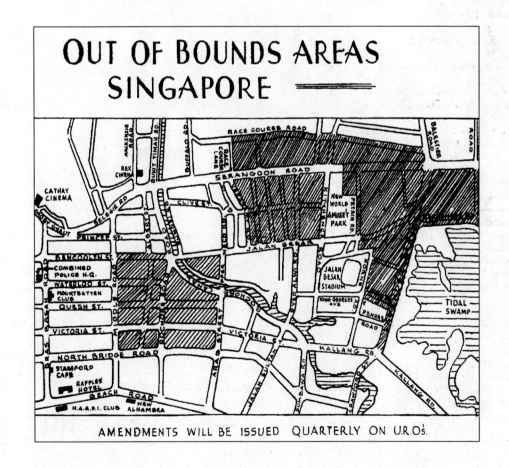

RAF Seletar from the air, probably late 1958 judging by the number of Sunderlands on the Straits compared with those on the dump.

Jim Brown

Could this be the original "Pedalo"? Designed & built by a Flt/Lt Wilson, this 1946 "Aquabyke" - a pedal-powered plywood affair christened Zinkabonk - made an entrance at Seletar long before they appeared at those swish Mediterranean resorts. **Malcolm Lancaster**

The only snakes seen around Seletar – apart from the highly poisonous but very timid sea snakes (they would swim away unless threatened, so they say) - the python, although not poisonous, did have a very healthy appetite. This one has swallowed a baby deer, though it could just as easily have been a child. **RA "Scotty" Powell**

Piccadilly. Seletar's main thoroughfare ran from Piccadilly Circus - the roundabout just past the guardroom - all the way down to join the Embankment, along the waterfront. **Ron Wilkinson**

Much more serious stuff. Boat fabricated from the float of a Japanese Zero aircraft - could this have been the Chevrolet-powered beast? Note the Japanese labour force. **Malcolm Lancaster**

Chinatown when they still had trishaws. A popular form of transport, but boy, you did need to be fit! **John Smith**

Seletar school 1940 **Joan Booth**

The RAF leave centre at Tanjong Bungar, Penang. The building itself was known as Sandycroft. **Author**

205 Sqn line up, almost in numerical order.   RA "Scotty" Powell

PP127 - Lima.   Author

A sad sight. De Havilland Hornets of 45 Sqn gather at Seletar in late 1955. When the squadron converted to the DH Venom, these aircraft were flown down from Butterworth to await destruction.   **Ed Noonan**

Short Rangoon, probably 203 Sqn on a visit from the Persian Gulf.   RA "Scotty" Powell

The West Camp Spitfire that ended up on East Camp's parade ground on Christmas Day 1955.

100 Squadron and their Vickers Vildebeest aircraft line up for an official photograph.   *100 Sqn Archives*

A Mosquito awaits the axe, literally.

A Meteor PR10 experiences a spot of bother with the undercarriage. A successful belly landing was made on the grass.   **Ed Noonan**

Hawker Audax.   RA "Scotty" Powell

Numerous types visited Seletar - Hawker Tempest.

The Beaufighter cockpit.

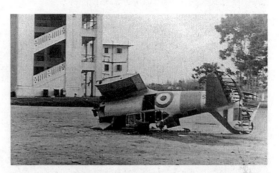

Scrap Harvard that was manhandled onto the West Camp parade ground during Christmas 1958. **Peter A Hughes**

Engine fitter and helper get their hands dirty on the R-R Kestrel of a short Singapore III. Note bags for catching wayward tools. Small prop on cross strut drives an air compressor.   **Ken McLean**

Quite large, these barrack blocks. Lining up for the start of a Corgi Grand Prix?

What could well be the Sgt's Mess Xmas draw. The person standing is the SWO, Warrant Officer Booth.
Joan Booth

Members of the Far East Flight, complete with "solar bowlers," pose before S1127, the replacement aircraft, in the yet to be completed hangar at Seletar, late 1928. **Vernon JW Lee collection**

The entrance today. *Author*

This Japanese flag flew over Seletar until the RAF return in 1945. 'acquired' by Cpl Jenkins, it now resides at the Yorkshire Air Museum. [Author]

Two 34 Sqn Beverleys at Seletar, one of them the only camouflaged version in the Far East. [Michael Murden]

One of Seletar's blocks as they were in the year 2000. *Author*

DP198 undergoes a final servicing in preperation to flying back to the UK for preservation. Shortly after leaving the hangar the plans changed, the aircraft was struck off charge & scrapped. Tym Paige Dickins